WHAT CANADIANS ARE SAYING ABOUT PETER KINCH
AND THE REAL ESTATE ACTION PLAN:

"A must-read for anyone contemplating investing in residential real estate as a means to achieving their personal financial goals. Informative, provocative and engaging. Peter's early roots as a teacher are clearly evidenced as he navigates the earnest group of sample investors through their journey of investing and financing the doors to their future."

> —John Webster, Head, Real Estate Lending and Scotia Mortgage
> Authority, President and CE0, Scotia Mortgage Corporation

"You don't become the #1 mortgage broker in the country by accident. Peter Kinch has earned that distinction by consistently helping his clients succeed. Simply put, he excels in the real estate industry. In this terrific book, Peter expertly outlines a practical action plan that will help you avoid the pitfalls that unsuccessful investors fall into, ensuring you prosper in the years ahead."

> —Les Hewitt, author of the best-selling *Power of Focus*

"Peter Kinch can break down complex terms and conditions so that everyone can understand them. His advice to my radio listeners is current and to the point."

> —Russell Byth, Business Editor, News1130 Radio, Vancouver

"Peter's review of possible exit strategies was great, as it gave me a much better understanding of the future benefits of my investments if I were to buy out my JV partners."

> —C. Misener

"Thank you, Peter, for all the great insights you provided. To be quite honest, I was a bit lost, but now that I have my 5-year action plan, I'm confident that I will succeed."

> —O. Sandhar

"Peter Kinch's 5-year planning workshop is one of the most worthwhile things my partner and I have ever done. The information he shares and the planning process itself are outstanding."

> —K. Muzin

"We now clearly see the big picture and have come to understand just what it's going to take for us to become successful real estate investors. Thank you, Peter, for challenging us to be realistic and reminding us to stay focused on the end result—the lifestyle choice that we have envisioned for ourselves and our family."

> —Brian and Beverley Gauntlett

"It has taken seven years to get both of us excited about and believing in real estate investing, and it took Peter one evening—I think that this type of consultation is going to help a lot of people out there!"

> —A. McLaren

"We are so empowered to have been a part of your passion and commitment, and the sharing of your knowledge and expertise in this planning adventure. By being a part of the workshop we were able to clarify our 5-year plan!"

—Bruce Yorga B.E.S., M. Arch.
—Jan Hollingsworth, B.A., M.C.S.

"The most amazing part for me was realizing what I need to accomplish my goals and that I have more seed capital than I thought I did. I also realized that I've earned some of my stripes already and I know more than I thought I did."

—Michele Dedora

THE CANADIAN REAL ESTATE

ACTION PLAN

THE CANADIAN REAL ESTATE

ACTION PLAN

Proven Investment Strategies to **Kick-Start** and **Build** Your Portfolio

Peter Kinch
Foreword by Don R. Campbell

John Wiley & Sons Canada, Ltd.

Library and Archives Canada Cataloguing in Publication Data

Kinch, Peter
The Canadian real estate action plan : proven investment strategies to kick-start and build your portfolio / Peter Kinch.

Includes index.
ISBN 978-0-470-15801-2

1. Real estate investment—Canada.   I. Title.

HD316.K56 2010   332.63'240971   ·   C2010-900900-2

Production Credits
Cover design: Pat Loi
Interior design: Pat Loi
Typesetting: Thomson Digital
Cover image: istockphoto.com
Printer: Friesens

John Wiley & Sons Canada, Ltd.
6045 Freemont Blvd.
Mississauga, Ontario
L5R 4J3

ENVIRONMENTAL BENEFITS STATEMENT

John Wiley & Sons - Canada saved the following resources by printing the pages of this book on chlorine free paper made with 100% post-consumer waste.

TREES	WATER	SOLID WASTE	GREENHOUSE GASES
63	29,014	1,762	6,024
FULLY GROWN	GALLONS	POUNDS	POUNDS

Calculations based on research by Environmental Defense and the Paper Task Force. Manufactured at Friesens Corporation

Printed in Canada
1 2 3 4 5 FP 14 13 12 11 10

Contents

Foreword
by Don R. Campbell

"YES." That is the magic word in real estate investing. Hearing "Yes" from a vendor, "Yes" from your bank or mortgage broker and then a "Yes" from a tenant moving in. All of these "Yeses" are critical, receiving too many "Nos" in the investing process stops everything. I learned this many decades ago when I first started investing in real estate, so I went on a mission to help people hear "Yes" as often as they need.

In my book, *Real Estate Investing in Canada*, I showed investors exactly how to pick a great investment property and how to get a "Yes" from the property seller at the price and terms you want. However, that is only the beginning of the process. The next stage is what the book you have in your hands is all about: **How to help your bank to say "YES."**

Whether you're just beginning with investment real estate or have been building your residential or multi-family portfolio for years, you understand that a major part of the magic of real estate comes from using smart leverage. Leverage of up to $4 for every $1 you invest. Leverage that banks, brokers and other financial institutions are glad to provide you . . . *if* you know how to minimize their risks.

In *The Canadian Real Estate Action Plan*, you will discover that what you believe gets a bank to say "Yes" is often VERY different to the reality that has come out of the 2008–2009 recession. The financial world has become less risk tolerant and that means only a select few deals are getting approved.

That means, beginning in 2010, if you continue to try to build your investment portfolio based on old assumptions or strategies, you will hit the financing brick wall called "No." The rules of the game have changed and you need to know the truth behind the curtain. And Peter is the man to throw open that curtain and force us all to take a close look at our portfolios, our plans and our financing strategies.

Peter's sole focus for years has been opening financing doors for real estate investors, and he is so successful at it that in 2008 he was named "Canada's Top Mortgage Broker." His track record and reputation with banks is second to none and he has access to the upper floors of the banking industry. In other words, he knows exactly of which he speaks.

Through his understanding of how it all works, he has consistently been able to work magic for investors (large and small) across the country. Where once they were told "No," Peter and his team have been able to garner a "Yes" for investors who have their plan in place and follow the steps very clearly laid-out in this book. And, best of all, he does it all without ever entering the grey area. You'll discover that you can continue to hear "Yes" to your financing request without having to hide information, sign un-true documents or enter into fraudulent transactions. You can win by playing fully above-board.

By reading this book, you will witness financing myths being busted, investment lending becoming de-mystified and best of all, no matter what level of investor you are, you will discover the exact steps to getting the financing you need to build your strong cash-flowing portfolio.

Do not invest in another piece of real estate or approach a bank or mortgage broker without reading this book first. Unless, of course, you prefer to hear "No" to your next deals.

Go for "Yes" by learning from Canada's expert.

Sincerely,
Don R. Campbell
www.reincanada.com
Best-selling author of *Real Estate Investing in Canada*

> "Never doubt that a small group of thoughtful committed citizens can change the world; indeed, it is the only thing that ever has."
>
> —Margaret Meade

Mission Statement

To teach, coach and empower individuals to accomplish goals that will positively impact the world.

It is my personal belief that, through the process of accomplishing the goals you have set for yourself, the world around you will be a better place. I was told something years ago that really struck a chord with me—making more money in itself doesn't make the world a better place or you a better person—it simply amplifies your character, good or bad. Well, I'd like to help amplify the character of some of the good people I've met through the course of working with real estate investors. The truth is, the more people I meet and the more I learn about their goals and aspirations, the more I realize that the majority of people really do want to make a difference in this world. In fact, if the majority of people were not preoccupied with the rat race of the 9-to-5 world, they would live a life that positively impacts others. Ultimately, I believe most people want to live a life of significance. They want to know that the world is a better place because they lived in it. The problem is that most people go through life so caught up in survival mode, they can't help but think of themselves and are never able to step back long enough to realize their true potential. But when they do, I'm always amazed and inspired by the many visions I see though their eyes.

I am absolutely convinced that every person who accomplishes a worthwhile goal will positively impact at least 100 people in their lives.

It is important to understand that your goal doesn't have to change the world in order for you to make a difference. Sure, your goal could be to fund an overseas charity or create world peace, but it can also be as simple as creating enough financial freedom within your own family to allow a father to spend more time with his son. Perhaps it's as simple as creating a family environment that is not burdened by financial stress. Perhaps it's giving your children the opportunities in life that allow them to grow and prosper and, in doing so, create a lasting and positive impact on the world.

In the end, the steaks can only be so thick, the houses so big and the cars so fast—the true sign of success is *significance*. And the accomplishment of your goal, no matter how big or small it may be, is significant. My own goal is to help 10,000 people in this world achieve their goal so that they will positively impact at least 100 people around them. Together, we will be able to positively impact over one million people and, in the end, the world will be a better place because we lived.

Sincerely,
Peter Kinch

Introduction

In the early 1990s, I was teaching English in Japan for the Board of Education—certainly a long way from the world of mortgage financing in Canada. But surprisingly, it was there that I had my first introduction to the world of finance and real estate. A Japanese businessman who wanted to buy real estate in Canada asked for my advice. At the time, I didn't have a clue where to begin to help him—but I did know one person who probably could. He was a friend/mentor of mine who lived in Victoria, B.C. I didn't entirely understand what his job was, but I knew that he was a mortgage broker and that had something to do with mortgages, which had something to do with real estate and, therefore, he was eminently more qualified than me to provide advice and service to our Japanese buyer. In short, I soon found myself in the midst of a deal that would see our Japanese friend purchase, among other things, a ski resort in the Kootenays.

While on a break from teaching in Japan, my friend asked if I would consider becoming a mortgage broker and come work with him. The concept was both intriguing and exciting, so I went to the University of British Columbia the following day and registered for the correspondence program. As soon as I returned to the land of the rising yen, I set out on my course to become a mortgage broker.

I would teach English during the day and then, at night, in my small *tatami* room 150 kilometres north of Tokyo, I would pour over my textbooks studying and learning about the world of mortgages. As I sat in that small room trying to understand terms and concepts that were completely foreign to me, I realized that this is exactly how my students must feel about learning the English language. The key, I realized, was to break it down into its basic fundamentals and begin with a core understanding. For some of us, the world of mortgages can be just as confusing and just as foreign as learning a new language.

Over the following years I was introduced to a world within the world of mortgages and finance—the world of the real estate investor. I found the world of real estate investing both fascinating and challenging, but I realized that there was a void in the information and education available for the average Canadian investor when it came to finance options. I took a teaching approach to working with investors and quickly developed a niche in providing knowledge and education that was lacking in the marketplace. I started to ask questions in an effort to better understand their unique needs. Throughout this process of asking questions and getting to know my clients better, I came to realize two things:

1. Virtually every real estate investor was using real estate as a vehicle to allow them to accomplish a larger goal, but they were seldom clear as to what that goal was. Therefore, they needed a plan.

2. Neither the investor nor the broker had the luxury of treating their investment real estate transactions the same way they would treat a simple home purchase.

I soon learned the importance of helping the investor identify why they wanted to invest in real estate and, more importantly, help them discover that real estate was simply their investment vehicle of choice. Once they knew what results they needed from their real estate, the action plan simply became a case of reverse engineering the process: Start with the end result and work backwards. Identify the obstacles and then put a three-phase action plan together to overcome the obstacles and accomplish the goal. And so, the *Canadian Real Estate Action Plan* was created.

After years of consulting and educating real estate investors, I have discovered some of the critical keys to success—why do some people succeed while others do not? The answer is not simply that successful people have set goals. It's far more than that. It's because they understand the importance of being able to obtain financing and they have learned how to structure their real estate portfolio in such a way that they've ensured their own success. And that is exactly what this book will teach you to do.

This book is not designed to convince you that buying real estate is a good thing—I'm assuming that you already believe that. This is also not a simple "mortgage book" that explains all your financing options—it's much more than that. This is the definitive guide for all real estate investors to map out a game plan, business strategy and financial plan to accomplish their goals.

Inside you will meet Brian and Michelle. They are a typical Canadian couple. They both have jobs that keep them busy and kids who keep them even busier. Brian wants to buy real estate but has no plan. Michelle is extremely apprehensive and has little or no faith in their ability to make the right decisions and is afraid to make a mistake and risk losing their hard-earned equity. For both of them, the land of real estate investing is foreign and quite intimidating. So they take that all-important first step and attend one of my real estate action plan workshops. There they are introduced to other Canadian real estate investors of various levels of experience. Together as a class, they spend the day identifying all of the different obstacles that arise and develop their own personal action plans to overcome them and accomplish their goals.

This book is intended to be interactive, not passive. So whether you are a seasoned real estate investor or the whole idea is still a foreign concept, I challenge you to discover what is really important to you, and I show how you can achieve it through developing your own real estate action plan.

Part I
CREATING
YOUR LIFE ON
PURPOSE

Chapter 1

Why Are You Buying Real Estate?

"Oh no, no. I was just wondering
if you could help me find my way."

"Well that depends on where you want to get to."

"Oh, it really doesn't matter, as long as . . ."

"Then it really doesn't matter which way you go."

—Conversation between Alice and the Cheshire Cat,
Lewis Carroll's *Alice in Wonderland*

BRIAN: Can you help me get financing for my next real estate investment?
PETER: Well, what is your goal over the next five years?
BRIAN: I want to buy real estate.
PETER: Why?
BRIAN: So that I can make more money.
PETER: What is your definition of "more money"?
BRIAN: Well, I'm not exactly sure . . . .

Brian was quite surprised when he first walked into my office asking for a mortgage and I started by asking him about where he wanted to be in five years. Much like Alice, he wasn't clear on the direction he was heading. The truth of the matter is, for many Canadians, it is not uncommon for them not to know where they want to head either financially or otherwise. People know that buying real estate is a good thing to do—after all, that's what all the financial experts say. We've all heard the quote "The greatest number of millionaires have been created through real estate." The fact that you are reading this book indicates you believe real estate would be a good addition to your financial portfolio. The question isn't "*Should* you buy real estate?" but rather the question is, "*Why* should you buy real estate?" The more I could learn from Brian about his goals, the more I could help him achieve them. There is a big difference between simply buying one rental property and building a rental portfolio.

During a television interview in the summer of 2009, the question posed to me was whether or not it was a good time to buy a cottage or recreational property. I found this question quite interesting. When I probed a bit further, the interviewer suggested that many Canadians have become disenchanted with stock portfolios and were turning to real estate as a safer, more secure investment. The thinking was that since we were in the middle of a recession and prices had fallen off a bit, now might be a good time to purchase a cottage in the lake country or a cabin at the ski hill. That was when I realized something that I've taken for granted for many years—many Canadians don't realize that real estate "investing" can be much more than simply securing a recreational property for your family's future. In fact, the term "real estate investment" conjures up different impressions and definitions for various people. This was also when I realized just how valuable "goal-oriented" planning is before taking your hard-earned money and throwing it against the proverbial wall, hoping that this investment would work out better than the last one. Exiting the stock market to enter the real estate market can produce equally poor results if you do not have a plan. This was the reason I needed to ask Brian some questions before I simply processed a mortgage for him. The first thing I asked him was, "Why are you investing in the first place? What results do you want or need from your investment?"

It's important to note that I wasn't attempting to turn Brian into the next Donald Trump and he didn't need to show me a plan to conquer world hunger. In fact, it didn't matter how aggressive or conservative his goals were, but what was crucial was that he had a clear goal that his real estate investments needed to produce for him.

Brian's answers helped me to clarify what type of investor he was and, therefore, how I could best structure his real estate portfolio. Having worked with investors for over a decade, I've discovered that there are three basic types of real estate investors:

1. The "Mom and Pop" investor who likes to buy one or two rental properties as a way of diversifying their financial portfolio and supplementing their retirement pension. Also included in this category would be the couple who want to buy a cabin on the lake or a recreational property that will provide an immediate lifestyle benefit for their family, as well as appreciating over the long-term, adding to their net worth and, ultimately, passing it on to future generations. These individuals see real estate as an important, but complementary, part of an overall financial and retirement strategy.

2. The second group is made up of those individuals who use real estate investment as their primary vehicle for wealth creation and a major component of their retirement plans. These individuals want to increase their net worth, move towards financial independence and create wealth that can be passed on to future generations. They are not full-time real estate investors, but focus on creating sufficient cash flow from their investments over the years to potentially replace one of their incomes.

3. The third group comprises those individuals who not only see real estate as their primary vehicle for wealth creation, but also as their full-time job. These individuals want to build their real estate portfolio to the point where they will be able to quit their current employment and devote their energies full time towards developing a large real estate portfolio. The majority of the individuals in this group not only see real estate as a way to create financial independence, but also as a way to achieve larger goals, some of which are charitable in nature and go beyond just a larger house or a nicer car. These individuals will need to build a large portfolio with a significant number of properties that include both the potential for increasing their net worth and developing a significant monthly cash flow.

It really doesn't matter which of these three groups you fall into—you may, in fact, see yourself evolving from one group into another. The point is, regardless of which category you fit into, it is critically important that you are honest with yourself about what you require the real estate investment to produce for you. For example, if you see yourself in either category two or three above, then the answer to my television question would be no—this is not a good time to buy the cottage on the lake. That type of real estate investment would not be the best use of your investment dollars based on your goals. If, on the other hand, you fit into category one, then now may very well be a great time to buy that cottage/family investment property. The key is understanding that there is no right or wrong answer—it's simply a matter of determining what role real estate can play in order for you to achieve your goals. Not sure? Don't worry—that's the whole purpose of this book.

This book will walk you through a process I have developed over the years called the Real Estate Action Plan. It will not only help you to determine which category of real estate investment you are in, but will also help you clarify why you are buying real estate, what results you need to achieve from your real estate investments and allow you to put together a three-phase action plan to achieve those results.

WHY YOU NEED A PLAN

Generating wealth through real estate is not about simply purchasing one piece of property then sitting back and relaxing. Creating wealth through real estate requires a serious commitment to developing a portfolio that will produce long-term results.

To successfully accomplish this, you must have clarity—a thorough understanding of what you are doing when you buy real estate. You must also have purpose—a set plan based on clear goals. Without clarity and purpose, you're simply taking your hard-earned money and saying, "Okay, I've got this money but I'm not really sure what I'm going to do with it. This sounds good, I sure hope it works." You're throwing mud against a wall, then sitting back and praying that some of it sticks!

With the real estate action plan you won't have to "throw mud against the wall." The plan provides you with the knowledge and understanding you require to make sound real estate investment decisions. You will gain a clear understanding of:

- **Why** you are buying real estate; and
- **How** you are going to accomplish the goals that you set.

Before you start to roll your eyes and say "I don't need to read another book on goal-setting or creating a business plan," let me share with you the background on how the real estate action plan was developed.

Originally, I came from a teaching background and was not in real estate. What is obvious to me today was not obvious to me when I was studying for my mortgage broker's course in Japan. When I returned to Canada and began brokering, I realized that many people were in the same boat. They had a concept of what mortgages are, but their knowledge was really nebulous—almost a necessary evil. You know you need to get a mortgage to buy a house or property, but you probably don't really understand a great deal about it. After two to three years in the brokering field, I came across a company that bought townhouse or condo projects at wholesale, stratified them and then sold them at retail to investor clients—much like buying a whole pizza and then reselling it by the slice. I agreed to work on one project with this company and, before long, I became one of their key brokers. Without even realizing it, I had entered the world of financing for real estate investors and nothing would ever be the same for me.

As a broker, typically when I receive an application from a client, I plug in the numbers based on textbook formulas and ratios to determine whether the client qualifies for a mortgage. I approached these "investor projects" the same way, but then two things happened that would change my career forever.

The first happened when I received an application from one of these condo investors. I did the formulas using the textbook method that I had been trained to use, and the result concluded that there was no way this client should qualify for a mortgage—the ratios were totally out of whack. I decided to send the application off to the bank anyway, and was completely shocked when it came back APPROVED. I didn't want to question how they approved it; certainly, I didn't want them to realize their mistake and reverse their decision, but I had to know why. I asked the underwriter, why her ratios differed from my calculations; after all, being the good student that I was, I had followed the textbook calculations to a tee. She simply said, "Well, we have this thing called a 'rental cash flow analysis,' which calculates the debt coverage ratio. It's a system used for real estate investors only." It all sounded quite complicated, so I asked some of my broker friends if they knew anything about rental cash flow analysis and the majority of them had never heard of it before—and those that had, knew very little about it. That's when I knew I was onto something. I could create a niche specializing in brokering for real estate investors. So, I decided to study, learn and write about financing for real estate investors. In the process, I began to learn that real estate investors were unique. That's when a second significant event happened in my mortgage career.

Randy, another investor client, came to me one day and said, "I've got this great deal, but I don't have much money to put down." He was very excited about the deal and I was trying to figure out how to arrange financing for that particular property. The ratios wouldn't work with a conventional lender, so I looked at some of the sub-prime options and, sure enough, I was able to find one. The interest rate was higher and he had to pay some fees, but he got the mortgage. We managed to arrange the financing and Randy was able to purchase the property, so everyone was happy—right?

Well, we were happy until Randy returned three months later because he had just found another property and needed another mortgage. Suddenly, I realized that due to the higher interest rate charged on his previous deal, the lack of cash flow wasn't helping his debt service ratios, and now it was even harder for Randy to qualify for a conventional mortgage. The sub-prime lender we had used for the previous mortgage would only allow one mortgage per client (something I didn't know while arranging the previous deal), and due to the poor cash flow on his existing property, any subsequent high-cost solutions would only serve to create a downward spiral—especially if he ever wanted to buy more real estate in the future.

Then I asked the magic question: "How many purchases do you plan to make over the next few years?" Randy answered, "As many as I can afford." If I had asked Randy that question when he first came to me, I would have structured his first mortgage differently. By not taking the time to ask the right questions in the first place, I had inadvertently put Randy in a mortgage situation that made it extremely difficult and complicated for him to get another mortgage. And that's when it dawned on me: I can't simply treat a real estate investor the same way that I treat a regular home buyer. Investors have unique needs and it is critical to determine their goals before forging ahead with their financing. How you structure each deal can have a major impact on their ability to accomplish their goals. It was a painful lesson, but a valuable one.

These two events shaped my mortgage career. First, I realized banks have different programs for investors, but more importantly, not every bank and not all brokers are aware that these programs exist. This is what motivated me to step into the world of real estate investors, creating my niche area of expertise. Second, I realized the importance of learning more about my clients' goals and looking beyond their current deals. From that time forward, I have made a point of asking every single client questions.

It started with sitting at a Starbucks and asking my clients how many properties they planned to buy in the future. The more questions I asked made me realize that, although each individual was unique and had different goals, they all faced similar issues and challenges. By asking questions and writing down the answers, I was helping my clients really analyze where they were going (or where they wanted to go) and what their unique needs were. I asked questions such as, "Where do you see yourself in five years?" It quickly became apparent from their responses that everyone had their own individual story and plan. I was quite amazed by the fact that the majority of their goals, dreams and visions were not simply materialistic in nature. I met people who wanted to help their aging parents. Some were very passionate about their church or a charity that they supported. Others simply wanted to provide their children with better opportunities. There were many examples among the investors I met, but one thing they all had in common was the fact that they all looked to real estate as their investment vehicle of choice to generate the cash flow necessary to finance their visions. I began to come to the realization that this was about something much greater than simply getting a mortgage, and my role as a mortgage broker took on a much deeper meaning. If only half of my clients actually achieved what they hoped to do, then they could make a positive impact on the world.

Put simply, it wasn't about the real estate or the mortgage—real estate was just the vehicle—it was the result that real estate could achieve for them that was really important. The mortgage was just a necessary instrument to accomplish something far greater, but without it, their goals would be unattainable. So, if I could figure out a way to help them build a portfolio, they would be able to achieve their desired results and, in a small way, I would be a part of helping their dreams become reality. And, I discovered, the larger my client's goal—the more impact it would have on the world—the more I wanted to help make it happen.

The process of analyzing the goals of thousands of investors across Canada and coming to understand how the cause and effect of today's decisions impact tomorrow's options evolved over time into the creation of my real estate action plan. This is the reason why the first question I asked Brian when he came into my office for a mortgage was, "What is your goal for the next five years?" and why I will spend the remainder of this book teaching you the lessons I've learned from financing thousands of mortgages for Canadian real estate investors.

Some Interesting Statistics

Before I delve into helping you create your own real estate action plan, I feel that it is important for you to know the following statistics:

- Roughly 4% of all Canadians will ever buy real estate as an investment. That's a number that is surprisingly low for most people I talk to. That means if you've bought even just one investment property, you are in the 96th percentile of the country.

- I estimate that roughly half of that 4% only buy two or three properties as a way of supplementing their pension plan. So, if you have bought or are planning to buy more than three investment properties, you've gone from being among 4% of the population to the top 2%.

- Taking this one step further, how many people do you think take the time to become educated, either through a real estate network such as the Real Estate Investment Network (REIN) or other real estate investment programs around the country? My guess is that it is about half of that 2%. Now we are down to 1% of the population.

- Finally, the number of investors who understand the need to make a plan and treat their investment portfolio like a business, actually taking both the time and money to learn how to accomplish this, is probably only 10% of that 1%.

That's 10% of 1% of 2% of 4% of the entire population, if you're keeping track. I say this a little tongue-in-cheek and the actual number is not important—the point is, the number of people who actually educate themselves to this degree (such as reading and learning the material in this book) is a very small percentage. What's equally important for you to know is that if sophisticated, well-informed real estate investors represent such a small percentage of the population, so too are the number of brokers and bankers who understand how to work with them. The truth is, the average mortgage broker and banker is trained to think in what I call, "transactional terms," whereas working with investors requires a "portfolio approach." (I will be explaining these terms in more detail later in the chapter.) In other words, if you go to your regular broker or your regular bank, don't be surprised if they have difficulty understanding your unique needs. The danger, of course, is that just as in Randy's situation, neither you nor your broker will realize this until it's too late.

CREATE YOUR FUTURE ON PURPOSE

The fact that you are reading this book tells me that you have come to the conclusion that you want to buy real estate for investment purposes. My job is not to convince you that real estate is a good alternative to the stock market—I'll leave that for you to decide. In fact, you can use every exercise in this next section and apply it to whatever investment vehicle you choose. But for the purposes of this book, we'll assume that you have chosen real estate.

Whether you are just starting out and looking to make your first investment purchase or you already own a number of investment properties, you will need a plan of action. My goal is to help you create that plan on purpose. Now I know some of you are shaking your head: What do you mean by creating a plan on purpose? Well, think about it. What's the opposite of doing something on purpose? Doing it by accident. How many times have you heard someone say that they did something by accident? Unfortunately, the truth is that the majority of people you know will, five years from now, find themselves living a life which is simply the result of reacting to people and circumstances around them. Very few will have designed a purposeful life. Very few will take the time today to analyze where and what they want their future to look like. Very few will take the time to create a vision of what their life will look like five years from now. Very few will create a future on purpose.

So you've decided you want to buy real estate. Now I'm going to ask you the same question I asked Brian at the beginning of the chapter—why? What's your reason for wanting to buy real estate? We've already talked about the fact that it's not really the real estate you want so much as the results that real estate can achieve for you. So what do those results have to be for you? For some people, the answer is very clear. For others, it is more of an intangible. For still others, it is a complete mystery. When I think of why people buy real estate, I'm reminded of the book *Rich Dad, Poor Dad* by Robert Kiyosaki and Sharon Lechter. I read this book years ago, and the one concept that struck me was the idea of creating assets or investments that would eventually create a cash flow to finance your lifestyle. The ultimate goal is that you are no longer dependent on income from a job, since virtually all of your lifestyle is paid for from the cash flow created by your investments.

I've met a lot of investors who have adopted a variation of this strategy, but when I started to analyze the investors' thought processes I discovered one flaw. Basically, the process worked like this:

- You start with a job or business from which you use any excess money to purchase investments.
- These investments create a stream of cash flow.
- This cash flow is what you use to live your lifestyle.

Here's where I started seeing the problem:

- The average investor has a limited amount of excess cash to invest.

- The amount of money they have to invest determines the nature and type of investment they make.
- The type of investment they make determines the amount of cash flow they produce.
- The level of cash flow they produce, in turn, determines their lifestyle.

Correct me if I'm wrong, but this scenario sounds a lot more like a lifestyle lived by default, rather than one created on purpose. At the end of the day, you end up living a lifestyle based on whatever cash flow you receive from whatever investment you can afford. That's why many investors wake up five years from now wondering why it didn't work.

Don't get me wrong—I believe the person who buys "whatever kind of investment they can afford" is infinitely better off than the majority of Canadians who do not invest at all and simply wait to retire hoping to collect their old age pension. But that's not who you are—we've already determined that statistically, you're not the average person. You wouldn't be reading this book if all you wanted to do was simply buy one more property. So, what if we took a different approach and started with the end result in mind?

As I mentioned earlier, I believe it's not the real estate that you want, but rather the results that real estate can produce, and with those results, you'll be able to create the lifestyle you want. If we're completely honest with ourselves, what real estate investment is really about is attaining your desired lifestyle at the end of the day. So, why not start with the end result in mind?

1. Determine what type of lifestyle you would like to have in five years from now.
2. The type of lifestyle you want to have will determine the amount of cash flow you will need.
3. The amount of cash flow you need to live the life you want will determine the type and nature of investments you will need to make.

4. This will bring you back to where you are now—your current job or income.

I know some of you are saying that sounds all good and well, Peter, but it still doesn't address the question "How much real estate can I afford to buy? It's all fine and dandy to create some fantasy vision of an ideal lifestyle, but given my current circumstances and with the amount of money I have in savings, I can't afford to buy the number of properties I need to create the cash flow required to pay for my ideal lifestyle. Maybe I'm better off creating a more 'realistic' goal based on what I can afford."

I know exactly what you mean. But in reality, all you've done is identify an obstacle. And that is precisely why you need an action plan. You need to clearly define your obstacles and then put a plan of action into place to overcome them.

By starting with the end result and working backwards, you will be amazed at how much clarity you get by identifying and then overcoming the obstacles you will encounter en route to accomplishing your goal. You will be able to clarify exactly the kind of lifestyle you want to live, figure out how much cash flow you will require, figure out the type and nature of investments you'll need, identify your obstacles based on your current realities and figure out the solutions to overcoming these obstacles.

A NOTE ON REALITY

Understanding "reality" is crucial. It doesn't matter how grandiose your vision is, there is no such thing as a realistic or unrealistic goal. People often have a lifestyle vision—a dream—but don't think it's realistic.

A goal cannot be realistic or unrealistic, but what's required of you to accomplish that goal may be unrealistic given your current circumstances, or sometimes the goal is realistic, but the time frame is not. You don't have to change the goal—just the time frame.

Chapter 2

What Is the Goal for Your Real Estate Investment?

In my first appointment with Brian, it was clear to me that there would be no way to answer all of his questions in a brief half-hour meeting. Initially, Brian was completely focused on what interest rate he could get and how much he had to put down on his purchase, but then in the very next sentence he was talking about maybe buying one property a year for the next 20 years. Sitting there politely listening to his questions, I felt like Obi-Wan Kenobe, waiting for the right moment to use my Jedi skills, telling Brian, "These aren't the mortgages you're looking for." I know that may sound arrogant, but after working with as many investors as I have, you quickly start to see patterns. That doesn't make me better or smarter, it's simply a fact of what I do. If I went down to Brian's workplace on Monday morning, I'd be completely lost. I wouldn't have a clue what to do. So I certainly don't expect Brian to know all the ins and outs of real estate investing, especially when he hasn't bought a rental property before.

This is why I find it quite surprising (sad really), when the majority of would-be investors strike out to start their investment careers, the first thing they do is go down to their local bank or broker and shop for the best mortgage rate. And what does that broker or banker typically do? They answer the question the investor asks and the client gets the best rate on a mortgage that the bank can give them on that particular day. But did they get the right investment advice? The truth is, Brian had far more important things to worry about than saving $100 on his next mortgage. To start with, he wasn't clear on the direction he wanted to go. I recognized five minutes into our conversation that although he had a sense of wanting to get involved in buying real estate, he wasn't quite sure of the results he was looking for. To further complicate things, his wife, Michelle, was not entirely on board with his idea to invest in real estate. During our short meeting, I was able to surmise two things:

1. Brian had a strong desire and ability to build a real estate portfolio, but needed more clarity on what that meant.

2. His chances of being successful would be far greater if Michelle was on board, or, at the very least, had the confidence that Brian was not simply spending their hard-earned equity on some "hot-tip" from a friend, but rather following a proper plan of action.

I told Brian about my real estate action plan workshop and explained that if he were truly serious about using real estate to accomplish his goals, it would be in his best interest to attend it with Michelle. "Instead of simply throwing mud against the wall and hoping it sticks, wouldn't it be better to start with a plan? Wouldn't it be better to start with the end result in mind, working your way backwards, identifying your obstacles and then putting a three-phase action plan together to overcome those obstacles and achieve your goal?"

"More important than that," he said, "Michelle would be on board and we could create a plan together. The only concern I have is that it might be hard for me to convince her to spend the money and take the time to attend another workshop."

"Let me ask you a simple question, Brian. Based on what you know right now, how many properties do you think you will need to buy in order to accomplish your goal?"

"I'm not sure, anywhere between five and twenty, it all depends."

"Well, let's just assume that it's five. And let's assume that each purchase is $200,000 on average. That's a million dollars of real estate and likely $800,000 in debt. Do you think it's possible that if you're not clear on what you are doing and you don't have a plan, you could make a mistake that would be far more costly than the cost of a one-day workshop?"

"Good point. We'll be there!"

· · ·

When Brian and Michelle showed up for the workshop, the room was already half full. I hold these workshops all across the country and the sizes can vary, but this particular workshop was designed to be smaller and more intimate to allow for more interaction between my guests and myself. This was perfect for Brian and Michelle. I knew they would get a lot out of the day and I was excited for them. Part of what makes these workshops worthwhile for me is the knowledge that a day like this can change a family's life forever.

Brian was self-employed, having tried his hand at various things over the years, some more successful than others. He had started a small business a few years ago installing kitchen cabinets and doing small-scale home renovations. It had been a struggle to get the business up and running, but once he'd developed a good reputation along with a solid database of referral sources, his income became steady and he was doing quite well. The problem Brian had was that the more business he got, the harder he had to work. Although he could've hired more people, it can get to a point where you have so much overhead that you are working just to keep people employed. Like many small business owners, Brian worked long hours. He knew that due to the physical nature of his job, he didn't want to be working until he was 65. He and Michelle had two young boys, and he struggled between working hard to provide them with a good lifestyle and future, and spending more time with them while they were still young.

Michelle had a good solid job working in government. She did a great job of balancing home and work, but was frustrated by Brian's long hours. And now, on top of everything, he wanted to take on buying real estate. She had trouble seeing where he was going to find the time to fit in creating a real estate business when they were already busy with one business, a full-time job and two young boys who required a full-time taxi driver between school, soccer and hockey.

I knew before we began that, if nothing else, this young couple would spend a valuable day talking and thinking about their future. And as simple as that sounds, how often do you take the time to plan your future. When was the last time you took half a day out of your busy life to truly focus on your future? Sadly, the answer for most Canadians is seldom, if ever. Is it any wonder that most people end up living a life by default? I didn't care if Brian and Michelle ever bought a single piece of real estate. In fact, they may very well decide at the end of the day that real estate investing is not for them, or not something they are prepared to do at this moment in their lives. However, they may well decide that, although it will require more work and more sacrifice up front, and it may mean they need to make adjustments to how they currently have their life structured, it will be worth it in the end. Either way, my goal for Michelle and Brian that day was for them to be honest with themselves and each other so that whatever decision they made, they did so with the knowledge that they were creating their future on purpose, with clarity and with no regrets.

As the room filled up, I knew that both Brian and Michelle would benefit from meeting the other people in the room. Sometimes you have conversations in your head and think you're the only one with these issues or these visions, and then you get into a room with like-minded people and think—hey, my ideas aren't that far-fetched after all. It can be very comforting and reassuring to know that there are others out there who are going through the same struggles that you are. I don't advocate seeking people out simply to have someone to commiserate with, but rather find people who have had similar challenges to you and discover how they overcame them. A room of people such as this should be a source of empowerment and give hope, which is exactly what I had envisioned it would be for Brian and Michelle that day.

This workshop turned out to be a perfect mix of clients. The group ranged from young couples, such as Brian and Michelle who were brand new to the concept of real estate investing, to a retired couple, a single mother and a young man who had just moved to Canada three years ago and had a job working in the oil fields up north in Fort McMurray. We had professionals in the room (one couple were both doctors, originally from India) while others were self-employed. There were even two women there who wanted to form a partnership to buy real estate. They were both married, but their husbands were not involved in this particular venture—this was their own thing. They were friends and wanted to learn how to build a real estate business together. I knew that there was a wide variety of individuals in the room, but I also knew that they were all here for one common reason—they all wanted to create a future on purpose. All of them needed to determine what role real estate could play in that future, and they all needed to find out how they were going to do it. Each individual (even within the couples) had their own unique set of circumstances, but as a group, I knew exactly where they needed to start. They all had to answer one question—*why?*

THE WORKSHOP

"Why are you here today?"

I began the workshop like I always do, and was not surprised as I watched Michelle dart her eyes over to Brian as if to say, "You dragged my butt down here for this?" I almost expected her to shout out, "I don't know Einstein, you tell me," but alas, she didn't, and Brian chose to keep his eyes focused forward, hoping that I'd help answer the question for him. I proceeded to walk the guests through the same process I did with you at the beginning of this book. I shared my concept of living a life on purpose and the importance of starting with the end result in mind. As a group we talked about the real reason they were there—not about investing in real estate, but creating the results that real estate could produce for them—and that, ultimately, it is those results that would create the lifestyle that they wanted. It was at this point that I saw Michelle start to relax, uncross her arms and allow herself to think about what it was she truly wanted in life. And that's where it has to begin—with the end result in mind.

Visualization

"If we all agreed that the reason you're here today is ultimately to create a lifestyle that you desire and real estate is simply the investment vehicle of choice to produce the desired end result, then you will need to start with clarity as to what that end result should look like. So, let's begin by projecting five years into the future and visualizing what life you want to live."

The process of looking into the future is a tricky one. First of all, there is no way of truly knowing what the future holds. Life is capable of throwing a curve ball at you at any point, which can derail the best-laid plans. But that is no excuse for not creating a vision. I learned a long time ago that if I were to sit across from you and ask you where you saw yourself five years from now, it would be very difficult for you to answer; unless of course, you are one of those rare individuals who have already mapped out their future. Sure you'd have a vague sense of what you wanted, but if pressed for details, it would likely be difficult to have clarity. One of the challenges in gaining clarity for your vision is that you seldom, if ever, take the time out of your busy schedule to just sit and think about it. If you're married, when was the last time that you sat down with your spouse (without the children around to interrupt you), poured a glass of wine and had an honest conversation with each other about the future, and where you want to be in the next five years. The truth is, with our busy lives and the pressures of day-to-day life, we may have great intentions, but it is very difficult to do. Something always seems to get in the way. And that's exactly where Brian and Michelle were when we began this exercise. In fact, 99% of the room was in that proverbial boat—and my guess is that you are too.

I'm going to challenge you, just as I challenged the room that morning. Take a minute and let me walk you through a visualization exercise that will help you create more clarity for what you want your future to look like. I consider this exercise one of the most significant parts of the process, if done properly, so take a moment to put this book down and grab a pen and paper. The more effort you put into this exercise, the more useful it will be for you. The results you create from it will form the foundation of more to follow, so take the time to treat it seriously.

Looking around the room that morning, I knew that if I simply asked everyone to think about where they wanted to be in five years, half of the audience would drift off, thinking about work, kids, their dentist appointment, the guy who took their parking spot an hour ago, etc. I had taught long enough to know that just because you are speaking doesn't mean the students are listening. I had to find a way to shut out the noise of the rest of the world (including the noise in their own heads) and get them to become completely focused on being present. Actually, I wanted them to be completely focused on being in the moment—five years from now. As I walk though the following exercise with the room, I want you to put yourself in that room with Brian and Michelle, and allow yourself to create your own vision.

Seeing Your Future

"For the next exercise, I need everyone to be fully engaged. For now, I'm giving you permission to let go of all the thoughts and worries of the world outside these four walls. At this point, you cannot do anything about what is going on out there—so just let it go. Allow yourself the freedom to be present." As I spoke these words, I could see the change in body language around the room. Even Michelle started to relax. "Now I want you to start thinking about your current life. What are you excited about? What do you like about it? What would you like to change (if anything)? Do you have children? If so, how old are they today? All other things being equal, what would you like your life to be like five years from now? How old will you be? How old will your children be?"

I could see heads slowly start to nod as everyone in the room shifted their focus to the questions and started to envision their futures.

"Now close your eyes and picture yourself waking up in the morning—five years from now. What year is it? It's 8:30 a.m. on a Tuesday morning. You get up, get dressed and make your way downstairs to the kitchen. You walk over to the kitchen counter and pour yourself a fresh cup of coffee. See yourself pouring the coffee . . . look down at your coffee mug and breathe in the fresh aroma. Take a sip then a deep breath, and say to yourself, 'Wow! This is it. Five years ago I sat down and created a five-year plan for myself and my family, and here I am. I am in the place where I always wanted to be. I'm living the life that I always wanted to live. This is the house that I've always wanted to be in, and my family is growing up in the neighbourhood where I always wanted to raise my children . . . this is it. Five years ago I created a vision and now I am living that vision.'"

As I scanned the room, I couldn't help but notice the different looks on everyone's face as they sat there, eyes closed, visualizing their futures. Some did look confused, but for most, you could start to see the formation of smiles spread across their faces as they slowly began to allow themselves the freedom to dream and visualize their future.

"Now picture yourself walking to the back door. You open it up and walk outside. Take another sip of coffee and then take a deep breath of fresh air as you lift your head and look around. What do you see? Look to the left and take in your surroundings, then slowly pan to the right and start to grasp where it is that you are. Take in all the sights and smells, the colours, the sounds. Take the time to truly be in this moment and be as detailed as you can. And as it dawns on you that this is your life five years from now, think to yourself, 'Wow, this feels awesome. I absolutely love being here. This is exactly what I always wanted to create.'

"Take another deep breath, have another sip of your coffee and then turn around and walk back into your kitchen. What does that look like to you? Is it different from what you currently have? Has anything changed?

"As you take in your surroundings and begin to fully realize what you've created, look down at your watch and recognize it is now 9:00 a.m. What happens next?

- Do you have to slam down that cup of coffee because you're late for work and have to rush off?
- Was that part of the vision?
- If not, what *are* you going to do today?
- What do you do for work?
- What do you do to make money?
- What do you do for fun?
- Who do you surround yourself with?
- What's your home environment like?
- What kind of car do you have in the garage?
- What's important to you today?

"As you start to think more and more about the future you are currently creating, what else comes to mind?

- Has your health changed?
- Are there charities that you are able to help?
- What's really important to you?
- What opportunities are you able to provide for your children today that you were not able to provide before?
- What are you able to do for your parents and family members today that you were not able to do before?

"As you start to grasp a vision for your future, finish this sentence: The biggest thing that's changed in the last five years is _____

_____."

I then asked the room to open their eyes and write down their vision. It was amazing to see the transformation in the room. Some people were so into the exercise that they didn't want to come back. Barb, one of the two ladies who were forming a partnership, is a Type A personality and found the whole exercise rather frustrating. She wanted to get to the numbers and didn't see the purpose behind everyone closing their eyes and creating visions. "I already know what I want," she stated emphatically.

"Well, thanks for being patient with the exercise. Now, take the time to write down what that is," I responded.

What was interesting was to see how the couples reacted when I asked them to write down their visions. Some of them had a very clear picture and started to write furiously. Others were looking at each other as if to say, "You go first," as they peered over at each other's papers, much like schoolchildren cheating on an exam. One older gentleman appeared to have writer's block and couldn't get started. Eventually, after some poking and prodding, everyone, even Barb, was busy writing out their vision.

What's Your Vision?

I'd like you to do the same thing. Now I know from personal experience that a large percentage of people reading this right now (mostly the men) will make a mental note, "Yes, I'll do that later. Right now I want to finish this chapter." Well, you and I both know that "later" seldom happens. Do yourself a favour and take the time to do it now. In fact, I'm even going to give you some space right here in this book to write it out. If you don't want to write in the book in case you lend it to a friend, then go grab a pen and paper and start writing.

Having trouble coming up with what to write down? Here are a few pointers:

- Avoid judging yourself and editing your vision—you can do that later.
- Let the ideas flow naturally.
- Don't edit your ideas based on what you think is realistic—we can decide what's realistic or not later.
- Effective visualization involves all of your senses—sight, sound, touch, smell and taste.

- Think about all of the non-physical conditions or circumstances.
- Put feelings and emotions into what you are doing.
- Stay positive.
- Include the non-material aspects of your ideal lifestyle—family, charities, health, etc.

Note: This is not a one-time exercise! Visualize your lifestyle often to reinforce or alter your goals and plans.

Exercise: Write out the visualization of the lifestyle you'd like to be living five years from today.

For example, start with the view you saw when you opened the door to your deck.

_____

_____

_____

_____

_____

_____

_____

_____

_____

_____

_____

_____

_____

_____

_____

_____

_____

_____

Now answer this question: The biggest thing that's changed in my life in the last five years is . . . ?

_____

_____

_____

_____

_____

_____

_____

_____

_____

_____

Note: Go to www.peterkinch.com to download copies of these worksheets to work on.

As the exercise at the workshop began wrapping up, I observed that conversations were starting up, especially among the couples in the room. The most interesting comment was from Nicole, a teacher. She was attending with her husband Marc, who worked in health care. "I never knew you wanted that." I heard her say as she leaned over his paper reading what he had written. They were not alone. A lot of other couples in the room, including Brian and Michelle, were having the same conversations and learning things about their spouse they didn't know before. The truth was, for most of them this was the first time anyone had given them the opportunity to really explore and visualize their futures, and for some couples, what their partner had written down surprised them.

We took the time to explore what they had learned. For some people, the view they saw from their back door off the deck was crystal clear. For others, less so. Nicole made the comment that when she opened her eyes, she had conflicting visions. She'd see one home and landscape, and then suddenly another came into her head. Marc suggested to her that the second vision was their summer home. For many in the room, the exercise was an awakening. They had allowed themselves the freedom to really explore. Sean and Candice, a young professional couple, saw a life of financial freedom complete with world travel and international vacation homes.

John and Liz, an older couple close to retirement, already lived in their dream home and had no reason to change where they lived or how they lived. The future they saw included looking after their grandchildren and creating a legacy. Liz envisioned being able to devote more time and money to her favourite charity. Ryan, a young single guy, was flying his own jet. Shelley, a single mother, saw a future where she wasn't controlled by money and was able to make decisions for herself and her children on her own terms—not her boss's. Jasmine and Gill, two doctors, saw a future with enough money to fund a foundation that would help a certain type of gifted child with a unique disorder. When I asked them about this, they explained to me that their son was very gifted and quite intelligent, but he had been born with a certain disorder that made it very challenging for him within the public school system. In spite of his extremely high IQ, he was looked upon as stupid in school. They wanted to create a foundation to work with children like him—both in Canada and back home in their native India. They explained to me that by helping them to achieve this plan, I was, in my own way, helping each of those children. I can't tell you how much that moved me and made me want to do whatever I could to help them.

Not all of the visions were on that same scale. Nicole and Marc simply wanted to find a way to supplement the pensions they would receive from the school board and the hospital. Barb and Kathy were forming a partnership to buy real estate, so they each had to write down a vision or goal. Although they each had their own goal for their family, I also encouraged them to write down a vision and goal for their partnership. If you are building your real estate business with a partner who is not your spouse, it is important to remember that the results from your real estate investments have to serve both parties. It is critical to be clear on your expectations before you enter into a partnership with someone, in order to avoid conflict in the future.

And as for Brian and Michelle, well that was truly interesting. Brian had written many things down. It was clear he had some pent-up ideas for his future that needed to come out. He just needed permission to be allowed to set his visions free. In fact, he had some very aggressive goals. Michelle, on the other hand, had a more difficult time with this exercise. She couldn't move past thinking about what was realistic. "I'm just not the type of person who can create some fantasy without seeing how it's going to happen. I just don't see how we're suddenly going to start buying all of this real estate and become millionaires overnight. Not unless we win the lotto." I knew exactly where Michelle was coming from and, in fact, she had good reason to be skeptical. Brian had been guilty of chasing after a few rainbows in his life and, in Michelle's mind, he was still looking for that illusive pot of gold. But so far, all the hot stock tips and business ventures seemed to be more like black holes that sucked in their savings. Now all they had left was the equity in their house and Michelle was going to make darn sure that didn't get squandered as well.

If you are married or in a long-term relationship and have just finished this exercise, I strongly encourage you to sit down with your spouse or partner and share what you have written, asking for his or her feedback. You may be pleasantly surprised by the results of your conversation.

Before moving on, ask yourself the following questions: When you went through the visualization process, what was the biggest thing that had changed for you in five years? Were you surprised by this?

BOX SEATS FOR HOCKEY

I remember going through this exercise with Stephen, a young man from Calgary. When I asked him what his goal was, he told me, "My goal is to have box seats at all the NHL rinks across Canada—Vancouver, Calgary, Edmonton, Ottawa, Toronto, Montreal!"

I didn't say it out loud, but I thought to myself that this was kind of silly. He couldn't possibly attend all those games. In my mind, it was simply an excessive goal, but I was curious, so I asked Stephen why he wanted this.

"When I grew up, we didn't have a lot of money so I could never go to see the Canucks or the Flames and I remember always wanting to be able to see a live NHL game. What I would like to do is to have box seats and enough money so I can work with inner-city kids or children who are underprivileged. I'd like to set up a charity foundation to fill those seats every night with underprivileged children who would otherwise never have an opportunity to watch a live game."

I was impressed, "Wow, okay, that's cool." I told Stephen I would be happy to work with him to help accomplish his goal. A goal like that gets me excited and I was ready to jump on his bandwagon. One of the most fulfilling things I hear when travelling across the country and working with investors is their different visions and goals. I love finding out what people want to accomplish and why. I know that if I can help them to create and finance their real estate portfolio, which in turn will finance their goals, then, in a small way I'm part of the process that achieves those goals. And that gives me, my staff and our PK-Approved partners a greater sense of purpose in our business. Helping you to accomplish your goal gives us a chance to positively impact this world.

Your dreams and goals don't have to be grandiose or materialistic. You could simply be a couple who have done the math and figured out that, at the current rate, you won't be able to retire in the lifestyle you want. Your goal could be something simple—such as the need to look after your parents or a family member. In fact, the one thing that constantly amazes me while conducting these workshops is the number of dreams and goals that involve families and charities or something that isn't related to a person's own material well-being. When people focus on doing something for others, making more money simply becomes a by-product—not their focus.

At this stage in the planning process, I need to make a disclaimer. It is perfectly fine to set a goal for yourself and to have a vision. I obviously believe this or I wouldn't be teaching it. But it would be irresponsible of me if I didn't take the time to remind you that this is going to be a journey, and along the way there will be bumps in the road. Don't become so focused on achieving the goal that you forget to enjoy the journey in the process. Don't wait until you reach your destination to start looking after your health. Who cares how much money you make if you drop dead of a heart attack in the process? And remember, your nine-year-old son doesn't want to wait five years before Dad has the time to play catch. By the time you've accomplished your "goal," your son won't care about playing catch anymore. This is not to say that you have to live every day in balance. In fact, I think that in order to accomplish something great, you will definitely be out of balance for a short period. But the key is to do this in spurts—each time with an end result in mind and always maintaining your health.

A Tip for Reaching Your Goal

In 2009, I was awarded the top volume-producing mortgage broker of the year award. In the same year, I also won coach of the year for coaching my son's hockey team. I also found the time to write this book and create a new business venture. How? I worked in spurts. During hockey season, I really focused on not taking on any extra projects and minimized my travel so that I could focus on being there for my family and kids. In the spring, I sat them down and told them, "Dad is going to be doing a lot of travel over the next few months, but this is part of the reason we're able to do certain things." I had a crazy spring (and an amazingly wonderful and understanding wife) and then created time in my schedule to make sure we had a great summer as a family. I strategically chose to be completely out of balance that spring, but because it was on purpose and my family knew that there was a beginning and an end to my very long hours, they were fine with it. Yes, there were a few ball games that were missed as well as the odd dance recital, and we had to practice some delayed gratification along the way, but I (and my family) decided that the ends justified the means. I know that the future I am creating for my family will require a little sacrifice along the way, but the emphasis is "a little" and your health should never be, and doesn't have to be, part of that equation.

At the end of the day, your vision, the goal you have just created, is what it is all about. It is the reason you want to buy real estate. This is the "result" that you need to create. In the next chapter we'll take this a step further.

THE IMPORTANCE OF WRITING DOWN YOUR GOALS

A study at Yale University asked the graduating class to write down their goals. Only 3% of them actually wrote their goals. What was amazing, when they went back 20 years later and did an analysis of the net worth and income of the graduating class, the 3% who had written down their goals had accomplished more of their goals and had a higher cumulative net worth than the remaining 97% combined. A similar study was conducted at Harvard with similar results. That is the power of the written goal!

Chapter 3

What Will You Need to Support Your Lifestyle?

At this point in the workshop, everyone in the room had completed the visualization exercise and, for the most part, had a much stronger vision of what they wanted their life to look like in five years. As simple as it was, for some, this visualization exercise was a major breakthrough. There were a few couples who had never sat down together and done this before, and they could have left the workshop then and gone home happy. For Brian and Michelle, it was a major breakthrough. They still weren't on the same page, but at least they now knew what the other had written down.

"When we started the day, we all agreed that it wasn't real estate you wanted so much as the results real estate can create," I reminded them. "The exercise you just completed allows you to begin with the end result in mind. You now have a clear vision as to *why* you are investing in real estate. The next question is how much?"

"You should all have a much clearer picture of how you want to live your life five years from now," I stated, beginning the next section of the workshop. "But having a vision of your future is only one part of the equation. If we stop right there and do nothing else, then all you have created is a fantasy. The key now is to dig a little deeper and find out what it would cost to live the life you just described. The difference between a fantasy and a goal is a plan." I could see some of the men in the room begin to look a little uneasy—they wanted to return to the vision exercise. "You may recall earlier that I told you there is no such thing as a realistic or unrealistic goal. But what can be realistic or unrealistic is your willingness to do what it would take to accomplish that goal. In this next section we're going to find out exactly what it would take to achieve your goal."

At this point, I challenged everyone in the room to take a look at the goals they had written out in the previous exercise and determine how much it would cost to live the life they just described.

"If you were to live the life you just drafted out on paper, how much money would you need on a monthly basis to live that life?" At this point, I had to lay some ground rules for people like Michelle and Barb. If I simply asked that question and left them to their own devices, a person like Michelle would sit there and try to figure out how much money she currently had and how much she was likely to have five years from now, and then calculate how much she would reasonably need based on what's realistic.

Barb, on the other hand, already had her calculator out and was factoring how many properties she thought she was going to have and, therefore, how much money she's going to be making or needing to make.

That wasn't the point of the exercise, so I needed to come up with a way to get everyone to focus on how much money they would need, on a monthly basis, to live the life they had just described.

"Imagine that you just won the 'Set for Life' lottery and they are going to pay you a set amount every month for the rest of your life. You do not have a job and you don't own any real estate. The only source of income you will have is from the lottery. Here's the catch—they will determine the amount of your winnings based on what you wrote down on the previous page. If this were the criteria, how much would you need monthly to live the life you described in the previous chapter?"

Nicole raised her hand and asked, "Do I still have a mortgage on my house?"

"I don't know; it's your vision. Do you? The key to this exercise is to be as honest with yourself as possible and be as consistent as possible with what you wrote." I stated.

I saw Ryan scratching his head. "What if I don't know some of the numbers? I mean, it's hard to know what things are going to cost five years from now."

"Don't worry about that, simply try your best to be as accurate as possible, but if you have to, for the purposes of this exercise, guess and then make it a homework assignment to look into the actual costs. I should also note that this number is intended to be after taxes and in today's money. It will be far too difficult to try to index this amount to inflation or determine your tax bracket five years from now, so let's just work off a net number in today's dollars."

I was pleased to see Michelle reach over and grab the calculator away from Brian and start to crunch some numbers. Then I noticed the conversation at that table started to get a little heated. "There's no way we need that much money, that's unrealistic."

"Michelle, you're supposed to stretch yourself and come up with a number for your ultimate lifestyle."

"Yes, but not a fantasy number."

At this point I stepped in and suggested that they develop two parallel plans with two sets of numbers—one would be Brian's "stretch target" and the other would be Michelle's "realistic target." This seemed to work for the two of them.

Now it's your turn. Complete the following exercise.

ALL THINGS BEING EQUAL

Exercise: How much money will you need to be able to live and maintain your chosen lifestyle five years from now?

Here are some tips:

1. Be as accurate as you can with what you write. Remember to count everything that's in your vision and calculate the cost for everything.

2. It's all about being real. Everything else that follows will be based on this number, so the more accurate you can be the better.

3. You may or may not have paid off all your debts or you may be carrying a mortgage, so include these in your calculation.

4. Take into account all of your normal expenses plus those that occur from your new lifestyle changes.

_____

_____

_____

_____

_____

A. Total: $_____ monthly income required to achieve personal goals.

"Now that you know how much money you will likely need to live the life you want to live, the next step is to look back at your written vision and ask yourself, 'What will I be doing for work five years from now?' The next number to calculate is how much money you will be earning from a job or non–real estate–related business five years from now."

Whenever I do this exercise, I invariably have to challenge some people to be consistent. This time it was Ryan. "Hey Ryan, I noticed that you put down $3,000 a month from employment income five years from now."

"Yeah, I figure that's probably what my current job will be paying me." Now having had the opportunity earlier to walk around and look over some of their visions, I reminded Ryan, "Correct me if I'm wrong, but wasn't quitting your job part of your earlier vision?"

"Oh, that's right. I forgot about that. So what do I put down if I plan to be a full-time real estate investor five years from now?"

"If that's your sole source of income, then in this section you would put zero," I explained.

Remember, it makes no difference to me whether you keep your job or not, I just want you to be accurate and consistent. For those of you who are planning to use real estate as your sole source of income, it is important to become very clear on what that will involve. For the record, I am not an advocate of quitting your day job to buy real estate—but we'll talk about that when we get to the section on obstacles.

Exercise: How much money will you probably be earning from your job or business five years from now?

Some tips:

1. Remember, it is five years from now, so what are you going to be doing for a job or business in five years?

2. Do not count real estate in this figure.

3. If your vision stated you did not have a job five years from now, then don't put down any income from a job.

4. This number cannot be higher than the first number (A Total).

_____

_____

_____

_____

B. Total: $_____ monthly income from job/non-real estate business.

Note: If you are just starting up a new business and have allotted a certain amount of monthly income in your plan, then you should have a separate business plan and cash flow analysis for that business.

As I walked around the room, I came to Jeff, who had just started up a new business and noticed another common error that happens when doing this exercise. Jeff's B total was higher than his A total. "Jeff, how can you expect to make more money from your job or business five years from now, than the amount you would need to live the ultimate life you want to live?"

"Well, I'm really excited about this new business I just started and I think this number is realistic."

"That's fine," I replied. "I believe you. I'm just challenging you on whether you were possibly a little too conservative on the previous number, or you didn't understand the question. It is impossible for the second number to be higher than the first. If it is, then you have to start dreaming bigger." Once he realized his mistake we both had a chuckle and moved on.

"Now that you know how much money you will need to live the life you want to live and you know how much you plan or hope to earn from your job or business, the last source of potential revenue we want to look at is non-real estate investments. These would include, but are not limited to, income trusts, stocks, bonds, mutual funds, etc., but would not include RRSPs, unless you plan to retire within the next five years.

"Personally, I believe in diversifying your portfolio, so it may well be a good thing to have other investments in the mix, but if you currently don't have any stocks or bonds, and you have made the commitment to build a real estate portfolio, then I wouldn't recommend running out and buying some now."

I have learned to look for certain inconsistencies when I walk around the room, in what people write down. And sure enough, I noticed Chad had put down $2,000 a month in the investment category. But when I asked him how much he owned right now, he told me, "None right now, but I have some excess cash, and I really think oil is set for another spike in prices."

"Well, that's fine Chad, but let's think about it. In order to get $2,000 a month in revenue, you would need an initial cash investment of $240,000, generating a 10% annual return. Once you've spent the $240,000, how much money do you have left over to buy real estate?"

"Not much," he said, rather embarrassed.

Again, I'm not telling you that you should buy real estate and not invest in something else. I'm simply challenging you to be consistent.

Exercise: How much money will you be earning from non–real estate investments?

Here are tips to follow:

1. Remember, earnings from non–real estate investments can be in many different forms, such as income trusts, stocks, bonds, and mutual funds.

2. Do not calculate retirement or pension (RRSP) money, unless you are qualified to receive it.

3. If you have some money to invest in the stock market, is that the money you were planning to invest in real estate?

_____

_____

_____

_____

_____

C. Total: $_____ monthly income from non-real estate investments.

"Now that you have created three sets of numbers, let's do some simple math. Add B and C together and subtract that total from A. Don't worry, it's easier than it sounds. You're simply taking the amount of money you think you will need five years from now to live the life you want to live, and subtracting the amount of money you expect to be earning from your job or non-real estate investments."

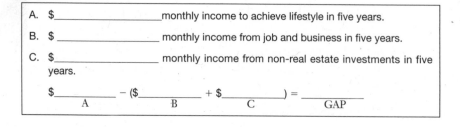

A. $_____ monthly income to achieve lifestyle in five years.

B. $_____ monthly income from job and business in five years.

C. $_____ monthly income from non-real estate investments in five years.

$_____ − ($_____ + $_____) = _____
  A   B   C   GAP

THE GAP

"The number you just came up with is what I refer to as "the gap." The gap is the difference between what you need to live your ultimate life and the amount of money you are likely to be earning five years from now."

As soon as I said this, I could see all the Type A personalities in the room (you know who you are) roll their eyes and think, "This sure isn't rocket science. I can see why he taught English, not Math."

And you know what? It's true—it is simple math. In fact, the beauty is in its simplicity. Napoleon Hill once said, "All great truths are simple in final analysis, and easily understood; if they are not, they are not great truths." My goal is not to reveal something new or earth shattering to you, but to guide you though a process whereby you discover simple truths about yourself. Yes, the above exercise was incredibly simple, but what you may not realize is that you just discovered why real estate is important to you. You just discovered what role real estate has to play in your financial future. And for some of you, that was a revelation.

Assuming that you had a gap (there are about 1% of you who don't), you now need to figure out one of two things:

1. Find a way to fill the gap; or

2. Change your goal.

I suggest we figure out the former.

"I'm going to make a few assumptions about everyone in this room. One, I'm going to assume that everyone had a gap. Two, I'm going to assume that you are choosing to find a way to fill that gap as opposed to giving up on your goal." At this point, I saw Nicole lean over to talk to Marc, but it didn't look like he was too willing to pull out the eraser just yet.

"The third assumption I'm going to make is that you have chosen real estate as your investment vehicle of choice to overcome the shortfall and fill the gap. Now again, I know the math is simple, but whether you realize it or not, you have just defined what real estate has to produce for you." I could see that the majority of the room was starting to get it.

"Let me give you a hypothetical example—these are simply hypothetical numbers I'm using for illustration purposes, don't copy them down. You need to use your own numbers. Let's say, for example, that I need $10,000 to live the life I described in the first exercise. I plan to still be working five years from now, although maybe not as much as now, so I expect to be earning $5,000 a month. I've created a few non-real estate investments that should be earning $1,000 a month by then, so I'll have a total income of $6,000 a month five years from now. Since I need $10,000 to live the life I want to live, my gap will be $4,000."

THE GAP—A HYPOTHETICAL EXAMPLE

1. I require $10,000 a month to achieve my personal goals.

2. I will generate $5,000 a month from my business.

3. I have been investing money regularly, so my income trusts will probably be about $1,000 a month.

Since my vision requires $10,000, but my income only totals $6,000, I have a $4,000 gap.

At this point in the workshop, everyone had discovered their gap. Granted, some were larger than others, but even Michelle had loosened up enough to allow herself to see a future for her family which she might not otherwise have seen before. I could tell by the look on her face that she was starting to think, "What if . . . ?" The best part was that by working through this simple exercise, she had not only created a vision and a goal, but had attached a dollar amount to it. Not as much as Brian's vision, but an amount nonetheless. And although the vision would cost more than the amount she and Brian were likely to be earning five years from now, she was beginning to see that if they did invest in real estate and that investment produced the results necessary to fill the gap, then maybe, just maybe, she'd be willing to consider coming on board. The day was still young.

It was interesting for me to look at all the different gap figures. There was quite a range. As was typical in these workshops, Chad and Ryan had the largest gaps. I learned a long time ago not to judge these numbers, no matter how fantastical I thought they were. After all, who am I to judge or say that you can or cannot do something? In fact, the exact opposite is true; I've never had a client's goal, no matter how aggressive, that I have not been able to map out a plan for. Remember, the goal cannot be realistic or unrealistic—it's a question of whether you are willing to do what it takes to make it happen.

Chad needed $30,000 a month to fill his gap. Ryan was not far behind with a gap of $25,000 (jet planes are expensive). Jasmine and Gill had a large gap, but they also had large incomes to replace, since part of their vision included stepping away from their medical practice to devote more time to their charity. Jeff was starting a new business and Linda wanted to be working at their real estate business full time, so their gap needed to replace her income. Shelley, the single mom, had what I would call a very manageable goal. Her gap was $3,000 a month, an amount that would allow her to quit her job if she wanted to, but more importantly, she would be in a position to provide for her children on her own terms. Nicole and Marc simply wanted to make enough to supplement their pensions, so they actually changed to a 15-year goal. It was very conservative, but one that they knew would be manageable with their lifestyle and consistent with their family values.

John and Liz struggled with the whole thing. As I walked over to chat with them, they were concerned that they didn't have much of a gap. They live a very good life—they have the home of their dreams, they are sitting on a large amount of equity and with the pension John will start receiving in a year, they don't have a large need for more revenue. So I took a few minutes to dig a little deeper and look at the vision they had created in the first exercise. Not surprisingly, it revolved around their children, grandchildren and Liz's charity. We talked about the need to create income to fund the charity, but also the ability and desire to create a financial legacy that could be passed on to future generations. John wanted to know that his grandchildren would have something to inherit. I explained to them that this was perfect. "You've just identified what purpose real estate has to provide for you. In fact, you're the type of person I have the most concern for."

"Why's that?" John inquired.

"Because the more money you have, the more important it is to be very clear on the results you need from your investments. Otherwise, you are vulnerable to making poor investment decisions based on what someone else believes is a good deal. I worry about you more than Shelley. She can't afford to make a poor decision, you can. But don't worry," I assured them. "I'll be covering all of this in the next section."

"Whether you realize it or not, what you've just done is identify why real estate is important to you and, more specifically, what results you need real estate to produce for you—it has to fill your gap," I announced to the room. "Again, assuming you had a gap figure, another important item you have identified is that your real estate must produce a positive cash flow in five years in order to fill that gap. I know this sounds obvious, but let me explain to you why I spend so much time focusing on something that seems so obvious. The fact you are in this room today would indicate that you are, or want to become, a sophisticated investor, but statistics show that for many Canadians, their definition of being a real estate investor involves buying a 'pre-sale' condo and hoping they can flip the paper before they have to take possession. Or perhaps they think being an investor means buying a recreational property up at the lake. Or maybe it is the person who lives in Vancouver who bought another house in Vancouver because it was close to their home and they were comfortable managing it themselves, even though it was very expensive and it will not generate any cash flow for a very long time. Or it's the individual who bought a piece of raw land on Vancouver Island because it had 'great upside potential' for future redevelopment.

"None of these are 'bad' purchases. I simply question whether they were decisions made with an end goal in mind. Or, were they simply random purchases because the person knew buying real estate was a good thing to do. The point I'm trying to make is, don't underestimate the power of knowing what results you need from your real estate. Now that you have a clear vision of what your end result or goal is, and you have a better understanding of what role real estate has to play in accomplishing that end result, you will be far less susceptible to being 'sold' something because someone told you it was a good deal."

I like to tell the following story at my workshops, because I think it really illustrates this point.

A GOOD DEAL AT THE HARDWARE STORE

A guy goes to the hardware store looking for a drill. He meets the salesperson who starts telling him, "Did you know our power saws are on sale for half price? Boy, look at the bells and whistles on this puppy. It dices and slices, it's the best thing since sliced . . ." Well, you get the idea. The guy gets caught up in the power saw, which is on sale for half price, and he can't imagine passing up such a great deal. So, he ends up buying the power saw and goes home.

When he gets home, he realizes that he had completely forgotten why he went to the hardware store in the first place. What he needed in the first place was to make a hole in his wall. The drill was simply the tool he needed to accomplish the end result—to put a hole in the wall to complete his project. He forgot his purpose in going to the hardware store, and got sold on a good deal for something he didn't really need. More importantly, he bought something that didn't allow him to accomplish his end result. Now theoretically, a power saw could still make a hole in the wall, but here's the question: Was the power saw a good deal or a bad deal?

It is neither. What makes something a good deal or bad deal is determined by its ability to create the results you need to accomplish your goal. The question should not be whether it's a good or bad deal—the question is: Will this help me achieve my goal?

If you forget your purpose, you can be sold anything!

How many people do you know who have fallen victim to sales pitches under the pretense of a 'good deal'?

If you are not clear on what real estate has to accomplish for you, if you don't know what your purpose is behind building a real estate portfolio— what your gap is—then how will you ever know what represents a good deal or bad deal for you?

IF YOU FORGET YOUR PURPOSE, YOU CAN BE SOLD ANYTHING!

"So, was the power saw a good deal or a bad deal?" I asked the class.

"It was a good deal for a power saw," Jeff chimed in.

"But it wasn't what he needed," Shelley stated. "So it doesn't matter how good the deal was, if it didn't help him accomplish his goal." I knew right then that Shelley "got it." I had realized when I met her earlier in the morning, that if she got it she would run with it. The thing about single moms is, they simply don't have the time or luxury to mess around trying something out. They are driven by results (most often) and when you get a woman like Shelley who zeros in on what she wants, watch out. This was the first time Shelley had said anything all morning, so I knew that a light bulb had just gone off.

"Shelley's bang on. It doesn't matter how good the deal is, if it doesn't help you accomplish your goal. That's the whole point. By doing that simple gap exercise, you all now know your goal. You know exactly what real estate has to do for you, so you should never fall victim to a sales pitch. The next time you hear someone tell you 'this is an amazing deal,' simply ask yourself: For who? Amazing for me—or you? The more clarity you have on what real estate has to produce for you, the more you'll be able to determine if it's a good or bad deal for you. And like I said to John and Liz earlier, the more disposable income or funds you have available, the more vulnerable you are to someone else telling you what is or is not a good deal. It is critical that you develop this filter for yourself. Remember, you're either moving closer to, or further away from, your goals. You are never standing still.

"I'll share one last story that really illustrates this. One of the most common questions I get is: 'Peter, I'm thinking of buying this . . . Do you think it's a good deal for me?' To which I always answer, 'I have no idea—I don't know your goals.' The best example I had of this was on a trip to Calgary a number of years ago. I was meeting with two separate couples. The first couple wanted to get my opinion on a piece of property they were looking at on Vancouver Island. The property was 10 acres of raw land, which had great long-term potential for rezoning and could eventually be developed into a sub-division. They were an older couple who were getting close to retirement. They owned their own business and were in the process of selling it. As it happens, the company that was planning to buy their business had offered them a very sweet deal to stay on as management consultants for a healthy sum of money over the next 10 years. In fact, when we did their gap analysis, the amount of money they needed was the same amount that they were going to be receiving as a management fee. So, their gap target was zero.

"Naturally, I asked them, 'Well if your gap is zero, what role does real estate have to play for you? What results do you need from your real estate investments?' I'll never forget their answer. 'We want to create a legacy for our children and grandchildren. We want to make investments today that will increase our net worth and position us to be able to transfer wealth to the next generation. We don't need it to create cash flow today.'

"Wow, what a great vision. Now let me ask you a question. What are some things about raw land that might make it a poor investment decision for most people?"

Jeff was quick to jump in. "They're not easy to finance; you have to put more money down and you have zero cash flow until you convert it into something else."

"Sounds like the voice of experience, Jeff?" I asked.

"Oh yeah."

"Jeff's absolutely right. Now, knowing what you know about this couple from Calgary, would you say that this is a good investment or a poor one?"

"Potentially, it's a good one," Sean said. "They don't need the cash flow today and it has the upside potential to meet their long-term goal of creating a legacy for their children."

"That's right. Now we don't know anything about the actual deal, but on the surface, it would appear to be consistent with their goals. So that is the first filter you use when analyzing any deal—is it consistent with my goals. Now, could we have answered that question without knowing their goals? No, of course not.

"Later that same day, I met with a younger couple. Their goal was to create enough positive cash flow from their real estate investments so that Joey could retire. Joey made $5,000 a month at the time, so obviously their gap target was to earn at least that much from real estate in five years so that Joey could have the option to walk away from his job. Would the same piece of property on Vancouver Island make sense for them?"

Fortunately, the response from the group was a resounding "no," and I knew that they were all starting to "get it."

"What about flips? Where do they fit in?" Ryan queried.

"Well, here are two things about flips. First of all, I'm not a big fan of them, because they tend to be more appropriate for people with a short-term mentality, and it's just a matter of time before you get burned. But, if you know what you are doing and have a skill set, like Brian here, to add legitimate value to a property, then buying, renovating and flipping a property can be a good way to build up more capital. However, you still are not addressing your gap target. And Ryan, I've looked at your numbers. Somewhere along the way you will need to have long-term buy and hold properties to achieve your target.

On that note, let's take a short coffee break."

Chapter 4

How Much Real Estate Will You Need to Buy to Reach Your Goal?

The break gave everyone a chance to mingle and share war stories. I could see Jeff and Linda talking to Brian and Michelle about some of the properties they had bought previously, and how not having a proper plan almost created a disaster. I overheard Michelle saying that she could now see that buying real estate with this kind of approach was totally different from anything she had read about or heard of from her friends. At that point, Candice came up to me and commented, "I can see where having your gap figure before you start buying makes sense now. A friend of mine bought two pre-sale condos in downtown Toronto, but wasn't able to flip them before closing. She is now carrying both of them, but can't get enough rent to cover the payments and they are costing her over $600 a month."

"Yes, and if your gap target was $2,000 a month, how many condos losing $600 a month do you need to reach $2,000?" I said, tongue-in-cheek.

"It sure puts it into perspective. If you're aware of your gap target at the beginning, you would never get yourself into those situations in the first place," she surmised.

"I'm glad you get it, Candice. Just remember that unfortunately, you still represent a small percentage of the population. There are a lot of people out there making poor investment decisions every day."

As I turned away from Candice, I bumped into Dr. Gill almost spilling my coffee on him. "Peter, can I ask you a quick question about using the equity in my home to buy investments?" he asked.

"I'll be covering that a little later, so why don't we round everyone up and get started on the next section." I knew we had a lot to cover and I wanted to get right back to it.

CAUSE AND EFFECT

"Well, now that we've had a short break, let's take a moment to go over what we've covered so far. You will recall that we started the morning by deciding that the single most important place to start is with the end in mind. Our goal today was to identify the life we want to live five years from now, then determine how much cash flow we would need in order to live that life, which would, in turn, determine the type and nature of investments that we would need in order to create that cash flow. That, in turn, would lead us back to the obstacles we face today. In the second part of this workshop, we will create individual business plans to help you overcome those obstacles.

"Each of you took the time to visualize your ideal lifestyle. You then identified the amount of money that would be needed, all things being equal, to live that life. The next exercise identified the gap target—the amount of money that is needed to bridge the gap for you to achieve your goals. The next step is to determine how you are going to use real estate to bridge that gap. It's actually quite exciting when you think about it. You now know how much money you will need to live your ideal lifestyle, so the next step is to take a look at how much real estate you need to buy to make that happen."

"Actually, it can be quite depressing," Linda chimed in. "Now that I know how much I want to make, I don't see how I'm going to be able to buy enough real estate to make it happen."

"That's why you're making a business plan today," I reassured her.

The truth is, Linda's, or for that matter, anyone's plan or goal may be more aggressive than their willingness to make it happen. But, I would rather see them build a plan that works towards tangible results, than not have any plan at all and, five years from now, be disappointed with their results.

As I went through my introduction, I could tell by the look on the faces around the room that most of them were starting to piece the puzzle together. It was now time to move things along and shift the focus to real estate.

"As you can tell by now, a major theme you'll be hearing all day long is 'why?' Why are you buying real estate? What is your purpose for buying real estate? What results do you need your real estate to produce for you?" My goal was to get everyone thinking about the results they needed from their real estate.

"Real estate produces one of two things—*cash flow* or *capital appreciation.* Ideally, you get both, but not always. For some of you in this room, the goal is to increase your net worth by creating 'equity,' in which case your focus may be different than those of you who are dependent on cash flow to finance your goals. One client I had wanted to build up a certain amount of equity and then liquidate the properties in five years, taking the cash and re-investing it in secure funds on which to retire. If that's your vision, then how much equity will you require in five years?"

"How many of you have bought something in downtown Vancouver, Calgary or Toronto this past year?" I queried. A few hands shot up, some enthusiastically, others less so. "Are you getting positive cash flow?"

"I will be," Linda stated with a sense of dogged determination.

"Well, a lot of people have purchased pre-sale condos on the premise that they could flip the paper or that they will simply keep going up in price, and now they're saddled with a negative cash-flow property, which is something Candice and I were talking about on the break.

"One of the most important concepts I teach is 'cause and effect.' My daughter is a great example of this. She always fights putting on her jacket to go outside—I'm sure my daughter is unique and none of you have children like this. And sure enough, what happens? She gets cold and complains because she doesn't have her jacket. Eventually, the consequence becomes the teacher and she learns there is a cause and effect—if I don't wear my jacket I will get cold. Your real estate decisions are no different. 'I'm thinking of doing such and such . . . well, that will impact this.' It's critical that we learn to analyze the consequences of our actions. Every action has a reaction. Every decision you make in real estate will have a consequence. To be successful you simply need to analyze the 'cause and effect' of your decision-making process. Before you make your next investment, simply ask yourself, 'How does this decision impact my overall plan and portfolio?' I like to think of this in terms of playing chess."

The puzzled looks returned to many faces, especially the Type A people who were wondering what real estate had to do with playing chess.

"How many people in this room have played chess?" A fair number of hands went up. "How many of you have gotten beaten badly in chess?"

The same hands were still up. "Is it safe to say that the person who beat you was able to think two or three moves in advance, if not more?" Again, those with their hands up were nodding in agreement.

"A good player can see the whole game before making even one move," added John knowingly.

"Absolutely, and what we are doing here today is arming you with the tools to be able to approach buying real estate and building your real estate portfolio with the same strategy as a chess player. You're developing the ability to think one or two moves in advance, so that you don't paint yourself into a corner. It's like coming up to a 30,000-foot view. We know exactly where we're going and can clearly see the roadblocks up ahead. We know the exact purpose of our real estate purchases so we can anticipate the roadblocks ahead of time; and because you're anticipating them, you can make moves to avoid the obstacles, just like in a chess game. The way most people buy real estate is equivalent to playing a game of chess at eye level, instead of looking down at the board. Not only is it impossible to know your next move, you can't even tell the consequences of your current move." Some of the puzzled looks in the room were now starting to nod, giving me the sense that they were beginning to understand.

I have two rules of chess that I apply to buying real estate:

1. Never make a move unless you know what the next move is going to be.

2. Plan out your next three moves in advance.

"Remember my story about Randy at the beginning of this workshop? I inadvertently gave him the wrong advice because I wasn't thinking more than one move at a time and we got painted into a corner. It's the difference between what I call the 'portfolio approach' versus the 'transactional approach.' Whenever somebody comes into our office, I no longer see their mortgage as a simple transaction. I look at their goals and analyze how this transaction is going to impact the next, because I know their goal is to develop a portfolio. Just ask Brian. That's how he ended up being here today."

"Well, now I know who to blame," Michelle added jokingly. It was good to see that she was starting to feel more comfortable. I think the idea that

Brian would actually be following a plan, in which she would also have input and understand its goal, made a big difference.

GAP ANALYSIS

Everyone now knew how much money they would need in order to live the life they wanted to live, so the next step would be to find out how much real estate they needed to buy in order to cover their gap amount. To do this, we have to make some simple calculations. Simple math tells us that, if you can figure out the amount of net profit you make per door on each rental property you own, then it wouldn't be difficult to determine how much real estate you would need to buy. Again, very simple math, but surprisingly few people have done it.

"What if you knew the exact number of doors you needed to buy in the next five years in order to achieve your goals?" I could see a few eyebrows rise and heads start to nod.

"That would certainly make it a bit easier," said Jasmine.

"Or scarier," added Shelley.

"Well, let's do some simple math. What is the average cash flow per door that you would expect to earn net, after all expenses on any given property?"

"When you say 'door,' do you mean property?" Linda asked.

"Not exactly. I use the term 'door' because if you say you want to buy three 'properties,' I don't know what you mean. That could be three small apartment units or it could mean three apartment buildings. That's a pretty big difference. So I prefer to talk in terms of 'doors' just to make it consistent. For example, if you are buying a fourplex, that would be four doors."

I asked everyone to brainstorm what the average net income per door would be. This is the net amount, after you've paid out all expenses, including servicing the cost of the line of credit that was used for the down payment. This sounds like a simple exercise, but you'd be surprised at the range of answers you get in a group such as this.

"So if you were to go out today and buy a property, what would be the average cash flow per door that you could expect to earn?" I asked people to shout out some of the results they were currently getting.

"$200."

"$150."

"$500," Chad exclaimed.

"$500 a door—wow, that's quite a bit!" I responded. "Where are you getting that?"

"Fort McMurray," replied Chad.

"Now here's a good example of something I want to point out," I paused to use Chad's example. "Chad's getting $500 a door up in Fort Mac. For those of you who are just starting out, that is unusual, but not impossible. It is usually in towns like Fort McMurray or Grand Prairie where there is a big demand for labour to feed the oil industry, and it creates a housing shortage resulting in very expensive rents."

Chad had immigrated to Canada three years ago from South Africa. He was a young, single guy in his late 20s and worked in the oil industry. But unlike a lot of his peers, he had his act together and recognized that there was no guarantee that the high wages and great income he was earning today would last forever. He understood the importance of creating a plan and "living life on purpose."

Chad arrived in Canada with enough money to buy a house right away and he was able to pick up a rental property a year later. He was determined to take advantage of the extra income he was earning now, to build his "exit strategy." I was actually quite impressed with Chad, because most young guys his age don't "get it." They don't realize that they could be only a $5-a-barrel drop away from having their current project cancelled. They believe the good times will last forever and half of the money they make gets completely wasted on weekend frivolities. Those are the individuals who wake up five years from now thinking, "woulda, coulda, shoulda." This outlook isn't unique to the oil fields. I see the same thing happening in Vancouver's film industry, where a group of young actors or stunt men are living their dream, oblivious to the fact that the Canadian dollar at par could wipe out half of their contracts. Or the young professional athletes who don't seem to realize that they are one "blown knee" away from heading back to a small-town factory job. There are a lot of young people in their 20s right now who are making enough money to set themselves up for life with a few smart investments, but the Chads of the world are not as common as they should be.

Having said this, it is these same peers that may end up helping Chad achieve his goals, and in the process, he will be able to help them in ways they don't even know. I didn't tell him at the time, but I had already figured out a version of Chad's real estate action plan—a way for him to achieve the ambitious goals he had set for himself in the first exercise. I could see the entire picture unravelling before my eyes, but I couldn't share that with him—not at this point. Chad would have to discover it for himself as the day went on—and I was confident that he would.

I turned to Chad and cautioned him, "Now the key here is actually two things, Chad. If you are going to use $500 as an average, then all your future purchases have to be at that rate as well."

"That might be tough, because the prices have gotten so high up there. I don't know if I can continue to keep buying in Fort Mac," he explained.

"Well, Chad," I continued, "the second thing you need to take into consideration is becoming heavily invested in one town and/or industry. Fort McMurray is obviously heavily dependent on oil, so if there is a prolonged recession such as the one we had in 2009, you will need to factor in a higher vacancy rate than normal. The main thing is to be consistent. If all your properties will be like the one you bought last year, then use $500. But if you are planning to make purchases in different cities, then you can't use the same cash flow projection."

"What else do we have out there?"

"$850," Kathy beamed proudly as she shouted out an unusually high number. I knew right away that whatever they were doing was different, because you don't normally make that much net profit per door unless you've owned a property for a number of years.

"So what's the catch?" I asked.

"We super-suited it a year ago," she said with a half smirk, knowing that I had clued into the fact that it wasn't a normal rental property. I could tell by the look on both Michelle and Candice's faces that they had no clue what "super-suite" meant.

"'Super-suite' is another name for renting out a 'fully furnished' unit. Basically, you furnish the apartment as if it were a hotel. There are a lot of oil companies in Alberta, especially in Edmonton, who will have employees stay in a unit for several months at a time, in lieu of buying a house or apartment. It ends up being significantly cheaper for them to lease a fully furnished 'suite' rather than paying for a motel every night, and much more comfortable in most cases."

"Absolutely," Barb added. "We own two of them and the amount of rent we get is way higher than our one non-furnished suite."

"Now I'm going to give the two of you the same caution that I gave to Chad. You can use those calculations as long as every unit you plan to buy from here on is a fully furnished unit."

"Actually, they are a lot more hands-on for the maintenance and property management," Kathy volunteered, "so we don't plan to be doing any more of them for a while."

"Perfect. That's a good example of where you would have to adjust your numbers. The key here is that you are making future projections. You can only use current or past numbers if you are confident that you will be able to get the same amount in the future," I reminded the entire class. "Now, there must be a few people out there with negative numbers?" I asked, looking for a few brave, honest souls to share some less-than-perfect stories. And sure enough there were.

"Negative $150."

"Negative $250."

"Negative "$50."

As the numbers started to come out, including a few negative cash-flow properties that I had, there was a whole range, including one that Dr. Gill was looking at with negative $350 a month. Again, the purpose of this exercise was to create a more accurate picture of what you can expect to make on a monthly basis in real estate. It never ceases to amaze me how some people seem to have a vision of how much they plan to make per month, but what they are buying is totally inconsistent with that vision. I remember talking to one young man in my office who had just purchased a property in New Westminster, B.C. His gap figure was $4,000 a month and the property that he had just put an offer on was producing negative $348 a month. He was absolutely the poster child of the "mud against the wall" strategy. He had a strong sense that buying real estate was a good thing, but no one had ever taught him or challenged him to actually calculate the numbers. To this day, I will never forget his puzzled look when I asked him straight-facedly, "How many doors at negative $348 a month will you need to purchase in order to make a net profit of $4,000 a month?" You could literally see his brain churning and he actually pulled out a calculator and started to crunch some numbers before suddenly realizing that I was being facetious. He wasn't a foolish investor; he simply had not been challenged to "think it through." I wonder how many Canadians are out there today buying pre-sale condos because they either feel the need to get into the real estate market or a marketing company is blowing out a hundred new units at 40% below the list price?

If you've done the math up to this point, you know how much money you need real estate to produce for you on a monthly basis and, more importantly, you know why you need it to produce that amount. Now ask yourself: "If you are currently looking at an investment property, how much net profit will you be able to put into your jeans at the end of every month, after taking into consideration all the expenses?"

The truth is, if you can get $100 a month in positive cash flow across the country, that's not a bad number. As we've seen in the examples above from the workshop, there are plenty of cases where you can get more than that, but there are equally as many where the cash flow is negative. In some cases, you may choose to buy a property with negative cash flow today, knowing that you have the opportunity to raise the rents in a year, which would move the property into a positive cash flow position. Some savvy investors have the ability to create positive cash flow from renting out the garage as a separate "storage unit," or, as we saw with Kathy and Barb, renting out a fully furnished unit. There are plenty of options, but I want you, the reader, to take a moment and ask yourself, "How much money do I plan to earn per door five years from now?"

$ _____ monthly cash flow per door expected in five years

Caution: You may very well intend to raise the rents every year and create a high number, but keep in mind that if you also plan to access any equity from any of your properties in order to finance future purchases, you will be eating into your future cash flow projections. Again, try to be as real, accurate and consistent as possible.

For the purposes of this exercise, I will use $100 a door. Not only does it make the math simple, but it is also a number I have consistently seen in workshops across the country.

As I moved on to the next exercise, I could see that Barb was well ahead of me and had filled in the blanks already. "Now that you have an average cash flow per door," I announced, trying to bring the group back from all the various conversations that were sprouting up (mostly arguments around what was the "true" amount of monthly cash flow). "You can do the next calculation easily. For those of you like Barb who have already looked ahead, you simply divide the monthly gap figure you had from your earlier calculations by the cash flow per door to come up with the total number of doors you will need to buy in order to accomplish your goal."

$ _____ / $ _____ = _____
Monthly gap   Cash flow per door   # of doors

Once again, no rocket science here. The gap is the amount of money you calculated earlier that you need real estate to produce for you in order for you to accomplish your lifestyle goals. Simply divide your gap amount by the average amount of cash flow per door that you project and you will come up with the number of doors that you will need to buy over the next five years. I refer to these as gap doors.

I then shared my numbers with the group, based on the hypothetical scenario I had created earlier. I used $100 a door in my example, for the purpose of both keeping it simple and keeping it conservative. Again, you can use a higher number if you wish, but I want to make sure that the plan I create is a conservative one.

CALCULATING DOORS NEEDED TO FILL THE GAP

My gap is $4,000 per month (the shortfall amount I need to live the life I want).

I estimate I can get $100 per door, per month.

So, how many doors do I need to fill or bridge the gap? The answer is 40.

$$\$4,000 \div \$100 = 40$$

Simply put: I would need to buy 40 doors at $100 per door net cash flow to generate a monthly income from my real estate of $4,000.

This is the point in the workshop where I inevitably have to do a lot of policing among the couples. I knew what the numbers were going to be for most of them before they even started, so I wasn't surprised when

Michelle looked at Brian as if to say, "No bloody way we're buying that much, bud."

There were a lot of expressions of concern around the room as that stark realization of what it would actually take to accomplish the dollar figures some of them had written was staring them in the face. Ryan, the other young guy in the room with very aggressive goals, was looking a little shell-shocked. His monthly target for living the life he wanted to live was $25,000 and he wanted to be a full-time real estate investor. Although the math seemed simple enough to me, this was the first time he had actually done the calculation for himself, and the idea that it might require 250 doors at $100 a door seemed rather intimidating. Unlike Chad, who had an equally aggressive goal, Ryan didn't work in the oil fields earning a strong six-figure income. In fact, he was in construction and didn't even own his own home yet. He was looking at real estate as a ticket out, a way to short-cut the system. I can't help but be skeptical with young guys like Ryan, but I've also learned not to pass judgment. I knew there was a way for Ryan to accomplish his goals, but time would tell if he was willing to do what it would take to make it happen. Again, as I noted earlier, the math was very easy, but for some reason, Ryan hadn't figured on having to buy that many doors in order to create the money he needed. And Ryan is not unique. I run across a lot of people like him throughout my travels. They're not all looking to make $25,000 a month, but sometimes even those who are looking to make an extra thousand dollars per month have never sat down to do the math and determine exactly what they would need to buy. I often think they prefer not to know—ignorance is bliss sometimes.

Nicole and Marc, on the other hand, were very pleased with their numbers. They had a goal of making an extra $3,000 a month 15 years from now and, as such, determined that $1,000 a month in positive cash flow was quite realistic in that time frame. Therefore, they simply needed to focus on buying three single-family homes over the next few years and then shift their focus to a debt-reduction strategy. (I will talk more about this later.)

Sean and Candice were busy re-calculating numbers. When I glanced over Candice's shoulder, I noticed that she was doing something I see often in these workshops. As soon as she saw how many doors were required to accomplish her goal, she started to rework the original numbers and change the goal. This is something that I don't like to see—your goal is your goal. Why would you immediately discount your ideal lifestyle because the task at hand seems daunting? I totally understood where she was coming from, but I encouraged her to work through the rest of the plan; and then, at the end of the day, if she still felt that the number of doors required was unachievable, she could re-evaluate her goals. Personally, I'm a firm believer in the "Law of Attraction." Once you let the universe know what it is that you truly want, it has an amazing way of bringing it to you. But you need to be clear on what you want and then have the faith that it can happen. Candice decided to leave her original goal unchanged for now and work through the rest of the workshop with that number intact.

Jeff and Linda were busy crunching their numbers. "I really don't think $100 a door is realistic for us, Peter," Linda commented. "We currently have five doors and are making an average of $225 per door."

"That's fine," I responded loud enough for everyone to hear. "Remember, I'm simply using $100 a door for my example. You can use any number you wish to as long as you are confident that you can earn that amount five years from now. In fact," I announced so that everyone would listen, "you can make the dollars per door any amount you want. You can change any of the numbers in the formula, you just can't change the formula. The money you will be earning from real estate five years from today will always be determined by the dollar amount per door times the number of doors you own."

I could tell that this made total sense to Jasmine and Gill. They weren't smiling per se, but they definitely had a strong look of confidence that their numbers were doable.

"Now I know that was a sobering exercise for some of you, especially if you haven't bought any real estate before and you're basing your calculations on $100 a door," I felt the need to address the group as a whole and instill some much needed reassurance at this point. "But let me remind you of something. Fifteen to twenty years from now, what happens with all of those mortgages if you keep your units fully rented?"

"They get paid off," Barb chirped in.

"That's right, and what happens to your cash flow?"

"It goes up," she added.

I reminded everyone that over time, the mortgages will get paid off and the cash flow will go up. Now keep in mind that doesn't mean that you will get to keep 100% of the rent (unless you are buying triple-net commercial real estate). You will still have taxes, property management fees and, in the case of apartments, condo/strata fees to pay. In fact, your cash flow per door could go as high as $1,000–$1,500, but again, in keeping with my very conservative numbers, let's assume that your net profit per door jumps from $100 a month to $500 a month once the mortgage is paid off. I then asked everyone to re-calculate their numbers based on an income of $500 a month instead of $100 and used my hypothetical numbers as an example:

$500 per door × 40 doors = $20,000 a month

"Just by letting the tenants pay off my mortgages over time, my income went from $4,000 a month to $20,000 a month. Not a bad pension plan if you ask me." I could see some smiles return to the faces of a lot of people in the room as some of them grasped the true power of real estate for the first time. Once the mortgages were paid off, there was the potential for some significant cash flow. For some, that created a whole new vision, for others, it allowed them to re-evaluate some timelines. Either way, it sure got everyone thinking.

Chapter 5

Overcoming Obstacle One— Qualifying at the Bank

OBSTACLES OVERVIEW

We began the day talking about how most people end up living a life by default and our goal was to live a life on purpose. In order to do this we needed to clarify exactly what end result we wanted to have for our lives. We then determined how much money we would need in order to live that life. This allowed us to define the role real estate would play in accomplishing that goal. And, more specifically, we now knew exactly how much real estate would be required in order to create the necessary results. The next step for everyone was to look at the obstacles that were in their way.

"At this point, there are a few things that you should be very clear on," I continued.

1. You should have a clear vision of what your ideal lifestyle would look like.

2. You should have a clear idea what that lifestyle will cost you on a monthly basis.

3. You should have a clear vision of what your monthly shortfall is and, more importantly, what role or results real estate has to play in your ability to achieve that goal.

4. You should have a clear sense as to how many dollars per door your real estate will produce.

5. You should have a clear sense of how many doors you will need to buy at "X" dollars per door in order to produce "X" dollars a month in order to live the life that you envisioned.

"Gee, you make it sound easy," quipped Sean.

"Conceptually it is," I responded. "But remember, if you are not clear on any of these numbers, then make it a homework assignment to figure them out, and for the purposes of this workshop, work with your 'best guess' numbers for now. That way, you'll be able to make a plan today, you just need to remember to adjust it as you become clear on your real numbers."

At this point, I encourage you, the reader, to take some time to make sure you have done the exercises as well and have a clear vision for yourself. All of the following exercises are built on these numbers, so it is imperative that you take the time to analyze your own numbers in order to get the most out of reading this book.

"Now that you have clarity around these numbers and a good sense about why you need to buy real estate and what you will need to buy, the next step is to answer the question *how*."

"That's exactly the question I was asking," Shelley laughed.

"Well," I carried on, "the next step is to look at the obstacles that each of you will be facing. And this is where we begin the process of building your personal real estate action plan."

I then explained to the room that after many years of working with real estate investors and analyzing thousands of investors' portfolios, I have narrowed it down to only two obstacles. Now, don't get me wrong, every individual is unique and has their own special set of circumstances, but in the big picture, it always comes down to one or both of the following two obstacles:

1. Qualifying at the bank.
2. Coming up with the down payment.

This reminds me of an old joke:

"I've got some good news and some bad news."

"What's the good news?"

"The good news is that your future lies in your own hands."

"Well, what's the bad news?"

"Your future lies in your own hands. . . ."

So I announced to the workshop: "Class, I've got some good news and some bad news."

"The good news is that there are only two obstacles that you will need to face in building your real estate portfolio. The bad news is that there are two obstacles that you will need to face." Everyone had a chuckle and then I added, "After working with thousands of real estate investors, at the end of the day, outside of emotional and psychological issues, these are the only two obstacles you will face in building your real estate portfolio."

My belief is simple. If I can help each investor come up with a strategy for overcoming these two obstacles, then I will be able to pave the way for them to accomplish their goals. Perhaps even Michelle would start to see the possibilities.

> **Obstacle One:** You are going to have difficulty qualifying for a mortgage at the bank because of debt service ratios (DSRs); or
>
> **Obstacle Two:** You are going to run out of money for down payments.

OBSTACLE ONE: OVERCOMING THE DEBT SERVICE RATIO BANK REQUIREMENT

There are rules that the banks have for lending you money. I refer to them as the "Rules of Engagement" because when you choose to engage in building a real estate portfolio, you will need to understand and learn to play within their rules in order to be successful. Simply put, "He who has the gold, makes the rules." You can either choose to complain about the rules or you can learn how to work within them.

Unfortunately, there is no magic wand that can be waved to automatically qualify you for a mortgage. But there are ways to develop your portfolio to help you qualify. The first step in overcoming any obstacle is learning more about it.

I will discuss some simple formulas that all banks use for DSRs, starting with your gross debt service ratio (GDS).

Gross Debt Service Ratio (GDS)

Typically, a bank doesn't want you to spend more than 32% of your verifiable income on servicing the mortgage payment, taxes and condo fees (if applicable) on the subject property that you are buying. In other words, whether it's for a principal residence or a revenue property, banks want to make sure that the mortgage payments, the property taxes and condo fees do not consume more than 32% of your total verifiable income. The GDS is simply the ratio of your monthly housing costs against your verifiable income. Housing costs would include the mortgage payment, the property taxes and the condo/strata fees (if applicable).

At this point, Brian raised his hand and asked me to clarify what I meant by the word "verifiable." Although he knew what the word meant, what he was really asking me was, "Is there a way around this for self-employed individuals?"

"I know, I know, the word 'verifiable' is villified by all you self-employed individuals in the room," I joked. "But unfortunately, regardless of how creative your accountant gets or how justified you are in claiming those expenses, the average bank will look at the two-year average of line 150 on your tax return."

"That doesn't seem fair," added Jeff, as it suddenly dawned on him that the fact his accountant was able to show enough "write-offs" after his first year in business that Jeff didn't need to pay taxes, may not be such a positive thing when it comes to getting a mortgage.

"Here's rule number one, Jeff," I said, meeting his concern with a very specific and deliberate message. "What's fair or not fair has nothing to do with it. Your job is to understand the rules and work with them."

"But how can they do a two-year average when I've only been in business for one year?" he continued.

"Good question. I guess Linda will have to keep her job for at least another year," I answered with a smug grin. "Don't worry, I'll cover that in a bit." I wasn't trying to be cynical with Jeff, but knowing he had only started his new business a year ago and that Linda currently had a well-paying job, I knew that they would have no problem qualifying for a mortgage. But the key was Linda's job. I wanted both of them to be very clear that if she planned to quit her job any time soon to become a full-time real estate investor, their investing lives would become very difficult in a hurry.

I then went on to explain what total debt service ratio (TDS) is.

Total Debt Service Ratio (TDS)

Like the GDS, your TDS is a ratio of your debt to income. The key difference is that the "T" stands for total debt. The GDS only takes into consideration the housing expenses associated with the subject property (the one you are buying). The TDS takes those numbers into consideration and then adds all your other debts, such as any consumer debt that shows up on your credit bureau or any debts associated with other rental properties. Again, banks do not want to see you spend more than 40% of your verifiable income on your total debts. These debts include everything related to the principal residence, your mortgage payment, your taxes and condo fees (if applicable), plus anything else that shows up on a credit bureau, like credit cards, lines of credit, other mortgages, car leases, etc.

For example, if you are self-employed and write virtually everything off to the point where you show little or no income, one of the worst things you can do is go out and lease a BMW at $580 a month; that's going to chew up 40% of your verifiable income pretty quickly.

The bottom line is that every time you apply at a bank for financing, you will be faced with having to work around these two ratios. So, let's take a look at how these ratios are affected when you start to build a real estate portfolio.

PORTFOLIO STRATEGY—IMPACT OF CASH FLOW

"Regardless of whether you are self-employed or not," I began as we moved onto the next segment of the workshop, "this is probably the most important section of the workshop for you to understand. What I am going to describe to you is basically the way in which a bank will underwrite your mortgage application. And in so doing, you will learn how to create a 'portfolio approach' to building your real estate business as opposed to a simple 'transactional approach.' You will also learn about a concept that I refer to as the 'impact of cash flow,' which will illustrate how both positive and negative cash flow can impact your ability to qualify for a mortgage." The participants could tell by the shift in my tone that I treat this section very seriously and everyone listened intently.

DSRs are formulas that banks use to help them analyze your borrowing limits. I find that a lot of clients are intimidated by some of the terminology used in our industry when, in fact, they are really simple concepts. In a nutshell, a bank doesn't want you to spend more than 40% of your verifiable income servicing your monthly debt commitments. I refer to this number as your debt service limit or DSL. So your monthly DSL is simply 40% of your monthly verifiable income—simple, right?

Now you can calculate your own personal DSL:

(Verifiable income × 40%) ÷ 12 = $ _____ monthly DSL

Remember, if you're self-employed, your "verifiable" income will be a two- to three-year average of line 150 on your tax return (depending on the bank). If you have a job where you receive a T-4 or a pay stub (in other words you are not self-employed), then you can use your current "gross income" and do not need to worry about a two-year average.

Everyone at the workshop was furnished with two Excel spreadsheets prior to attending:

1. A rental cash flow analysis that auto-calculates the debt coverage ratio on their rental portfolio; and

2. An impact of cash flow worksheet.

Both of these are available to you, the reader, at no cost by going to www.peterkinch.com and registering your copy of this book.

I paused before launching into this next segment of the workshop because I wanted to make sure that I had everyone's attention. It's funny, as complicated as the world of banking, finance and real estate portfolio development is, after conducting dozens of workshops and teaching thousands of investors across the country, I have learned how to break this section down into its simplest form. Maybe it's the English teacher in me, but when it comes to finance, I like to keep it simple. As my good friend Don Campbell likes to say, "A confused mind always says no." So when I took a look at how the banks evaluate an application for a mortgage and I took a look at the client on the other side of the application, I asked myself: "What's really happening here?" Ultimately, the bank makes money by lending money and you want to provide them with an opportunity to "make some money" by lending it to you.

However, the bank also has to manage their risk and, as such, they have developed rules and tools such as the DSRs to do that.

I recall when I first started brokering in 1995 in Victoria, B.C. My friend and mentor, was a wise veteran named Chris Stewart. Chris had a small but very successful brokerage. On one hand, he had a small group of people who entrusted him with their money to be lent out in the form of first and second mortgages. They trusted Chris implicitly and he would, in turn, make very prudent lending decisions, thus securing a solid and consistent return on his investors' money. On the other hand, Chris had a handful of small builders (single-family spec homes and small residential developments) who, for some reason or another, just didn't fit the mortgage rules for the banks. They weren't necessarily high risk, but weren't able to fall within the strict rules of the banks. They were happy to pay slightly higher rates and fees to Chris, in exchange for easier access to capital, which, in turn, allowed them to focus on what they did best—build houses. It was a classic win-win situation; the builders were able to keep building and the investors received the return on their investment that they desired. Today, this type of structure is referred to as a Mortgage Investment Corp. (MIC).

I came along, fresh from teaching English in Japan and wanting to be a mortgage broker. Chris took me under his wing and chose to mentor me. I'll never forget one of my first lessons.

I had become quite accustomed to earning good money while living in Japan. We were paid well to teach English over there. In fact, it was not uncommon for a Japanese businessman to pay $100 an hour just for the privilege of having a "Western" English teacher to practice his English on, even if that meant your class was held at a local Karaoke bar—it's not as bad as it sounds. After spending a few years earning good money from my linguistic skills, I was quite accustomed to walking around with $100 bills in my pocket on a regular basis. So when I returned to Victoria and found myself working on 100% commission, which was based solely on my ability to find a few worthy souls to lend Mrs. Jones' money to, it was quite a shock to my system. That's when I learned what was perhaps the most valuable mortgage lending advice I've ever had.

I had saved a fair amount of the money I made in Japan and, after learning what Chris did for a living, I decided to hand my savings over to Chris to be added to the pot of money which was being lent out as second mortgages.

The return on investment was between 8% and 12%, significantly better than the rates I could get at the bank. As one month turned into two, I began to realize that making money in the mortgage broker game would be a lot harder than teaching English in Japan. My job was to find builders or individuals who, for whatever reason, could not qualify at the bank and needed to borrow money from us. It seemed easy on the surface, but as the days went on, I realized that it was much more difficult than I had anticipated. One day, after going a month or so without any success or paycheque for that matter, I was suffering from severe "cash-in-pocket withdrawal." I had an appointment with a builder who had built a series of spec homes, but couldn't move them. I had received his name and number from one of his creditors, which, as it turned out, was just one of many people in the city to whom he owed money. The guy had made a series of poor choices and the truth was, anyone who lent him more money would only be throwing good money after bad and further greasing the skids. He was not simply "down on his luck," he had a serious need to reverse the decision-making process that had gotten him into his mess. Now, do you think that I, as a young, hungry, commission-based salesman, took all of that into consideration? No, of course not. The only way I was going to earn a commission cheque that month was to find someone to lend money to and this guy fit the bill. So I met with him, filled out the application and hurried back to the office, where I proudly presented it to Chris with eager anticipation and waited for him to say, "Well done, we'll get the money out to him tomorrow and you'll be able to earn your first cheque as a broker."

Instead, what I got was a very valuable lesson that I have carried with me ever since. Chris looked over the application, and then started to ask me a few pointed questions. "What is this client's exit strategy? How do you think he is going to be able to pay us back." And the one I really didn't want to hear, "What if he can't pay us back?" These were all questions that I knew I needed to answer but my hungry, rookie mind was trying to ignore. Then Chris went for the strike, "Are you confident that this is a good risk? Should we lend our money to this client?" he asked as he leaned forward and looked me in the eyes, the way a parent does when they are asking a rhetorical question. I hesitated, knowing on one hand that a "no" would mean no paycheque, but in reality, I just wanted to abscond from the responsibility for the answer and place that back onto Chris' plate—after all, it's his business and he's the one who should be making this decision. I'm just bringing the clients to the table. So, I answered a sheepish "Yeah sure, I guess so." And that's when I got the lesson I'll never forget. Chris sat back in his chair and announced, "Well, if you think it's a good loan, then we'll lend him your money. I'll just take the money that you've invested here and give that to this client."

"Well, it's not *that* good of a deal," I heard myself saying, and that's when I understood the most valuable lesson I've ever learned in my mortgage career—treat every loan application as if you were lending your own money, not the bank's. Ask yourself, "Would you lend your money to this individual?" and if the answer is "yes," then you simply need to explain to the underwriter at the bank what your logic and reasoning is. Every bank has "risk" parameters. Our job as the broker is to package you, the borrower, in such a way that we help to mitigate those risks. I often wonder if the loan officers who structured all the sub-prime mortgages in the U.S. had bosses like Chris who instilled a sense of personal accountability into the decision-making process, how much of the global economic meltdown that followed would have been averted?

The Left Side, Right Side Equation

I know that banking, finance and mortgages can be pretty dry stuff, so I tried to make the point at the workshop that you need to keep it simple. Learn the rules that the banks have to live by and then structure your portfolio so that it helps them say "yes" to you.

In fact, the guidelines for understanding your DSL and how cash flow, or lack thereof, can impact it are quite simple. To start with, you need to separate your personal consumer debt from your portfolio debt. I often refer to this as the "left side, right side" equation. You simply tally up all your personal consumer debt on the left side, and then show enough verifiable income so that 40% of it can cover the cost of that debt. On the right side, you have all of your portfolio debt, and we simply need to find a lender who will "offset" that debt against the income earned from the rents. You are probably thinking, "easy for you to say." However, after many years of working with investors, I've been able to break the rules down and simplify them, and I knew that if I could help everyone in the class that day understand it in the simple terms that I did, then we would be halfway to helping them achieve their goals.

Complete **highlighted** fields only				

Annual Personal Income:	$ -		Client Name: _____	
Monthly Debt Services Limit (DSL):	$ -			
Postive/Negative Cash flow:	$ -			

Total Income (personal + positive cash flow):	$ -	
Total DSL:	$ -	

Personal		Portfolio	
Principal Residence Mortgage (Monthly P + I)	0	Total Monthly Rental Income (TMRI)	0
Monthly Property Tax / Strata Fee	0	TMRI x 70%	0
Credit Cards (3% of oustanding balance)	0	(minus) Total monthly mortgage payments (P+I)	(000)
Additional credit bureau debt (car loans, personal loans)	0		
Lines of Credits (Monthly minimum payment)	0		
Include Cash flow if Negative	0		
Total monthly consumer debt =	0	Total Cash flow =	0

DISCLAIMER:
The above summary of discussion and suggestions made at the time of your consultation are based on the notes taken from the meeting with you. The Portfolio Strategy Cash Flow Impact™ worksheet is provided by the Peter Kinch Mortgage Team, and is for informational purposes only and is intended to be used as a guide prior to the execution of real estate investment. This worksheet is only intended to be used in consultation with a legal and financial authority familiar with your specific investment and financial situation. Peter Kinch and / or Peter Kinch Mortgage Team are not engaged in rendering legal or other financial professional advice, and this worksheet is not a substitute for the advice of a professional financial advisor or legal attorney. This worksheet is not to be replicated or reproduced.

"By now, you should all have an idea of what your personal DSL is," I continued. "The next step is to figure out your total monthly personal consumer debt."

"I want everyone to split all of your debt from today moving forward into two separate categories: personal and portfolio. Pull out a blank sheet of paper and draw a line down the middle. At the top of the left side of the page write 'personal,' and at the top of the right side write 'portfolio.' Under the 'personal' column, write down all your monthly expenses that the bank will consider personal. These will include: your principal residence mortgage, taxes and condo fees (if applicable); 3% of the monthly outstanding balance on your credit cards; any loans, leases or lines of credit; and anything else that shows up on your personal credit bureau. When you add these together, you will have your 'total monthly personal consumer debt.' Now, in the right column, put down any income and expenses that are related to your rental portfolio."

It is our job as mortgage brokers to balance these two sides, I explained. The banks are going to want to see that you have sufficient income so that

40% of it will be enough to cover the total monthly personal consumer debt. We then work with you to ensure that the numbers on the right side don't negatively affect the ones on the left.

"But what if I pay off my credit cards every month?" Sean wondered.

"No worries, if the balance is zero at the end of every month, just put zero in there," I explained.

"What if your company expenses are under your personal name?" Dr. Gill had a lot of expenses that were actually for the clinic, but they were in his personal name.

"Good question, Dr. Gill. In that case, you would simply need to provide a paper trail that would help us explain that to the bank. Banks aren't totally unreasonable. They understand how business works, but the more paperwork you can provide, the easier it is for them to piece the puzzle together. Remember," I reminded everyone, "your job as a sophisticated investor is to make the underwriter's job at the bank easier. Anything you can do to make it easier for them to say 'yes' helps you in the end."

"On the right side of the page," I continued, "start by adding up the total amount of rent you are currently receiving from your rental properties, assuming you have rental properties that is."

"What about income from a basement suite in our house?" Linda inquired.

"Good question," I answered. "That's probably one of the most common misconceptions in this calculation. A basement suite in your home cannot be included when calculating your debt coverage ratio or your total monthly rental income from your portfolio. A basement suite is actually considered under personal income and will either be factored in as part of line 150 on your tax return, or a percentage of it will be 'added back' to your income, depending on the bank you are working with. So for the purposes of this exercise, only include income from any rental properties you own."

"What about the money we earn from our cabin?" John queried. "We don't rent it out all the time, but we do make a fair amount in the summer."

"Another good question. Cabins and cottages fall into that 'grey' zone. They are actually considered recreational property and unless they are rented out 'year-round' with lease agreements in place, which is highly unlikely, then they will fall into the same category as basement suite revenue and are included in your personal income."

OFFSET VERSUS ADD BACK

I now had to explain to the group that every bank will have their own way or system of how they treat rental income. Most investors would love it if the banks took the approach whereby they simply subtracted every dollar of expense from every dollar of rent. In a perfect world, if your rent was $1,000 a month and your expenses were $900 a month, you would have $100 a month net profit. In fact, many would hope that their bank would simply lend them money based on the fact that the rental property pays for itself. Would that it were that simple.

At this point, I am compelled to remind the reader of the statistics that were discussed earlier in the book. Many investors believe that a bank should feel more secure lending money to a real estate investor. "After all," they reason, "not only does the bank have me as security, they also have a tenant that is paying the mortgage, which should make it twice as secure." Good sound logic and reasoning for sure, but there is only one problem. If that were the case, real estate investment properties would represent the lowest amount of default and foreclosure on the books. Unfortunately, as logical as the investors' argument may be, they are betrayed by the statistics. The truth is, when a bank looks at their entire portfolio of mortgages on their books, those made for real estate investments represent the highest number of frauds, defaults and foreclosures. This is not a judgment, just a fact that the investor needs to be aware of. Combine this with the fact that mortgages for investors represent less than 5% of the overall mortgage market, and you can quickly see why banks are not overly anxious to relax the rules when it comes to working with real estate investors.

Now it should also be made clear that, because of these statistics, a large number of banks won't even play in this sandbox and those that do will apply one of two policies when factoring rental income into their calculations. They will either have a "rental offset policy" or a "rental add back policy" and the difference in policy could be the difference between whether or not you get a mortgage.

Rental Offset Policy

An offset policy simply takes into consideration a percentage of the total amount of rental income instead of the entire amount and then subtracts the expense or a portion thereof. If I seem rather vague in my explanation, it's simply because each lender has a variation of this policy, and it is not my intention here to lay out in detail lender policy for all of Canada's chartered banks. So, for the purpose of illustrating a rental offset, we will take the Scotiabank policy. They apply a 70% rental offset when calculating the rental income. This means that they will take the total rent, multiply it by 70% and then subtract the total amount of mortgage payments only. They are not factoring in the other 30% because it is being used to factor in miscellaneous expenses such as condo fees, property taxes, maintenance, management and vacancy ratios. Rather than calculate all of these separately, it is easier to assume that 30% of the rental income goes to take care of those expenses. What's left is 70% of the rent to "offset" the mortgage payment. Note that this will apply to a single property or an entire portfolio of properties. For example:

Rental income: $1,000
Mortgage Payment: $650
(Rent × 70% = $700) − monthly mortgage payment ($650) = $50 (Surplus)

Applying a "rental offset policy" will result in either a surplus or a shortfall. In most cases, any surplus is added back to income to help with servicing the personal consumer debt, whereas any shortfall is added on to your personal consumer debt as if it were a credit card payment.

Again, I'm oversimplifying this for illustration purposes and different banks will have different versions of an offset.

Rental Add Back Policy

An add back policy is significantly less appealing to the real estate investor who is trying to build a portfolio. Quite simply, instead of subtracting the mortgage expenses from a percentage of rent, the add back policy "adds" 100% of the total rental income "back" to your personal income. On the surface you may think, "Hey, that's not a bad policy—they're taking into consideration 100% of my rental income." Well, that's not really the case. You see, with an "add back" policy, we would also add 100% of your rental expenses back to your personal consumer debt. Logic would suggest that these should cancel each other out, but as you may recall, the TDS rule requires that we only use 40% of your verifiable income to service your personal consumer debts. So in essence, applying an add back policy only allows us to use 40% of your rental income, but still service 100% of your rental expenses—hardly a fair trade-off. If you are just buying one or two properties and you have a strong verifiable income, you may well be able to qualify using an add back policy, but once you move beyond three properties it is virtually impossible for the math to work in your favour.

As you can see, it is critical for anyone who is looking to develop a real estate portfolio to work with a lender who utilizes an offset policy once you have more than the first three purchases. The challenge is, every bank has a different application of these policies, and they are not always evident or obvious to the borrower. This illustrates perfectly my earlier caution to readers that the bank or broker who provided the mortgage on your principal residence may not necessarily be the one you should use to help you build a real estate portfolio. Not all brokers are aware of the different rental policies at the various banks, and not all banks are able to provide you with the right options. Therefore, it is imperative that you work with the right broker. It is highly unlikely that you will be able to accomplish your goals by getting all of your mortgages at the same bank. (I will cover this topic in the next chapter "Cap Space.") It is critical that you have someone on your team who can help you navigate through these policies. As I always tell my clients, "You need me to be sitting high above you watching the horizon for obstacles. If I'm sitting beside you in the driver's seat, neither one of us can tell if the bridge is out ahead."

Now that everyone had a good understanding of the difference between an offset policy and an add back policy, I could move on to explain how to balance the left side, right side equation.

NOTE

As of April 2010, all CMHC-insured mortgages for investment properties will apply a 50% add back policy as opposed to an 80% offset. This was not a positive change for investors and made the need for a strategic approach even more important.

BALANCING THE LEFT SIDE, RIGHT SIDE EQUATION

"By now, you should have two totals at the bottom of your page," I began, as the group was busy looking at charts and punching numbers on their calculators. Barb and Kathy were pulling out spreadsheets while others were referring to the cash-flow analysis that I had sent out prior to the start of the workshop (see example on the following page). Brian and Michelle had yet to make any rental purchases, so everything on the right side of the page was blank.

"On the bottom left, you should have a total for your personal monthly consumer debt. On the right side, you should either have a positive number or a negative number." Again I explained to the class that although there are various ways of calculating a rental offset, for the purposes of this workshop, we would be using a 70% rental offset. As such, they were instructed to multiply the total amount of their monthly rental income by 70% and then subtract the total amount of monthly mortgage payments in their current portfolio.

"What if I own some properties in a corporation or with a joint venture partner?" Kathy asked.

"Simple," I responded. "Owning property in a corporation does not protect you from a bank coming after your personal assets in Canada. Therefore, you need to provide a personal guarantee for each purchase you make in your company name; hence, you will need to include both personal- and company-owned real estate on the right side. But, as I'm about to show you, that could actually be an asset not a detriment, if built properly." I then explained that the same holds true for any property you own with a joint venture partner if you are on the title. Legally, you may only own half the asset, but if your joint venture partner left town overnight, try going to the bank and telling them that you're only responsible for half of the mortgage payment. Although you are 100% responsible for the mortgage debt, the good news is that you are also allowed to claim 100% of the rental income for the purposes of qualifying. So, for the purposes of this exercise, include all property owned wholly or jointly, personal or corporate in your calculations on the right side of the page.

Impact of Cash Flow

At this point, please take the time to fill in the following worksheet (excerpted from a spreadsheet available for download at peterkinch.com) for yourself:

Personal Monthly Debt	Portfolio Monthly Debt
Principal Residence Mortgage: _____	Total Monthly Rental Income (TMRI): _____
	If your name is on a Title, include it for both income and mortgage expense.
Property Taxes:_____	TMRI x 70% = (A)
	(A): _____
Credit Cards:_____ (3% of outstanding balance)	Total Monthly Mortgage P+I = (B) (B): _____
Debt on Credit Bureau (other than credit cards): _____	Total Cash Flow per month (C) (A — B = C): _____ * Could be (-) or (+) number
Lines of Credit: (monthly payments) _____	If (C) is a positive amount, multiply by 12 months to get your Annual Portfolio Income. This gets added to your verifiable income to calculate a new DSL.
TOTAL Personal Monthly Debt: _____	If (C) is negative amount, it gets added to your monthly debts.

Now you've divided your debt into two categories:

On your left side is all your **personal debt**—and—on your right side is all your **portfolio debt**.

Remember the banks' rule: 40% or less of your verifiable income must cover your total monthly personal consumer debts (the total on your left). Does your calculation meet the banks' rule? If not, here's the good news.	A good mortgage broker can help offset what's on the right side so that it does not have a negative impact on the left side.

Following is an example of a rental cash-flow analysis. This is a great tool to help you analyze your rental cash flow as you develop your portfolio. This is an Excel spreadsheet. If you haven't done so already, simply go to www.peterkinch.com and request a copy to be e-mailed to you directly at no charge.

Rental Property Cash Flow Analysis

Customer Name:

Mortgage Number	Property Address	Appraised Value	Principal Balance	LTV	Interest Rate	Maturity Date	Gross Monthly Rent	Condo Fees	Gross Monthly Expenses	Monthly P & I.	Taxes	Monthly Rental Surplus / Shortfall	Individual DCR
		$0.00	$0.00	#DIV/0!			$0.00	$0.00	$0.00	$0.00	$0.00	$0.00	#DIV/0!
		$0.00	$0.00	#DIV/0!			$0.00	$0.00	$0.00	$0.00	$0.00	$0.00	#DIV/0!
		$0.00	$0.00	#DIV/0!			$0.00	$0.00	$0.00	$0.00	$0.00	$0.00	#DIV/0!
		$0.00	$0.00	#DIV/0!			$0.00	$0.00	$0.00	$0.00	$0.00	$0.00	#DIV/0!
		$0.00	$0.00	#DIV/0!			$0.00	$0.00	$0.00	$0.00	$0.00	$0.00	#DIV/0!
		$0.00	$0.00	#DIV/0!			$0.00	$0.00	$0.00	$0.00	$0.00	$0.00	#DIV/0!
		$0.00	$0.00	#DIV/0!			$0.00	$0.00	$0.00	$0.00	$0.00	$0.00	#DIV/0!
		$0.00	$0.00	#DIV/0!			$0.00	$0.00	$0.00	$0.00	$0.00	$0.00	#DIV/0!
		$0.00	$0.00	#DIV/0!			$0.00	$0.00	$0.00	$0.00	$0.00	$0.00	#DIV/0!
		$0.00	$0.00	#DIV/0!			$0.00	$0.00	$0.00	$0.00	$0.00	$0.00	#DIV/0!
		$0.00	$0.00	#DIV/0!			$0.00	$0.00	$0.00	$0.00	$0.00	$0.00	#DIV/0!
		$0.00	$0.00	#DIV/0!			$0.00	$0.00	$0.00	$0.00	$0.00	$0.00	#DIV/0!
		$0.00	$0.00	#DIV/0!			$0.00	$0.00	$0.00	$0.00	$0.00	$0.00	#DIV/0!
		$0.00	$0.00	#DIV/0!			$0.00	$0.00	$0.00	$0.00	$0.00	$0.00	#DIV/0!
		$0.00	$0.00	#DIV/0!			$0.00	$0.00	$0.00	$0.00	$0.00	$0.00	#DIV/0!
		$0.00	$0.00	#DIV/0!			$0.00	$0.00	$0.00	$0.00	$0.00	$0.00	#DIV/0!
		$0.00	$0.00	#DIV/0!			$0.00	$0.00	$0.00	$0.00	$0.00	$0.00	#DIV/0!

LTV: #DIV/0!

DCR: #DIV/0!

Vacancy: 5%
NOI: $0.00

Gross Monthly Expenses (N/A if Condo)
Fire insurance 5%
Maintenance 5%
Management 5%

"Okay, so what does all this mean? You have three numbers that are important here," I explained.

1. You have your DSL or the maximum amount of money that a bank wants you to spend on your total monthly consumer debt;

2. You have the number on the bottom left, which is your total monthly personal consumer debt; and

3. You have the number on the bottom right, which could be zero if you don't own any investments, but it's positive if your portfolio currently has a surplus or it's negative if your portfolio currently has a shortfall.

"Here's the bottom line," I announced, loud enough to get everyone's attention. I knew we had just covered a lot of minor details and I didn't want the main point to be lost. "Think about this as a game. The bottom line is very straightforward. If your total monthly consumer debt is higher than your DSL, getting a conventional mortgage from a bank will be very difficult. It's simple—make sure your DSL number is higher than that number." I said as I pointed to the personal consumer debt number on the PowerPoint screen. "Once you understand how the game is played, it's easy," I reiterated. I needed to emphasize this point, because in my opinion, qualifying for mortgages as a real estate investor simply comes down to those two numbers on the right side and the left side, and once you understand that, the sooner you can start to develop a workable real estate portfolio.

"Now the next step is to look at the third component of this equation and see how cash flow, both positive and negative, can impact your DSL." This is where we were really getting to the meat of the matter. Now I was at a point where I could really teach the workshop participants the true impact of cause and effect as they began developing their real estate portfolio.

"If the number on the right side was positive, how would a bank that uses an offset policy treat it?" I challenged them.

"They'd consider it income?" guessed Chad.

"Yes, basically that's exactly how they would look at it," I said, assuring Chad that his answer was correct. "We can essentially multiply the monthly number by 12 to get an annualized amount and then add it to our verifiable income, thus creating a new DSL."

"So you're not actually getting credit for 100% of that surplus, only 40%?" asked John.

"Well you're getting 100% of the surplus added to your income, so now your annual, verifiable income has increased accordingly, but then we revert to the formula for calculating your DSL, which is to take only 40% of your verifiable income," I explained.

"Got it!" exclaimed John.

"Now let's look at how the bank treats a shortfall after calculating your offset," I asked the class.

"They'd subtract it from your income?" Dr. Gill answered in a manner that was really more of a question than an answer.

"Not exactly," I answered. "If there's a shortfall, it would actually get added to your monthly personal consumer debts."

"So it would increase the number on the bottom left?" asked Shelley.

"That's correct, it would be no different than adding a car loan to your monthly debt," I explained.

This was a very important distinction for everyone to make. It's easy to say, "Oh yes, positive cash flow is important." But how does it impact your ability to continue to be able to qualify for mortgages?

I had to explain exactly why this simple exercise was very important. If you're in a position such as Dr. Gill and Dr. Jasmine with two very high incomes that can be easily verified, and you have very low personal consumer debt, then your DSL is likely to be significantly higher than your personal monthly debt. If this is the case, you can actually afford to buy a negative cash flow property today, because you have enough "buffer room" in your DSL to absorb the negative cash flow. If, on the other hand, you are in a position such as Jeff and Linda where one spouse is self-employed and the other is looking to become a full-time real estate investor, then you likely have very little buffer room in your DSL and you will need to focus on creating a surplus in your portfolio. Or perhaps you are in Ryan's position where you are 100% self-employed and there is no spousal income to fall back on. In Ryan's case, his DSL was significantly lower than his personal monthly debt, simply because he has been focusing on not having to pay taxes. That's good when it comes time to pay your taxes, but bad when it comes to borrowing money from a bank. Ryan not only needed to focus on creating positive cash flow from his rental purchases, but he will likely also need some help in qualifying for his first few mortgages. I'll touch on that later.

As I went around the room, I looked over everyone's numbers and got a better sense of where everyone was at. Brian and Michelle were exactly where I thought they'd be—his verifiable income was low, but Michelle's job made up for it. Their DSL was higher than their personal debt and although they didn't know it yet, they would be able to buy a lot more real estate than they realized. I had seen enough of their numbers to know exactly what they were capable of doing, but it was still too early to share that with them. Michelle still needed to discover this for herself, which I knew would happen before the day was out. Nicole and Marc were bang on target. Their goal was very conservative and easily attainable. Given the fact that they both had strong verifiable incomes and were conservative in their spending habits, it didn't surprise me that their DSL was higher than their personal debts. The same was true for Sean and Candice—their personal debt numbers were significantly higher, but so was their verifiable income. Candice worked as a pharmaceutical rep and made very good money. She had an excellent base salary plus commission, which helped to offset the fact that Sean's salary was 100% commission based. They also had two kids and loved to travel, and I could tell by having just a few conversations with them that they had expensive tastes. I knew qualifying would not be an issue for them, but what would be interesting was to see how far they were willing to go with real estate. They certainly had the skill set and the knowledge to build a large portfolio, but the real question was whether they could devote the time required. Time would tell.

To further illustrate both the impact of cash flow and the importance of understanding cause and effect, I shared the true story of Joseph, one of our older clients who came to me with a dilemma about two years ago. The charts that follow graphically illustrate the result of what can happen when you don't get the right advice.

Joe was a long-term investor who had been investing successfully for a number of years. Our company had helped him finance some properties a few years earlier, but I hadn't spoken to him since. His portfolio was quite mature and he had managed to build up a fair amount of equity. In fact, the total monthly rental income from all of his properties amounted to over

$13,000 and the total amount of his mortgage payments was only $6,000. Therefore, even when applying a rental offset of 70%, Joe's portfolio still showed a surplus of over $3,400, which when annualized, amounted to over $41,000.

In addition to having a strong portfolio, Joe also had a verifiable income of $60,000 and had paid off a large portion of his mortgage (with the exception of the refinancing and line of credit that he had accessed for more down payment money). This meant his DSL was $2,000 and his total monthly consumer debt was only $1,875. On the surface, Joe would easily qualify for a mortgage on another rental property simply based on the fact that his DSL was higher than his expenses, even if we didn't factor in his positive cash flow. But when you also add the $41,000 of additional income from the surplus in his real estate portfolio, Joe's DSL shot up to over $3,300 a month.

Personal Monthly Debt		Portfolio Monthly Debt	
Principal Residence Mortgage:	$1,200	Total Monthly Rental Income (TMRI)	$13,520
Property Taxes:	$225	TMRI × 70%	$9,464
Credit Cards:	$150	Subtract Total Monthly Mortgage P + I:	$6,000
Debt on Credit Bureau (other than credit cards):	$150	Total Cash Flow per month:	$3,464
Lines of Credit:	$150		
TOTAL Personal Monthly Debt:	$1,875	Annual Portfolio Income:	$41,568

Impact of Positive Cash Flow

Portfolio Income of $41,568 + Verifiable Income of $60,000
= Net Income of $101,568

$101,568 × 40% ÷ 12 = $3,358 (new DSL)

A DSL this strong would even allow Joe to qualify for a high-ratio mortgage, even if it meant a slightly negative cash flow on the subject property. This is a very important point, because a little further along I will be talking about something called "cap room." Even though Joe would easily qualify with a lender who uses a 70% rental offset, he may run into the problem that, with a portfolio the size of his, he may well have already reached the "cap" or maximum that the bank is willing to lend to one individual (more on this later). Joe may well need a strong portfolio such as his in order to qualify at a lender who does not use a policy as favourable as this.

• • •

That's when Joe came close to making a very critical mistake. He decided that he wanted to buy some more properties, but did not have access to any more capital for down payments. In conversations with another broker, a solution was created that would definitely provide Joe with more capital for his down payments. Now I'd like to remind you of an earlier discussion we had about a concept called cause and effect. You may recall that I mentioned that every action has an opposite and equal reaction and that real estate investors can ill afford to make decisions without taking into consideration the cause and effect of their decision-making process. Well, Joe forgot to do just that, and he came very close to turning a very strong portfolio into a weak one.

The advice Joe received from the other broker was to simply refinance his entire portfolio back up to 80% of the market value. Now on the surface, this does seem like a very good answer to finding more cash for future down payments. But what happens when we play this like a chess game and think out three moves in advance? Let's see what the cause and effect would have been had Joe taken the other broker's advice:

- His monthly rent stays the same at $13,520
- 70% of his monthly rental income is still $9,464
- His new mortgage payment now becomes $10,000
- His total monthly portfolio income is now (−$536)

Do you recall how a bank treats negative cash flow from a portfolio? That's right, it gets added to his personal consumer debts. They now look like this:

- DSL based on annual income of $60,000 = $2,000/month
- Total monthly debts before refinance = $1,875
- New total when shortfall of $536 is added as personal debt = $2,411

Joe now had a problem. His total personal debt added up to more than his DSL. Yes, he now technically had created more money to use as down payments for future purchases, but his personal consumer debt was too high for him to qualify easily for a conventional mortgage. When this dilemma was presented to the other broker, his suggested solution was to go the route of sub-prime mortgages. Sub-prime mortgages, if available at all, would come at a higher rate and with fees. It's quite likely that the higher rates would also result in a negative cash flow property, which would, in turn, further exacerbate the problem. Before you know it, Joe would find himself caught in a downward spiral. And he would be sitting there a year from now, wondering: "How did I get into this situation, when a year ago my portfolio looked so strong?" To add insult to injury, Joe also was planning to use the extra funds to build a strong enough portfolio to quit his job and become a full-time real estate investor. Take a look at the numbers above again, and with the little I have taught you already about the mortgage game, eliminate the income from the job and re-calculate Joe's DSL. What would your answer be if you were the bank? He was about to give up the one thing he had going for him.

Personal Monthly Debt		Portfolio Monthly Debt	
Principal Residence Mortgage:	$1,200	Total Monthly Rental Income (TMRI)	$13,520
Property Taxes:	$225	TMRI × 70%	$9,464
Credit Cards:	$150	Subtract Total Monthly Mortgage P + I:	$10,000
Debt on Credit Bureau (other than credit cards):	$150	Total Cash Flow per month:	−$536
Lines of Credit:	$150		
TOTAL Personal Monthly Debt:	~~1,875~~ $2,411	Annual Portfolio Income:	−$536

Note: Register this book at www.peterkinch.com and request a free copy of the "Impact of Cash Flow Spreadsheet," which will automatically calculate the above numbers for you.

Joe could have had serious problems with his portfolio, because he was seeking advice from someone who didn't take the time to ask the right questions. The cynical side of me questioned the motive of the other broker, simply because I knew he stood to make a good commission on refinancing

Joe's entire portfolio as well as being paid a premium commission on placing Joe with a sub-prime lender. But I would prefer to think that it was a case of the broker taking the "transactional approach" to lending, instead of the "portfolio approach." Remember, the sad (and dangerous) truth is that no one teaches the portfolio approach. As you may recall, the only way I learned this approach was by making the same mistake with my client Randy. Fortunately for him, the consequences were minor. But the reality is, virtually every broker and banker are only taught the transactional approach to lending or brokering, and they typically don't learn the portfolio approach until they have first-hand experience of the consequences of cause and effect. Now that you know the difference, make sure that you have this conversation with your broker or lender before your next transaction.[1]

I should mention here that it doesn't have to be "all or nothing." The simple solution for Joe was to do a partial refinancing of his portfolio—enough to provide Joe with more cash for down payments, but not so much that his cash flow would be negative from the portfolio. Even if Joe's portfolio were to simply break even, as long as he doesn't quit his job, he'll be able to continue to qualify for more mortgages.

At this point in the workshop, Ryan was quick to ask, "So, what if Joe does want to quit his day job? How will he ever be able to do that?"

"Well, to a certain extent," I began, "it would depend on the market conditions. For example, if we were back in 2006 when the banks were being very aggressive, Joe would simply need to create enough surplus and report it on his tax returns for at least two consecutive years—the goal being that 40% of the two-year average of line 150 of his tax return would satisfy his personal consumer debts."

"So there's no way around that?" Ryan continued, hoping for the magic words that are only spoken when watching television channels with high numbers after midnight. "No, unfortunately Ryan, there is no magic wand in this case," I answered to his dismay. In fact, that was the answer when the banks were aggressive. If you look at the post–global credit crunch market of 2009, it is even more challenging to qualify as a full-time real estate investor without a joint venture partner."

---

[1]All PK-Approved mortgage brokers across Canada are trained in the portfolio approach to lending.

"Oh, and speaking of joint venture partners," I reminded myself, "it's important to note that if you have two people on title, everything I just taught you about the impact of cash flow applies to them as well. In fact, one of the most common misconceptions I see is that two people go on title and each of them thinks they are qualifying individually. If, for example," I looked to the obvious example in the room, "Barb and Kathy both apply for a mortgage, and both go on the title, then all the information for both of them are added together on the "Impact of Cash Flow Worksheet." Their incomes are combined, and so are their debts. It's no longer Barb *and* Kathy, the application treats them as one entity combined. Keep that in mind for later on when we talk in more detail about joint venture partners."

"We've already experienced that," Barb interjected, "and it caught us off guard. I thought we would only need one of us to qualify, but we were both on title."

"That's right, and while I'm remembering things, I also need to make a note for those of you who are self-employed in the room." Little things kept popping into my head and I didn't want to forget them, so I threw them out as little reminders. "A lot of people ask me what happens when you've got a creative accountant and you write everything off. Well, it's simple. Do the math: zero x 40% = your DSL," I said, hoping to discourage anyone from either writing everything off in the future, or quitting their day job prematurely. "We do have the ability to approach banks with a degree of common sense. They know that as a self-employed individual, you will be writing a lot of things off, so just be prepared to provide a paper trail that allows us to show some legitimate add backs. But it's important to keep in mind that while I have no problem going to a bank and saying that Joey here makes more money than he declares, he's just got a creative accountant, it may be a problem if the bank then turns to me and says: "Then explain to me why Joey can't pay his Visa bill on time and he has all these other outstanding debts." What am I supposed to say to them?" I posed the question hoping to make a very strong point. "If you're self-employed and want to build a portfolio, it is critical that you get everything on the left side of this equation under control. That means paying off your credit cards and keeping your unsecured lines of credit in check.

"Remember," I continued with a slight smile, "there's a difference between self-employed and don't declare versus unemployed and don't have. The main point is to be prepared to provide a paper trail or evidence to back up your claims. This may also mean having a discussion with your accountant about not writing everything off, because sometimes it's actually better to show a little bit more income to qualify for mortgages," I suggested. "Yes, you increase your taxes, but you've got to do some analysis to see if the tax increase is worth it in order for you to have the ability to keep buying real estate."

"What if you are retired?" asked Liz. This was the first time we had really heard from Liz all day, so I was pleased to hear her asking questions. It was a sign to me that the wheels were turning as she and John were obviously getting close to making retirement decisions.

"That's simple," I responded. "Will you have a pension?"

"Why yes, it should be a good one," she answered matter-of-factly.

"Well, then all you need to do is apply the exact same formula and replace your current income in the equation with your verifiable pension income," I explained. "That's another reason why any purchase you make now, while you are still employed, should create a positive cash flow. You'll need it down the road when you're retired." I felt the need to really emphasize this point with them, because with John's current income and assets, they were actually in a position where they could easily qualify, even if they purchased a negative cash flow property. Again, it is a case of cause and effect, playing out the chess game so that you are taking into consideration not only the short-term but the long-term plan as well.

"So what happens if you simply can't verify any income and your DSL is zero," asked Brian.

"Don't worry, honey, I'm not quitting my job any day soon," Michelle quipped, not missing a beat.

"Well, the truth is," I answered, "if you truly can't verify enough income in order to qualify under the conventional debt service rules, then you have two choices: .

1. You will need to become 100% dependent on joint venture partners, which we will talk about later on in the day; or

2. You will need to shift your attention to buying multi-family or commercial property.

"I get the joint venture part, but why multi-family?" Jeff asked with a puzzled look on his face.

"Glad you asked, Jeff, because that raises a whole new topic," I announced. Once again, I remembered another not-so-minor detail. "Multi-family properties are considered 'commercial' mortgages and that's a completely different sandbox. Everything we've been talking about to this point," I started to explain, "has been in regard to residential mortgages. As soon as you cross over into commercial mortgages, there is a whole new set of rules."

I explained that most lenders will treat a property with six units or more as commercial, rather than residential, even if there is no business or retail component to the property. So, for example, if you purchase a 12-unit apartment building in which all 12 units are residential, and there is no actual business component to the building, it is still considered a commercial mortgage, not a residential one. Once you move into this sandbox, the rules change.

"The best way to describe the difference is to think about it like this," I explained. "In residential mortgages the most important component of the application is you—the borrower. The bank will spend the majority of its time focusing on you to determine if you have the ability to qualify for a mortgage. With commercial real estate, the roles are reversed and the property is the main focus. Which is good news for some of you."

"You got that right," Ryan blurted out almost relieved that there seemed to be an option for him.

"But having said that," I cautioned, "I said that you, as the covenant, are *less* important than the strength of the building. I did not say you were *unimportant.* This is not a loophole for someone who is unemployed to be able to qualify for a mortgage, just because they found a positive cash flow apartment building. The bank will still want to see that you have the ability to service your personal debts; however, they will be less stringent in terms of following the 40% TDS rules."

"Why wouldn't more self-employed people simply skip residential real estate and move straight into multi-family?" Jeff asked.

"Simple," I answered. "Cost of entry. An apartment building costs a lot more than a single-family home and the commercial lenders often require a higher down payment. Add it up and the majority of investors are forced to stay in the residential sandbox. But for those who do step up, there are fewer players and more options."

"We'll talk a bit more about commercial mortgages later over lunch. But for now, let's summarize obstacle number one: qualifying for a mortgage," I announced to the whole group in an effort to wrap up the discussion on this obstacle and move on. "We've now covered exactly what you need to do in order to qualify at a bank. You simply have to keep that left side and right side balanced. Always make sure that your DSL is higher than your monthly consumer debt, and focus on developing positive cash flow properties—not only for the reason of qualifying for a mortgage, but also because it is consistent with your actual goals. And finally, if all else fails and you simply can't verify enough income to qualify for a residential mortgage, either learn how to attract a joint venture partner who can help you, or shift your focus to multi-family units and qualify for a commercial loan instead. Regardless, you should all now have a strategy for tackling obstacle number one."

By the looks on the faces in the room, I could see that a lot of them were really "getting it" and there was a quiet sense of excitement building as some of them, perhaps for the first time, were starting to think: "Hey, I can do this!" In particular, I noticed Drs. Jasmine and Gill as well as Shelley. Dr. Gill had a look of excitement because, having done the exercise, he was beginning to see that qualifying wouldn't be an issue for them. He was quite anxious to move on to the next obstacle to see if it would cause an issue or not. Shelley, on the other hand, had a very strong sense of determination on her face. She, too, had done the math and was both surprised and excited to see that even on her modest salary, she would be able to continue buying properties, as long as she kept her personal debts down and focused on buying positive cash flow properties. "I really wondered how it would be possible for someone with my income to be able to keep buying more properties," she had asked earlier. Now she knew.

I know that there are a wide variety of investors or would-be investors in the Canadian real estate landscape and it is impossible to cover off every individual scenario in this forum. But no matter what your personal scenario, ultimately, you should be able to overcome obstacle number one in one of the following ways:

1. Ensure that your Debt Service Limit (DSL) is higher than your personal consumer debt.

2. Use private money as long as it does not hinder your future buying options and the numbers make sense.

3. Utilize joint venture partners if you simply cannot qualify on your own.

4. Shift your focus to multi-family commercial mortgages.

Regardless of your personal financial situation, you should be able to overcome obstacle number one by utilizing one of these methods. If you are still unclear about your own personal situation or would like some clarity, please go to www.peterkinch.com and e-mail us a question.[2]

Once you've determined how you are going to deal with obstacle number one, the next step is to tackle obstacle number two: coming up with the down payment required to buy the number of properties you need to accomplish your goal.

"Now I know a lot of you have more questions about multi-family and commercial mortgages," I announced. "So, as a special treat, I have asked a guest to join us over lunch. Neil Shopsowitz is our PK-Approved commercial mortgage specialist and will be joining us for the lunch break. Neil is a commercial mortgage specialist and can delve into much more detail than I can, so if anyone has a specific question relating to commercial or multi-family mortgages you can ask Neil when he joins us.

"But in the meantime, before we break for lunch, it is important that we cover a very important topic that is often overlooked—something I call "cap space."

---

[2] There is a PK-Approved mortgage broker in most provinces in Canada who can help walk you through this process and analyze your personal situation. Go to www.peterkinch.com to be put in touch with the broker nearest you.

Chapter 6

Managing Your Cap Space

"Cap space is the most common issue that blindsides investors for two reasons," I explained. "The first reason is that the majority of investors are typically unaware that such a thing even exists, and the second is that 70% of all investors typically go to their bank first, and since most bankers are transactionally focused they seldom, if ever, even think about cap space becoming an issue."

So what is "cap space"?

Cap space is the lending limit that a particular bank will place on an individual borrower. In other words, one day you will walk into your branch and your banker, the same banker who has been so helpful and understanding with all of your previous mortgages, will sit there and say, "I'm really sorry, but our risk department has told me that they are no longer comfortable with the amount of outstanding mortgages they have with you." (Note that it is always "they" and not "me.") What your banker is really telling you is that you've hit your funding limit with that bank.

"So in other words, we can't rely on just one bank to finance all of our mortgages?" Dr. Gill inquired.

"Depending on how aggressive your goals are, no," I answered.

"How do we know what our limit is?" Dr. Gill continued questioning.

"Well, I wish I could hand out a chart right now that would easily outline the differences at each bank, but the truth is, this is not a hard-and-fast rule and that's what makes it even more dangerous for you as an investor. In fact, for the average investor, your banker probably won't even know that such a limit exists until it's too late. Then you feel like you've hit the proverbial brick wall," I explained.

"That's exactly what happened to us," Barb said.

"Yeah, we had a lady down at our local branch who loved us, and we were so excited because she did all of our paperwork and every mortgage was like a piece of cake. Then suddenly, boom—out of the blue she says that they can't do anymore, that 'her hands are tied,'" Kathy added in a very frustrated tone.

"Let me ask you this: Did you have a conversation up front with her about your goals and how many properties you wanted to buy over the next five years?" I asked.

"Not in so many words. I mean, sure we told her we were looking at a lot of properties and she knew that we had just formed a partnership, but the issue of a lending limit never came up," Barb offered.

"It usually doesn't, until it's too late—remember, as an investor with more than five rental properties, you are an anomaly at your bank. So don't be surprised to find out that your banker doesn't even know what cap space is. They just don't come across it that often during the course of their day-to-day transactions. That is why this is such an important topic and one that will completely set you apart from other investors once you 'get it'!" I explained.

"But why wouldn't a bank want to have more of your business?" Sean asked. "I mean, wouldn't they be excited to have clients like us who will continue to bring them more mortgages? Isn't that how they make their money?" he rationalized.

"Let's be clear. Banks don't make money by simply lending money. They make money by lending money that is repaid," I explained. "And every bank has what they call a 'risk' department, and it's the risk manager's job to establish guidelines or 'comfort levels' as to what degree of risk the bank is willing to take. In the case of one individual buying multiple properties, they will have a point where they begin to feel 'overexposed' to either the borrower or, in some cases, a city. I've had a situation where a bank has told me that they feel that an individual has too many properties in ABC town. The bottom line is, every lender will have their own comfort level with investors and that can literally range from zero rental properties to a dozen. Sometimes, it will be the number of properties and at other times it will be a dollar amount. For example, BMO will often have a policy that they will only finance up to five doors with you. After that, you have to work with their commercial lending department. Other lenders will have an overall dollar limit. For example, some banks will only allow an aggregate total of $1.5 million of insured mortgages.

It will vary from bank to bank, but rest assured, they will all have a cap at some point."

"Does that mean you can only get $1.5 million of mortgages insured through CMHC?" Barb enquired.

"Well actually, CMHC doesn't actually have a limit per se. The actual CMHC policy is that they will judge each client on a case-by-case scenario, and the determining factor will be the TDS ratio (maximum 42% at time of writing). In other words, it's not so much an issue of how much you have in outstanding CMHC-insured mortgages, as it is your ability to service your overall debt—which includes all of your mortgages. However, once they reach a certain 'comfort level' with you as a borrower, they will impose a cap. Again, the challenge is that their cap limit is not written in black and white," I went on to explain.

"I was talking to a friend who is also an investor and they just got a mortgage with a company called 'Merix' or something like that," Linda said. "Since they are a trust company, do they have more flexibility than a bank?" she asked.

"That's a great question Linda," I began. "Trust companies such as Merix, Street Capital or DLC Mortgage all fit into a unique category since they are essentially distribution channels for institutional investors," I went on to explain.

"Okay, you just lost me with all that," Sean threw out.

"Well, let's break this down a bit," I began, as I attempted to touch on the variances of the Canadian banking system. "At the risk of oversimplifying the banking system, there are two basic types of lenders in the marketplace today. The chartered banks are 'deposit-taking' institutions, which lend out their own money. In other words, you deposit your money into the bank and they lend it out. The bank makes money on the 'spread' or difference between the amount they pay you as interest versus the amount they charge as interest on your loans.

"The point is that a chartered bank can have more control over their decision-making process because, at the end of the day, they are lending their own money. A trust company that is not a 'deposit-taking' institution will rely on raising capital from third-party investors—typically large institutional investors such as Deutsche Bank or a pension fund. These institutional investors make pools of money available to trust companies to be lent out as mortgages to Canadians, but under very specific terms or guidelines." I hoped that I was not opening up a can of worms by trying to break down the multi-faceted world of banking.

"So, theoretically, the investor could control how a trust company lends out its money," Kathy said, trying hard to understand the process.

"Exactly, and further to the point of cap space and how all of this involves CMHC, the majority of those institutional investors insist that the money they make available must be insured by either CMHC or Genworth. And since Genworth is not currently insuring any rental properties in Canada, the rental programs at most trust companies are restricted to CMHC guidelines. But even though CMHC does not have an official limit on the number of mortgages one individual has insured, the institutional lenders' guidelines will place a restriction on how much the trust company can lend to any one individual," I explained hoping I hadn't lost half of my audience.

"Now don't worry if this all sounds confusing. You do not have to worry about the inner workings of the Canadian banking system. The bottom line for you, as investors, and really the only thing you have to worry about, is the fact that regardless of whether you are currently dealing with a bank or trust company, at some point or another, you will hit their cap, assuming you are looking to build a larger portfolio," I continued.

"Yes, but if we don't know what the cap space is at each bank, how are we going to know where to send our mortgages?" asked Chad with a real look of concern.

"Well, at the risk of sounding self-serving, that is exactly why you need to work with a broker who understands how to manage your cap space, while balancing your ability to qualify with each lender." This is a very important topic, so I wanted to make sure that everyone understood how managing their cap space tied into everything that had been taught so far that day.

"By now, a lot of you are starting to figure out that depending on the size of your goal, getting the mortgages you need to accomplish that goal may not be as simple as just walking into your local branch every time you buy a property," I began. "In fact, it all comes back to the theme I've been talking about all day long—are you transactionally focused or portfolio focused? I hope by now you are starting to understand just how important it is to work with someone who knows the difference. We just finished talking about obstacle number one and the importance of balancing your personal debt with your portfolio debt—or as I like to call it 'the impact of cash flow.' A clear understanding of this concept is critical to your ability to qualify for mortgages. But equally important is the need to manage your cap space," I explained.

"This seems a bit confusing," Shelley sighed, with a familiar look on her face. It was familiar because I could see the same look on quite a few of the faces around the room.

"Well, before you start being too hard on yourself for not understanding all of this in a half hour, take heart in the fact that there are probably quite a few bankers and brokers out there who don't understand this either," I answered, trying to give the topic some perspective. "The fact is, Shelley," I continued, "the majority of people never think of these things, but at the same time, the majority of people never accomplish their goals."

"Good point," she smiled.

I wanted to make sure that everyone understood this part before moving on. "Think of this entire exercise like a chess game," I started. "Remember what I said earlier? A good chess player can think two to three moves in advance. Well, that is exactly what I'm teaching you to do. The big difference is that you are now playing with a partner—us." As I started my explanation, I could see that many of the confused looks were starting to disappear. "Once you realize that we are your partner in this chess game, you will begin to understand that you don't need to know everything in detail—that's our job. You just need to know the basic concepts so you don't question us when we're moving you into position for checkmate.

"So how exactly will working with you help us with our cap space?" asked Dr. Gill.

"Well, to start with, you know that we know cap space exists, unlike many bankers. We also have a good understanding of how many doors you will need to purchase in order to allow you to accomplish your goal, from having helped you put your real estate action plan together. We will have a very good idea of where you will run into cap space issues at each bank and, therefore, we can help you build your portfolio strategically, to maximize your cap space."

"Can you give me an example?" he asked.

"Sure, let's say that your goal was to buy 20 properties over the next five years," I began.

"That's a good start," he chuckled, knowing that I already knew his goal was for many more than that, but I wanted to use a conservative example.

"We know right away that you will quite likely need a few banks to accomplish this task," I continued. "And let's say, for example, that you currently have a great relationship with the Royal Bank." I used RBC as an example for two reasons. One, they are an "investor-friendly" bank. In other words, they will lend on more than five properties, but they will have a cap. The second reason I chose RBC was that they do not work with mortgage brokers. They have their own "feet on the street" sales team and I wanted to demonstrate that I was not simply trying to bias the group towards only working with us as a broker.

"Let's assume that you have a great relationship with your personal banker down at RBC. Knowing that, I would expect they will be willing to do you 'favours' and will help you as much as possible," I continued.

"For example, once you have more than 10 properties and other banks start saying no to you, that's when you're really going to need to start relying on those favours. I know this might sound really simple, but this is where most investors make a huge mistake. They think that because they have a wonderful relationship with their local banker, they should start out by getting their first investment property mortgage with that bank. Well, let's take a look at that concept," I stated as I tried to emphasize the importance of having a "strategy" for placing your mortgages, rather than simply taking the easy path.

"Again, here's what we know. We know that there are probably four or five trust companies that will provide you with mortgages on your first two properties, as long as they are CMHC insured.[1] Now I must emphasize here that companies like DLC, Merix, Street Capital and Xceed will insure your investment property mortgage with CMHC even if it's a 'conventional' mortgage," I explained.

"So even though we put 20% down, it still needs to be insured?" queried Linda.

---

[1] Now that CMHC has reverted to a 50% add back policy as of April 2010, these trust companies will be limited to financing a maximum of only two rental properties.

"Yes, that's right," I answered her.

"But I thought you only had to use CMHC if your mortgage was a 'high-ratio' deal?" Sean challenged me, sounding confused.

"Usually that is correct, Sean, but do you remember when I was explaining that most trust companies use a third-party institutional investor to source their funds?"

"Well," I continued, "those third-party investors want all the mortgages in their portfolio insured by CMHC. That way, their investment—which is your mortgage—is more secure. In fact, it's totally secure, because it's insured by the Canadian government. So for that reason, most trust companies will insure your mortgage at 80% loan to value (LTV) and then cover the premium themselves. In many cases, you, as the borrower, might not even be aware that your mortgage was insured. But this is also the reason that all of the trust companies will have a cap after two mortgages in your portfolio. Quite simply, a 50% add back doesn't work once you have more than two rental properties. No matter how many combinations of these lenders you use, you will likely cap out.

"So now that you know this, here's your first test," I said with a wry smile. "If we know Dr. Gill will need twenty mortgages in total and he has a great relationship with RBC, but they may only do from six to ten mortgages with him, should he get his first two mortgages with RBC or with one of the trust companies?"

"That sounds like one of those math problems they gave us in high school," Marc joked.

"Yeah, if a train left the station at 5 p.m . . ." Sean laughed.

"I know it can seem that way, but hey, welcome to my world! Just be thankful that we'll take care of all of this for you. But the truth is, once you get this concept it is actually quite easy. Think about it. Dr. Gill needs up to twenty mortgages. We know that he can get two of them fairly easily through one of the trust companies, but once he has more than two somewhere else, he generally can't go back to the trust companies."

"So are you saying that if I got my first two mortgages with RBC I couldn't go to a trust company for my third property, even if it's the first one with that company?" Dr. Gill asked, trying to understand.

"Well, technically that may vary from lender to lender, and some of these trust companies may change their policy from time to time, but for the most part, that is true. At the very least, it's a good guideline to go by," I responded trying not to be too vague.

"What I'm trying to stress here, in a nutshell, is that properties one and two are significantly easier to finance than properties three through twenty, and that as your portfolio grows, your options become more restrictive. Again, using Dr. Gill's example of buying twenty properties, he has the most options when financing the first two purchases. Therefore, it makes sense that he should use a trust company for these first two purchases, and then use a different bank for the next few. In fact, depending on what your relationship is with your own bank, you may want to save them for when you really need a favour. For example, Dr. Gill could use a mix of RBC, Scotiabank and CIBC over the next ten purchases, but always preserve cap space at RBC for the last three or four purchases, since that's when he will need the most help from his bank," I went on to explain.

"I think I'm starting to get it," Dr. Gill announced with a confident smile.

"Great, now here's the bonus question," I stated.

"What should you do with the mortgage on your principal residence?" I posed this question to see if they were really starting to understand the importance of cap space.

"Well, my principal residence mortgage is over $500,000, so if my bank will limit me according to the total dollar amount of mortgages I have with them, I shouldn't have my principal mortgage there, should I?" Gill was half questioning, half reasoning it out.

"I think you're starting to get it," I said with a smile. "Now it's important to emphasize that what I'm teaching you is an overall strategic concept that will vary from bank to bank and individual to individual, depending on whether you currently bank with a chartered bank or a credit union. But the concept is simple. Be strategic about how you manage your cap space. To summarize, using the example we've been using all along, if I were Dr. Gill, I would *not* place my principal residence with RBC. In fact, I wouldn't place it with any of the main chartered banks, because all of them are what I refer to as 'investor friendly.' I would place my $500,000 principal residence mortgage with a lender that doesn't lend on revenue property. That way, I free up $500,000 of valuable cap space at RBC which can be, and will need to be, used to help me get properties 15 through 20."

"That makes total sense. I never thought of that," said Kathy.

"I wish I knew that about a year ago," added Barb, feeling excited about learning a new strategy and ticked that she hadn't known about it before.

"Well remember, before you beat yourself up, it's a strategy, and very few brokers and bankers think about this, let alone investors. So don't be surprised that you didn't know about it," I concluded.

NOTE

Although every bank will have a cap space or limit as to how many mortgages they will grant each individual investor, those rules are typically not written in stone and can vary depending on market conditions. Managing your cap space should be used as a guideline for investors—not a hard-and-fast rule.

"Is this something that we need to worry about?" asked Marc.

Knowing that their goal was to create $3,000 a month in extra/passive cash flow over the next 15 years and that they could likely achieve this by finding three houses that rented for over a $1,000 a month, I told him no. "Marc, the focus for you and Nicole would be totally different. You only need to focus on finding three good, quality homes, with good tenants and then shift your attention to debt reduction, paying off those mortgages as fast as possible in order to realize your lifestyle goal 15 years from now," I explained. "In your case, cap space will never be an issue, so you're free to choose any lender you prefer."

"Is cap space an issue if we are buying commercial properties or multi-family?" Sean asked.

"Good question Sean, thanks for reminding me. I keep forgetting to emphasize that we are talking about residential mortgages." I responded quickly as I noticed a few people in the room had started to change their notes. "Cap space, not to be confused with 'cap rate,' is really a residential mortgage issue. When dealing with commercial mortgages, lenders have a completely different set of criteria for risk. In fact, that would be a good question for Neil over lunch," I clarified.

"Again, the bottom line is to become more aware of the need to act like a sophisticated investor," I summarized. "As you build your action plan throughout the day, you will need to determine for yourself what degree of an obstacle 'qualifying at the bank' will be for you. And now, you also know how to factor in your cap space as part of the equation. As your broker, we'll be doing two things simultaneously with you on each mortgage. From a 3,000-foot vantage point, we'll be making sure that you can balance the left side and right side of your portfolio so that you can continue to qualify for mortgages. At the same time, we'll be managing your cap space at each lender, moving you along like a chess piece on the board."

"I can see now what you meant when you told me there was much more to this than simply finding the best rate," Brian said, recalling our initial conversation. I could see that some of the pieces were starting to fall into place for him. Michelle had been pretty quiet through this whole section, but she was beginning to see that there was a way to do this.

"That still leaves the question about how to come up with the money to buy all this real estate," Michelle stated, as if on queue.

"Great point, Michelle," I responded. "In fact, that leads us right to the next obstacle." And as I said that, the door opened and Neil Shopsowitz walked in, and I knew we were right on time for lunch. "Well now that Neil's here, lunch must be ready. Let's take a one-hour break for lunch, talk about commercial mortgages and then dive into the second obstacle—down payments—when we come back for the second half of the day."

The group was quick to bounce up. Their heads were filled with a lot of information from the morning session and many were eager to share their thoughts with each other. I could tell by the buzz in the room and the conversations that were taking place that the morning had produced as many questions as it had answers, but one thing was certain—it had got everyone thinking.

Chapter 7

Commercial Mortgages

LUNCH WITH NEIL

We laid out a spread of sandwiches, a veggie tray, some sushi and a fruit platter. As everyone settled back into the room and filled a plate, I introduced Neil Shopsowitz. I've been working with Neil for over two years now and have a great deal of respect for his knowledge. Neil actually comes from a legal background and was a lawyer in Toronto in a previous life. This gave him a very analytical approach and made him perfect for the commercial mortgage business. In addition to that, Neil also had experience in running a franchise, so he understood the art of being self-employed. He was a good fit with our office because I knew that it is impossible to be everything to everybody and there is such a difference between residential mortgages and commercial mortgages, that it warranted having someone completely dedicated to that one discipline. I learned a long time ago that if you try to be an expert in too many fields at the same time, you're ineffective at everything you do. So, to that end, Neil was our in-house commercial mortgage specialist.

Having Neil join us for the lunch hour was a great privilege for the workshop. His job was to answer any questions about commercial mortgages. My job was to translate his answers into English.

"While everyone eats their lunch, anyone who has commercial mortgage questions can pick Neil's brain for the next half hour or so," I began. "But before we get into specific questions, let's go over a quick summary of the 'commercial mortgage sandbox.'

"First of all, we need to clarify what a bank defines as a 'commercial mortgage.' Virtually every bank in Canada will treat a property with up to four doors as a residential property. There are a few who will treat a five-plex as residential, but with very few exceptions, any property with six or more units will be deemed a commercial property."

"What if there are no businesses on the main floor and all the units are residential tenants?" John asked.

"Your realtor may refer to that as 'residential,' but the bank would view it as 'multi-family' and, as such, it would fit into the commercial sandbox," I clarified.

"Now again, at the risk of oversimplifying things, let me give you a few overviews on commercial financing to help you put it into perspective," I announced, knowing that I needed to get everyone up to at least one level of commercial financing knowledge before Neil lost them on the technical stuff. "Now you may recall that I ended the last section on qualifying for a mortgage with a list of options if you weren't able to qualify for a residential investment mortgage. Included in that list was shifting your portfolio to 'multi-family' purchases. The reason multi-family properties becomes an option for you is that banks have a different set of criteria for financing them. Simply put, when you buy a residential rental property, the bank will look at *you* first and the property second. They will want to make sure that you have the financial ability to 'qualify' for the mortgage—then they'll look at the property to make sure it's something they would want to lend on, but the main focus is on you," I began to explain. "But when it comes to 'commercial' real estate, the relationship becomes inverted and the main focus is on the *property* and you are secondary'"

"Wow that's encouraging," a suddenly upbeat Ryan said.

"That certainly doesn't mean that the bank won't look at you," Neil was quick to add, making sure I wasn't setting them up for any false expectations.

"No, of course not, but it does mean that if you are self-employed and are having difficulty fitting into that 40% DSL box, you may have more flexibility in the commercial sandbox," I added

"Yes, you'll certainly have more flexibility, because at the end of the day, so much of it comes down to the cash flow of the building," Neil injected.

"We'll talk about the cash flow and how banks measure that in a moment, but one thing I want to do for everyone up front is to help 'manage your expectations' regarding commercial or multi-family mortgages," I interrupted, wanting to quickly cover some of the basic points that create the most problems in our office when dealing with new investors wanting to shift from residential to commercial.

"The first thing you really need to understand about commercial mortgages is that it really is a different set of sandbox rules. One of the most frustrating things we see in our office is someone who phones and says, 'Hey, thanks for arranging that wonderful mortgage last month on our duplex. We just bought another property and I want to put 5% down on that one as well and get the same rate.' I'll say, 'Great, what did you buy?' and he'll say, 'A 12-plex.' Then I have to go into the full explanation about the difference between the two types of mortgage sandboxes. So let's walk through a few basics right now, so that you can save yourself some frustration and you don't leave here today with any false expectations," I explained at the risk of over-emphasizing my point.

"To begin with, the players in the sandbox have changed. The banks and people you work with on your residential mortgages will not likely be the same people you will work with on your commercial mortgages. The second point to be aware of is that, although you can still get a high-ratio commercial mortgage through CMHC, you will have to put a minimum of 15% down, and I'll let Neil elaborate on that. The third point I need to stress is that there is a completely different cost structure involved in arranging and getting a commercial mortgage. When you get a residential mortgage, you can work with a broker and the bank will pay the broker. However, it doesn't work that way with commercial mortgages. Your broker will have to charge you a fee, and not only will the bank *not* pay the broker, they'll actually charge you a fee for the privilege of getting a mortgage from them."

"One of the most common issues I run into with investors who are used to buying residential properties is that they are put off by all the fees," Neil added.

"That's why I'm going over this part, Neil, so you don't have to look like the bad guy," I laughed. "In fact, the one thing you will find out about commercial real estate in a hurry is that everything is more expensive: the appraisals, the legal stuff, the inspections, things such as environmental reviews, etc.," I could tell by the look on some of their faces that I was starting to scare them. "The key is simply to be aware that there will be additional costs, but it can also be worth the added expenses," I added, trying not to put them off multi-family mortgages completely. In fact, multi-family investments can create an economy of scale for the investor. Buying one

25-unit apartment building with one roof, one boiler and one property manager, may be far more efficient and cost effective than buying 25 individual single-family units. So you shouldn't be surprised that the purchase itself will require significantly more time and up-front expense. The key for me was to manage their expectations and, in this case, cover off some of the obvious questions for Neil, while giving everyone a chance to finish off at least half a sandwich before grilling Neil with questions.

"How much of an issue is it that I'm self-employed?" asked Jeff. Given the fact that he was starting a new business, I was not surprised to hear this question from Jeff.

"Well, as Peter said," Neil began as I took the opportunity to grab some sushi, "there is more emphasis on the quality of the property with commercial borrowing. Banks will look at the creditworthiness of the borrower, but in the vast majority of cases, the personal guarantees of the principals will be required. For personal borrowers," he continued, "income verification is a factor, but it's not crucial."

"That should make some of you feel better," I threw in with a facetious laugh.

"Yeah, totally," said Jeff resoundingly.

"Now be careful," I cautioned, just in case everyone got excited about quitting their jobs too soon. "Like I said earlier, don't interpret the fact that the property is more important than you to mean that you are not important at all; it simply means that there will be less emphasis on your actual verifiable income."

"That's correct," Neil continued. "The key factors will be your net worth. They will want to see that you have a reasonable amount of net worth to support a sizable portion of your personal guarantees along with the ability to make the required down payment through tangible net assets."

"Gee, just when I was starting to feel good about this option," Ryan said with a smile.

"Keep in mind that everything Neil talks about goes for your joint venture partner as well," I reminded them, knowing that a young guy like Ryan may not have the assets to qualify on his own, but if he was to seek out the right joint venture partner, together they might. We'll talk more about that topic a little later when we cover down payment options.

"And of course, any prior bankruptcies or serious credit issues for any-one who will be on title will be a problem for commercial lenders," Neil added.

"Does it make a difference if I buy it in my personal name or a company name?" Sean asked.

"It depends on why you're asking," I interjected, knowing that many investors falsely believe that if they buy something in their company name, then the bank will look at the company—not them.

"All banks in Canada—whether we are talking residential or commercial mortgages—will require that you provide a personal guarantee on the mortgage," I continued. "So please do not believe some of the stuff you hear or see on late-night TV that buying your real estate through a corporation is a way around having to personally qualify for a mortgage. Or, for that matter, don't think for a second that your other assets are protected if you default on the loan. There is a lot of false information out there and you need to get the facts," I said with a sense of urgency, wanting to emphasize this point. "For the most part, whether you incorporate or not really has no bearing on how the bank views your mortgage, because you have to put up a personal guarantee regardless. Now there may well be some legal or tax benefits to incorporating, so before you make a decision about whether to incorporate or not, make sure you sit down with your accountant to get the facts and do it for the right reasons." That was my little side rant on the inevitable question: "Should I incorporate or not?"

Those of you who are still wondering whether you should incorporate or not, please send us an e-mail at clientcare@peterkinch.com and we will send you a list of contacts and references in your area. It is important to note that it is difficult to get good, unbiased advice these days and there are actually people who teach you to always incorporate before buying real estate. My question is: Who is benefitting the most from that advice? Remember, your accountant and your lawyer will earn additional fees every time you incorporate a company, so make sure you get the right advice from an accountant who specializes in real estate.

"Peter's right, when someone buys a property in a holding company or a shell company, the lender pretty much looks at the strength of the personal guarantees along with the cash flow from the property," Neil continued to explain.

"How much should we budget for a down payment on a commercial building?" Sean asked.

"Neil, before you answer that," I jumped in, "I think it's important to talk about the sandboxes within the sandbox," I said, knowing I'd get some strange looks. "Even within the commercial sandbox there are differences in definitions. For example, a 20-unit apartment building is considered 'multi-family' by CMHC and, therefore, 'insurable' as a high-ratio mortgage. Whereas an office building with multiple tenants or a warehouse/ industrial unit would not be insurable or considered a multi-family."

"That's correct," added Neil. "The amount of down payment required could vary greatly with commercial real estate. Generally speaking, the maximum loan to value that a bank will allow on a commercial property is 75% of the purchase price or appraised value, depending on which is lower."

"Note that Neil said 'maximum' loan," I added quickly, trying to stress this point since it is an area that differs greatly from residential. "In fact, it's not uncommon for a commercial borrower to have to put down more than 35% or 40% in order to get a mortgage."

"Now you're starting to depress me," Ryan said dejectedly.

"Don't worry, we'll show you how to overcome that obstacle in the next section after lunch," I added reassuringly.

"This is where there is a big difference between multi-family and office/industrial use," Neil said, carrying on while most of the class focused on finishing up their lunch. "If you're buying a commercial office space or an industrial unit, then there really is no high-ratio option. You will require at least a 25% down payment or more. And that will be determined by the net operating income (NOI) of the unit or building. If you are buying a multi-family building, however, there is an option to have the mortgage insured through CMHC, and if they agree to insure the mortgage, you may only have to put down as little as 15%," Neil explained.

"Note that Neil said as little as 15% and not 5%! I want to make sure we don't get any calls Monday morning from any of you hoping to buy something with 5% down," I stated emphatically. Can you tell I've had those calls before?

"Yes, and again, it comes right back to the cash flow of the building," Neil went on to explain. "CMHC will look at the NOI of the building based on the rent roll, and then apply a debt coverage ratio of between 1.2% and 1.3%."

"By the way, a debt coverage ratio, or DCR as we like to say, is simply a formula for factoring in your ratio of income to expense. Without going into elaborate detail or walking you all through a course on banking, simply think of it like this," I explained, interrupting Neil as soon as I saw the sea of confused looks in the room. Given my background as a teacher, I could always tell when the majority of my students were politely nodding but not really understanding.

"When we say that CMHC wants a property to have a DCR of 1.25%, think of that as meaning they want to see a $1.25 of income for every dollar of expense. Remember, 'You don't need to know how a motor works in order to drive a car.' And you guys don't need to know exactly how CMHC calculates their DCR formulas. What you *do* need to know is that they have a formula and the better your cash flow is, the better odds you have of putting less money down."

"And you're going to need at least a DCR of 1.25% in order to qualify for an 85% mortgage with CMHC," Neil added.

"What if I want to buy some raw land and build on it?" John asked.

"Anything I should know about dear?" asked an inquisitive Liz.

"Well, you never know, if the right piece of land came up . . ." John responded without quite sounding like he was backpedalling.

"Actually, raw land is very hard to finance," Neil stated. "You're likely looking at putting up to 50% down to purchase the land. And, since there is no cash flow from the property, they will place more emphasis on the borrower's ability to service the loan."

"So it would be treated more like a residential mortgage," Barb added.

"Yes, for the most part," Neil said and then added, "once you've secured the raw land though, you can arrange for a 'construction loan.'"

"Again, a sandbox within a sandbox," I said with a chuckle, "and you thought our job was easy."

"An appraisal will be required giving two values—one as-is, and the other as-completed. The lender will then create a 'draw-mortgage,' whereby they lend you a total amount for the whole project, but only advance it in 'draws' as you complete each phase. But financing for these types of projects is available for up to 80% of the cost of the project, and the borrower's existing equity in the land or property will be applied as part of the equity in the project," Neil explained.

"Well," John nodded, "I think I'll keep that in mind for down the road."

"Make sure you let me know before you head off to start building things in our retirement," his wife Liz was quick to add.

"Don't worry honey, you'll be the first to know," John told her reassuringly.

"It's almost time to wrap up lunch," I reminded everyone. "Is there anything else anyone wants to ask Neil?"

"Before we finish up, I'd like to remind everyone of a few items that always come up and tend to blindside borrowers who are new to commercial borrowing," Neil volunteered. "First of all, remember that the borrower is typically responsible for all the costs on commercial loans. Unlike residential loans, the borrower pays for appraisals, environmental reports, legal fees for both themselves and the lenders, lenders fees, and brokers commissions and fees. And, probably one of the most important items to address is timing," Neil added with a degree of urgency in his voice. "Because of the steps involved in obtaining commercial loan approvals and commitments, there is a great deal more time required to waive all conditions and proceed to closing. Ideally, you should allow six to eight weeks to remove subjects and an additional three to four weeks to proceed to closing."

"Okay, that's really important to note, gang," I said, making sure everyone got Neil's last point. "So there are two things I don't want to hear on Monday morning. Don't call saying you just bought a 12-unit building and want a mortgage with 5% down and you only have seven days for subject removal," I said with a smile, but my point was very serious and I think they all got it.

"I have one last question," Kathy said as everyone started to clean up from lunch.

"Sure, we have time for a quick question," I responded, knowing that our hour was up and we needed to get moving on to the second half.

"You mentioned that you can only get a 65% first mortgage sometimes, depending on the cash flow," Kathy continued. "Is it possible to get a second mortgage so that we don't have to come up with all of that down payment ourselves?"

"That's a good question and an avenue a lot of borrowers struggle with," Neil responded. "Ultimately, it will depend on the lender, but in today's market environment, most lenders will not allow secondary financing because of the emphasis they place on the cash flow in calculating their initial risk."

"I like the idea of buying multi-family units," Kathy told him. "But if I have to put 40% down every time, we'll run out of money in a hurry."

"That's a perfect segue into the next topic," I said jumping in, anxious to keep the day on schedule. "Now that we are finished with lunch, we'll get right into obstacle number two, which is 'coming up with the down payments.' So we'll be covering that Kathy, because I can guarantee that you're not the only person in the room who has thought about this issue."

And with that, we thanked Neil for joining us and took five minutes to stretch our legs before diving right back into the second half of the day.

Chapter 8

Overcoming Obstacle Two—Coming Up with the Down Payment

RECAP

I looked around the room as people trickled back in for the afternoon session, and I couldn't help but notice how different the room looked. It had only been half a day, but the difference in some participants was quite pronounced. Dr. Gill and his wife were beaming with excitement as they reviewed their notes from the morning and seemed quite anxious to learn how to overcome the next obstacle. Sean and Candice had spent a lot of time on the break talking with Barb and Kathy, and I could hear that they were swapping ideas back and forth. Nicole and Marc were comfortable with their goals and, more importantly, their ability to accomplish them within their timeline. They were actually quite interested in speaking with John and Liz to learn more about their vision of creating a legacy for their children and grandchildren. Jeff, Chad and Brian were being entertained by Ryan, who was regaling them with stories of flying and describing, in great detail, the make and model of his private jet. Linda, Shelley and Michelle were hitting it off wonderfully, telling stories of how they each balanced work and kids, while creating visions of what it would be like to have enough money from their real estate so they could do what they really wanted.

I could see that Michelle was slowly letting her guard down. She was certainly doing more of the listening when the topic moved from work and kids to dreams and visions, but she wasn't nearly as closed to the concept now as she had been in the morning—not so much because she suddenly had caught the bug to buy real estate, which was not my objective, but because she was starting to see that there might be a way for Brian to do this without risking their life savings.

"Now that you've all had something to eat and a crash course in commercial mortgages, think it's a good time to review what we actually accomplished this morning," I began, as everyone got settled in their seats. "You'll recall that we started out by everyone agreeing that our main purpose here was not to buy real estate, correct?" Everyone nodded as they remembered back to the beginning of the day.

"In fact, we all agreed that real estate was simply the vehicle of choice to accomplish an end result. So it isn't real estate that we want so much as it is the results that real estate can produce. And if we drill down deep enough, and we're honest with ourselves, we want those results because there's a lifestyle that we envision for ourselves. And at the end of the day, it's that lifestyle that is truly what's most important to us." Again, I could see everybody reflecting back to where the day began.

"So we started the day with the end result in mind. We began with the vision. Each of you visualized your future—a future to be lived and created on purpose. Once you clarified what your future lifestyle looked like, you calculated how much money you would require on a monthly basis to live that lifestyle five years from now. And once you had that number, you were able to calculate the gap between how much money you anticipate needing to live your future lifestyle and how much money you anticipate earning five years from now. The gap is the amount of money that your real estate has to produce for you over the next five years in order for you to accomplish that end goal. By identifying the role real estate has to serve, you were able to calculate how many doors you would need to buy in order to create sufficient cash flow to realize your lifestyle goal. And finally, we were able to work our way back to today, and identify two obstacles that stood in our way of purchasing the necessary real estate.

"Obstacle number one is qualifying for a mortgage, and we spent considerable time learning how to balance the left side and the right side of your portfolio balance sheet, while keeping in mind the cap space at each bank.

"Obstacle number two is coming up with the amount of money required for the down payment for each property."

By recounting the entire morning, the class began to realize just how much they had covered in a short time.

"And that brings us here," I concluded. "We are standing on the edge of obstacle number two—finding the money for down payments. So, let me ask you something," I challenged them.

"If I could write each of you a blank cheque right now and provide you with all the money you needed in order to buy the necessary property to accomplish your goals, and I emphasize that this is hypothetical," I added in order to lighten things up a bit, "how many of you would be confident in being able to go out and accomplish your goal?" I was not surprised to see that over 80% of the room put their hands up. "And I would hazard to guess that for those who didn't raise their hands, the remaining obstacle would be what, where and how to buy the properties? Is that accurate?" I asked looking directly at Sean.

"Absolutely, I'm still not sure what I should be buying," Sean offered.

"Well, assuming that you could join a group like REIN that can teach you those details, would you agree that between knowing what, where and how to buy real estate and having a blank cheque to pay for it, you should be pretty well set?" I asked.

"Sure, that would definitely help," he added.

"Then you would agree that the only thing separating the majority of you from your goal is the down payment?" I challenged them again. "If that's the case, on a scale of 1 to 10, with 1 being not important at all, how important is it to you to learn how to overcome this obstacle?"

"Eleven," shouted Chad.

"Exactly! So on that note, let's take a look at what your down payment options are," I stated, knowing that I now had their undivided attention.

Note: It is important again to point out that the obstacles referred to in this book are in relation to *how you are going to finance your portfolio*. This book is not designed to delve into how to find properties or research the best markets for properties, etc. There are plenty of books available that go into great detail on those subjects—including the book I co-authored with Don Campbell, *97 Tips for Canadian Real Estate Investors*. For our purposes, we will stick to the financing obstacles.

OBSTACLE NUMBER TWO: DOWN PAYMENTS

"The entire purpose of looking at your portfolio from a 3,000-foot view is to be able to identify the roadblocks or obstacles before you encounter them," I began, as we started working on what is quite likely the most common obstacle facing Canadians today. "The advantage that I have over the majority of you is that whereas you are looking at your own personal portfolio and situation, I have the benefit of having worked with thousands of investors across Canada. Therefore, I've seen the patterns and can start to predict outcomes. And the one pattern I've come across more consistently than any other is a surprisingly high number of false assumptions when it comes to analyzing down payment options for investors.

"Now a lot of this," I went on to explain, "is the result of either listening to too much late-night TV, attending too many American-focused seminars or simply not understanding that you are playing in a different sandbox, and the rules that applied when you bought your principal residence don't necessarily apply here." As I looked around the room, I could see that everyone was quite intent on learning more about this topic, mostly because they had all concluded that this was their biggest obstacle.

"So again, to clarify, please go back in your workbooks and look up the number of doors you wrote down as your gap doors." I wanted to confirm what I thought I already knew. (For the reader, go back to Chapter 4, page 54, for your gap doors figure.)

"Here's my question: Knowing that every one of you had a certain number of gap doors required to accomplish your goal, if you had to put 20% down to purchase each of those doors, how many of you would have enough money today to cover the down payments?" I asked, already sure of the answer, but wanting to ensure no one was kidding themselves.

"Oh, I'd have no problem," laughed Ryan, knowing full well that he had no idea how he was going to come up with sufficient funds.

"Actually, we're not too far off, depending on how much equity we can take out of our home," said Marc.

"Or, as we will soon find out, it may be more of an issue of how much you're willing to take out," I stated, knowing that would be a major conversation between Nicole and Marc.

Before I asked the question, I had pretty much figured out that Marc and Nicole would be close to being capable of accomplishing their goals, simply because they were only targeting three properties, which was a very tangible target. I also thought that John and Liz may very well have the resources to accomplish their objective with a little coaching, again depending on how aggressive Liz's charitable goals were. And sure enough, John was sitting there doing a few calculations before announcing, "Actually, we might be close, but then again, maybe I'm making some false assumptions too."

"Well, we'll soon find out," I responded. "I think it's safe to assume that this next section will be quite revealing for all of you, to find out just what you can and cannot do in terms of accessing money for down payments. But to start with, let's begin with an outline of what you will need in terms of a down payment for a rental property in Canada."

"The first misconception that real estate investors often have is that there is no difference between buying a rental property and buying your principal residence," I began as I expanded on a topic that we had covered earlier. I knew that by now, I was preaching to the converted and didn't need to elaborate too much on the fact that banks treat investors quite differently than they do homeowners, but nonetheless, there were some real estate basics that needed to be reviewed.

"We will be going over seven options for down payments shortly, but before I do, I want to start with some basics so that everyone is on the same page with some standard assumptions. First of all, there is no such thing in Canada as a zero-down purchase. You may hear a lot of people say that they purchased a property with 'nothing down,' but that's actually not true. Once you hear their story you will realize that what they meant was 'they' put nothing down. This is usually a situation where an investor used a joint venture partner to put up the money and they were the deal finder," I explained.

"The point I'm trying to make is that there are ways for you to personally put nothing into the deal, but for a typical purchase of a typical rental property in Canada, you will need to put down a minimum of 20%."

It is important to note that these are the rules and guidelines at the time of writing. These rules are subject to change at any point by both lenders and governmental regulations.

"But a guy I talked to up in Fort Mac bought two properties a few years back with zero down," Chad commented with some disappointment.

"He probably did," I answered confidently. "From early 2007 to mid-2008, CMHC actually changed their policies to allow zero-down mortgages for an 18-month period. But can anyone tell me what happened in August of 2007 in the United States that eventually led the Canadian government to put the clamp down on this program?"

"Oh, just a sub-prime crisis," responded Candice.

"Followed by a global credit crunch," added John.

"And rounded off nicely with a global recession," Jeff chimed in.

"Exactly, and that's one of the reasons it's become even more important for you to be aware of your options in this section," I stated. "Coming off three global financial issues in a row causes banks to be more cautious, it should cause you to be cautious as well. Again, the bottom line is, expect to put down between at least 20% and 25% for any purchase of residential real estate, and between 15% and 45% for the purchase of a commercial property if you want to do it right." I wanted to stress that no one was here to learn some late-night "quick flip, nothing down" strategies so this was a point worth repeating.

SEVEN OPTIONS FOR FINDING DOWN PAYMENTS

"Okay, let's jump right into it," I began. "Working with my clients over the years, I have compiled a list of seven different options for coming up with down payments for buying a rental property, whether it's residential or commercial." I then listed these seven options before going into detail on each of them:

1. Liquid assets
2. Real estate equity
3. High-ratio insured mortgages
4. Sub-prime mortgages
5. Private money
6. Vendor take-back mortgages
7. Joint venture partners

Option One: Liquid Assets

"The first option in this list is the easiest and most obvious—liquid assets. It's also the one thing that most investors have the least of," I said facetiously.

"Liquid assets can include money you have under your mattress or in the bank, such as savings accounts. But it can also include any asset you are willing or able to liquidate."

"Is that like an RRSP?" asked Shelley.

"No, I definitely wouldn't include RRSPs in this category unless you were really willing to pre-maturely liquidate them and pay the tax. Personally, I'm not a big fan of that. I think your portfolio should be balanced and, in most cases, if you have money in an RRSP, I would keep it in there. What I'm talking about are non-RRSP assets or investments in stocks, bonds or other funds that you feel would be better served liquidated, leveraged and used to buy real estate," I explained. "Now, understand that I'm not telling you to go liquidate your stock portfolio. I'm saying that it is an option when you are making a list of where the money for your next down payment is coming from."

"I had a ton of money tied up for years in mutual funds, which were underperforming and decided to move it all into real estate," announced Kathy proudly.

"Again, some of you may be very unhappy with the way a certain portfolio is performing and want to liquidate it—obviously Kathy wasn't happy with hers. Whether you do that or not is your choice. My point is that if you have your own cash to use as a down payment, it is the easiest source of down payment funds and the most attractive to the bank. If you use your own funds for the down payment, then the bank will view you as a stronger client," I explained.

"Would that include money from a line of credit?" Brian asked, expecting Michelle to remind him he wasn't allowed to touch that.

"Actually Brian, your line of credit, or LOC as it's called, is part of option two: real estate equity," I answered quickly so Michelle would have no time to get into it with him.

Option Two: Real Estate Equity

"As you may have guessed, real estate equity is the equity either in your principal residence or any other real estate that you own," I began. "This is probably the single, most common source of money used as down payments for rental portfolios. If you have more than 20% in equity of the market value of your home, you can apply to a lender to access it in the form of a secured LOC. The difference between a personal LOC and a secured LOC is that the secured LOC is 'secured' by the equity in your home. Since a personal LOC has no such 'collateral security,' it is deemed to be debt and is not allowed to be used as a down payment for a house in most cases."

"You'll note that I said at least 20%. Why did I choose that number?" I questioned everyone.

"Less than that and it has to be insured," Answered Linda.

"I thought it was 25%?" queried Dr. Gill.

"It used to be," I responded. "Up until 2007 Dr. Gill was correct; you had to put at least 25% down in order for your mortgage to still be considered conventional. But in 2007, the *Bank Act* was actually changed to make it 20%. Anything less than that and it will need to be insured, which we'll cover under the next option. But before we move onto the next option, I'd like to cover off a product that I think is very important to real estate investors if you are thinking of accessing equity in your principal residence," I said, trying to shift gears a little, because there were a few very important points I wanted to cover before we moved on. "So here's a question for you. If you're accessing equity in your residence, should you get a mortgage or a line of credit?" I challenged the group.

"Line of credit," Barb shouted out.

"What's the difference?" asked Michelle. I was glad to see she was starting to become engaged.

"Most of the time, Barb would be right. The real answer depends on whether you are going to spend all the money you are accessing right away, or whether you will be accessing a large amount and spending it in chunks along the way. The difference," I continued, "is when you get a mortgage, you start making payments on the entire amount of money that you borrow from the moment that you borrow, and it is usually principal and interest payments. For example, let's say that I have a house that is worth $400,000 and it is free and clear, meaning that I have completely paid off the mortgage."

"I like that idea," added Michelle, this time with a smile.

"So, knowing that you could access up to 80% of the equity in your home, assuming that you qualify to do so," I continued, "you would have a total of $320,000 in potential equity that you could access. Now, let's also assume that you were planning to buy three houses over the following year with that money, but were not necessarily planning to buy them all at once. If you had arranged a mortgage to access the $320,000, the bank would advance the entire $320,000 into your bank account from day one, and you would have to start paying principal and interest payments on the entire amount from day one, whether you used it all or not."

"But isn't the interest payment on a line of credit more expensive than a normal variable rate mortgage?" Chad asked.

"Usually yes," I responded. "But look what happens when I take the same money out in the form of a line of credit, instead of a mortgage. If it were structured as an LOC, our client would have access to the entire $320,000, but the money would not necessarily be advanced into his or her account. This is the critical difference between a mortgage and an LOC. A mortgage is fully advanced to you on day one.

"The LOC is made available, but you can choose to access as little or as much of it as you want, when you want it."

"So if you don't access it, you don't have to make any payments on it?" Michelle asked, trying to make sure she understood.

"That's correct. In the case of our client, if they wanted to spend their equity on three properties and took the entire year to access it all, they would only have to make payments on the amount of money that they borrowed, when they borrowed it. And to make it even more appealing, they could choose to make interest-only payments," I explained.

"So in the end, even if the rate was higher, you would save money with an LOC because you wouldn't have to make payments until you actually used the money," Chad said, confirming that he understood this concept.

"Plus, they could pay off any amount of the LOC with no penalty at any time," Linda threw in. This was a pretty sharp class.

"That's right," I said. "However, if the same client were planning to make a purchase that required the entire $320,000 up front with no immediate plans to pay it off, then I would recommend putting it into a mortgage and saving the money on the rate. Never pay a premium for a privilege you don't intend to utilize."

"Should we convert our existing mortgage into a line of credit?" Dr. Jasmine asked.

"Well that brings up a different topic," I answered. "First, if you are in the middle of a term on your mortgage, it would not make any sense to pay a penalty to convert a mortgage into a line of credit for the same reasons I just explained. However, it is important to analyze your mortgage options when it comes up for renewal to ensure you have taken advantage of the right mortgage product and mortgage tools for you as an investor," I explained, again making a shift in tone so that everyone was paying attention. I knew that virtually everyone in the room would find it challenging to come up with down payments in the future and there was a simple way of restructuring their mortgage upon renewal that would be beneficial.

"This is very important to you as a real estate investor," I began, trying to emphasize the importance of this next tip. "Since virtually every one of you will either need or want to access equity in your home at some point in the future to continue with your real estate investing, it is critical that your principal residence mortgage be structured in a way that affords you the maximum flexibility to do so. Therefore, every one of your mortgages should be a 're-advanceable mortgage'," I stated emphatically.

"What's that?" Dr. Gill asked.

"There are two types of LOCs available in the marketplace today," I began, breaking down this concept into basic terms that were easier for them to understand. "One is what I refer to as a static line and the other is a re-advanceable one. A static LOC is the type that most of you are familiar with—you simply go to your bank, have your property appraised and then set up an LOC for the difference between 80% of your home value and the amount of money owing on your current mortgage. And that's just fine, until five years from now, when you've paid off more of your mortgage and then you ask to have your LOC increased. What do you think the average lender will say or do?" I asked the class, making sure they weren't starting to drift away on me, as I was getting more technical.

"They'd look at how much equity you had built up and increase your LOC accordingly?" answered Sean with a degree of hesitation, assuming it was a trick question.

"Let's say that you had a commission-based job and had the ability to make lump-sum payments on your mortgage, and no, Sean, I'm not looking at anyone in particular, this is purely hypothetical," I grinned, knowing that he and Candice definitely had that ability. "And let's assume that you were able to come up with say, an extra $50,000 within that five-year period to reduce the principal balance on your mortgage. If you walked into the bank, and pointed out to them the fact that you had just reduced your principal balance by an additional $50,000, would they automatically increase your LOC by that amount?" I asked.

"They should," Marc stated emphatically.

"Perhaps they *should*, but the fact is that, with a standard static LOC, most lenders will have to: a) start with a new appraisal to confirm the current value; and then b) re-qualify you to make sure you can afford the new payments; and c) likely have to re-register the increased amount as a new mortgage, thereby incurring legal fees. Now, both point (a) and point (c) will obviously cost you more money, but the bigger issue for a real estate investor is point (b). What if your employment situation were to change in the interim and you had a challenge qualifying for the new mortgage?" I paused wanting them to think about this for a while.

"So what's our option?" asked Ryan.

"Well this is exactly why you want to structure your principal residence mortgage with a re-advanceable mortgage/LOC combination. With a re-advanceable mortgage product the lender will structure and register the mortgage in a completely different way. First, let's go back to our earlier example of our client who had a $400,000 home. Let's assume this time that they were getting a mortgage for $320,000 and they knew that they would want to buy real estate in the future; therefore, when that time comes, they will need access to down payment capital. Let's also assume that this couple had commission-based jobs where they often received large bonuses and had to decide whether to take the lump sum and invest it in savings or use it to pay off the mortgage. Sound familiar to anyone?" I asked, again thinking that this could very well be the type of conversation that went on inside Sean and Candice's home.

"So recapping, we have a $400,000 house and a mortgage of $320,000, which is 80% of the value of the home. If our client asked for a re-advanceable mortgage as opposed to a mortgage with a static LOC, the lender would register the mortgage this way." I then pointed to the chart on my PowerPoint showing the bank registering a "global borrowing limit" of $320,000. The chart showed the mortgage on the left side of the ledger and the LOC on the right, with $320,000 under the mortgage side and zero under the LOC side. "As you can see, the lender has advanced the entire amount of the global borrowing limit, in this case $320,000, in the form of a mortgage to start with. However, they have registered the mortgage with an LOC built into it from day one. The simple but powerful key to a 're-advanceable mortgage/LOC' combination is that every time you make a principal and interest payment on your mortgage, the amount of principal that is reduced in the mortgage, automatically becomes available to you in your LOC."

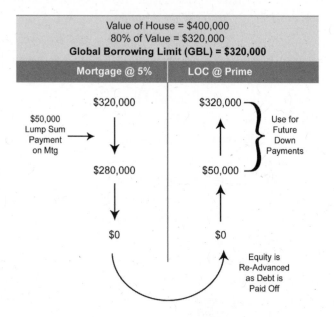

I paused, wanting to make sure that I hadn't lost anyone. "So let's go back to Sean's dilemma, or I should say our hypothetical client's dilemma," I said with a grin.

"If Sean and Candice had built up over $50,000 in equity just by making their regular monthly mortgage payments and a few lump sum deposits over the past five years, and they had set up their original mortgage as a re-advanceable one, then the $50,000 of equity would have been made available or 're-advanced' to their LOC. Quite simply, all they would need to do in order to access any of that money would be to write a cheque out of their

LOC. No need for another appraisal, no legal fees and, most importantly, no need to re-qualify."

"So every time I make a payment on my mortgage, the amount I paid off automatically gets re-advanced to my LOC?" asked Dr. Jasmine.

"Just to be clear, the amount of principal that gets paid off is re-advanced to your LOC, yes. Whether it is re-advanced automatically or whether you have to contact your lender to have those funds re-advanced is an issue that varies from lender to lender, as not all lenders have this product available and those that do vary as to how they structure it," I responded trying to cover all the bases.

"What is important here," I continued, "is that, as a real estate investor, you see the importance of this tool."

"Absolutely," Sean responded. "I don't have to struggle with what to do if I have a lump sum of money. I can use it to pre-pay my mortgage and then access it from my LOC at a future date if I came across a good real estate investment.'"

"You've got it!" I confirmed. In fact, it could be a good real estate deal, an alternative investment or even a family emergency—bottom line, it's just a prudent way for everyone to structure the mortgage on their home.

"Here's the bonus question: Let's say that Candice and Sean paid down their mortgage by an extra $50,000 which was then re-advanced to their LOC, and they then used that $50,000 from their LOC for a down payment on the purchase of a rental property—what additional benefit would they potentially receive?"

"It would be tax deductible?" Brian jumped in after quietly taking notes ever since the lunch break.

"That's right," I said, happy to see that he was grasping these concepts. "More specifically, the interest that they would pay on their LOC would be tax deductible. In fact, the actual Canada Revenue Agency guideline says that whenever you make an investment that has the intention of making money, then the interest you pay on money borrowed for that investment is tax deductible."

"If I used money from my regular LOC, would that be tax deductible too?" asked Linda.

"Absolutely," I replied. "The re-advanceable mortgage strategy doesn't make it tax deductible. In fact, any LOC or even a mortgage that is taken out for the purpose of making an investment can be tax deductible. That, quite frankly, is a bonus. The key thing to remember here is that you are essentially changing your regular mortgage into an equity-building, tax-deductible savings instrument that can be used to generate capital for future down payments," I explained. "Remember, we're still only on our second option for down payments."

I would be completely remiss if I didn't remind you, the reader, that whenever you read anything that talks about tax savings or tax deductible options, please refer to a qualified real estate tax accountant for professional advice pertinent to your personal situation. And yes, this is my form of a disclaimer. If you would like information on finding a qualified tax accountant or other professional in your local area, please go to www.peterkinch.com and send us an e-mail. We will be able to put you in touch with someone in your local area.

"Should we convert our regular mortgage and static LOC over to a re-advanceable mortgage a.s.a.p.?" asked Barb.

"No, I don't believe the tax advantages would out-weigh the penalty that you would have to pay to cancel your existing mortgage. Just keep this in mind as a tool that you'll be able to use when your mortgage is up for renewal," I told her.

"But if every time you make a payment on your mortgage, it gets re-advanced to your LOC, how are you ever going to pay off your mortgage?" Michelle asked in a frustrated tone.

"Good question, Michelle. In fact, that question is actually at the heart of one of the dilemmas many investors face. On the one hand you want to buy real estate and know you will need to come up with a down payment, but on the other hand there is a reluctance to touch the hard-earned equity in your house, right?" I asked, looking at Michelle.

"Well, yeah, I don't want to start risking all of our equity," she responded.

"Of course not, I wouldn't want you to 'risk' it either. But the key word here is *risk*," I said, trying to challenge her thought process. "Here's the interesting thing. If you go back a generation or two, the entire goal of most Canadian families was to pay off their mortgage. I mean, didn't we all get that message from our parents in one form or another, 'Get debt free.' Buy a house and then spend your entire working life to pay it off?" I could see a lot of people in the room nodding their heads. "And now we start talking about spending all that equity to buy more real estate and create even more debt. It seems to fly in the face of logic, doesn't it?" I said, trying to get everyone thinking.

"I can still remember how it was such a big deal when my parents paid off the mortgage," Nicole said.

"Absolutely, and now here I am, saying you can borrow that equity to buy more real estate." I added. "The truth is, you and the average Canadian investor are fighting against two internal conflicts. One is the way you were raised and the attitude about debt that you inherited from your parents, and two, your struggle and desire to create something better for yourself. Not just better than what your parents had or have, but a deep-down desire that is more an unwillingness to 'settle' for an average lifestyle. You don't want to settle for just getting by." I was now really challenging a lot of their deep-rooted thoughts and beliefs.

"And at the root of this struggle is your definition of debt and risk. On one hand, all debt is bad and all debt is risk. If you believe this, you will never be successful as a real estate investor. On the other hand, there is a different school of thought. One that says there is good debt and bad debt. Good debt is the money that is borrowed to create more money-producing assets. Bad debt is money borrowed to subsidize a lifestyle you cannot afford. A component of this school of thought is that a certain degree of risk is inherent in creating wealth. The difference is, there is controlled risk and there is the type of risk you have when you roll the dice in Vegas. It's important to recognize that difference. Because after all, how many people in this room have heard that the greatest number of millionaires has been created through real estate?" I asked, and 99% of the class raised their hands. "Now let me ask you, do those millionaires represent the majority of the population or the minority?"

"Definitely the minority," Chad was quick to respond.

"So, to try and answer Michelle's question, let's look at how those two groups think. The majority of average Canadians would definitely want to pay off their mortgage sooner and make becoming debt free their primary goal. The majority of the wealthy on the other hand, not including those who were born into it, want to pay off their mortgages as well, but they would utilize their equity and leverage it in a calculated risk to create more wealth. Thus, the rich become richer, not because of luck or circumstance, but because they think differently."

"That was a long answer and I'm still not sure I'm completely convinced, but it does make a lot of sense," Michelle responded as I took a breath.

"It is not my goal to 'convince you' of anything, just to get into your head and challenge some of the programming in there. In fact, I am not saying for one second that you should all change the way you think and strive to become millionaires. I'm simply asking you to go back to the very first exercise you did at the beginning of the day and think about the ideal life you visualized and then make sure your thought processes are consistent with the goals you are trying to accomplish. Remember these are your goals, not mine," I gently reminded them.

"It's hard to change the way you've been hard wired," John stated with a pensive look.

"Yes, but that's why we have programs like this. And think about it, we're still only on the second down payment option," I reminded him.

"Are you sure this is a one-day course?" Marc joked.

"Well, normally it is, but with this group, we might have to go a little longer," I laughed. "One final note on using equity as a down payment. Everything that we talked about with regard to the equity in your principal residence is true for your portfolio of rental properties as well. The key is, you have to take care when accessing equity in your rental properties so that you keep the left side and right side of the equation in check at all times. Remember Joe's story from earlier today?" I asked, reminding them that everything is connected and all part of the cause and effect of real estate investing.

Option Three: High-Ratio Insurance

"So, on that note, let's dive into down payment option three—high-ratio insurance," I announced, wanting to shift the focus back to the topic of down payment options.

It is important to clarify for the reader that the topic of high-ratio insurance is fluid and changes at different times. Up until 2007, the only choice Canadians had for high-ratio insurance for residential rental properties was CMHC, as Genworth felt the level of fraud and defaults associated with investment properties was too high. Because they had no competition in this sandbox, CMHC did not have to be overly aggressive with their policies. Personally, I found their policies so restrictive that we seldom, if ever, funded a CMHC-insured high-ratio mortgage for a residential rental property prior to 2007. In fact, they were so restrictive with their policies that I used to call it the 'Sasquatch mortgage'—you hear about them, but no one's actually ever seen one.

That all changed in late 2006, when AIG United Guaranty decided to enter the Canadian marketplace, along with a few other newcomers. One of the first markets AIG targeted was the residential rental market, coming out with 90% financing for investment properties. The maximum amount that CMHC would go to on a rental property was 85%, so AIG saw this as an opportunity to make inroads in the marketplace where CMHC had enjoyed a virtual monopoly. Meanwhile, Genworth Financial, fresh off a name change from GE Financial, stepped up to the plate, and in the face of new competition, entered the fray. Genworth essentially chose to match any and all products being offered by AIG and, virtually overnight, the landscape for Canadian investors had changed drastically. Then, in August 2007, not to be outdone, CMHC chose to trump any and all newcomers and reclaim its spot as the number one insurance choice for investors and offered a zero-down, 100% financing option on rental properties for the first time in Canada. The year 2007 saw a lot of change, as Canadian lenders and insurers were starting to bow to the pressure to relax the lending environment and allow more American-style mortgage options north of the border.

As you will recall, something else happened in August 2007. What started as rumblings from a hedge fund in France led to an avalanche called the "sub-prime crisis." As the financial crisis took affect south of the border, our previously stale and conservative banking policies in Canada were fast becoming the envy of the world. Although the Canadian mortgage and housing market was never exposed to a great deal of sub-prime risk and there was no legitimate fear of a housing or mortgage meltdown as witnessed south of the border, it was clear that Canada would not be able to escape the global fallout from the U.S. meltdown. As the global credit crunch led to banks around the world tightening their risk parameters, the Canadian banking system reverted to the safe and conservative systems that had enabled it to be relatively impervious to the sub-prime crisis.

The effect of all this on high-ratio mortgage insurance was threefold. AIG had to curtail their expansion plans into Canada and effectively became a non-player. Genworth re-evaluated their policy on rentals and chose to revert to their previous position and are, at the time of writing, not involved in providing high-ratio insurance on rentals. As for CMHC and their zero-down offer, the Canadian government actually stepped in and decided that, since CMHC was a Crown corporation and zero equity in real estate was at the heart of the sub-prime mortgage crisis in the U.S., it probably wasn't a good idea for Canadians to be buying a lot of real estate with nothing down either. This is an opinion I agreed with, by the way, given that there were a number of investors who thought that zero down was their ticket to riches in 2007, only to find out two years later that property values had dropped by nearly 20% and they were not getting positive cash flow—certainly not a good thing. By late 2008, policy was changed and you could no longer buy any real estate in Canada with zero down or have a mortgage insured by CMHC on a 40-year amortization.

And more change was coming. In April of 2010, bowing to concerns that the Canadian housing market had not only recovered from the recession, but was in fact getting overheated once again, the government stepped in and announced further changes. This time their target was real estate speculators. Although the government specifically stated that they were targeting speculators not investors, the rule change impacted anyone wanting to get a high-ratio mortgage for an investment property. Bottom line—they simply eliminated any CMHC-insured high-ratio mortgages for real estate investors with less than 20% down. Furthermore, they appear set to revoke the 80% offset policy that was so favourable to investors and revert back to a 50% add back on a borrower's existing portfolio. This rule change will make it difficult for anyone to get a high-ratio mortgage on their principal residence if they have an existing rental portfolio. Yet another reason you need to be working with a plan. Remember, this is for residential mortgages of five units or less. Commercial mortgages were not impacted by the April 2010 rule changes.

Again, this is a very fluid and fast-changing sandbox. By the time you read this, that may all have changed, again.

"One of the most common questions I get asked from someone new to investing is: How much do I have to put down?" I stated as we dove into option number three. "And then, of course, there's the guy who comes up to me and says, 'I was watching this show the other night about buying real estate with nothing down,' and I can pretty much tell what time of night he was watching and what station it was on. But here's the thing: I'll tell you what the options are and then I'll caution you why I don't necessarily like these options. And you'll start to see a pattern over the next three options, one that ties right into cause and effect."

"So," I continued. "For those of you looking to buy a residential real estate investment property, you will now have to put 20% down if it is CMHC insured. But, who can tell me why this is not necessarily a bad thing?"

"Well, the higher cost of a mortgage at 95% financing will make it difficult to get a positive cash flow property," Jeff answered.

"That's one thing for sure," I cut in. "Think about it. If you're having trouble getting your properties to cash flow at 20% down, what happens with 5% down? Does it get better or worse?" I asked rhetorically.

"Worse," was the chorus response.

"Yes, a lot worse," I echoed. "Now, Jeff, I've looked at the numbers for you and Linda, do you mind me sharing a little?" I asked, as if he had a choice.

"No, not at all."

"Jeff and Linda have a goal whereby Linda wants to be able to make real estate her full-time job. So that means, within the next five years, real estate has to produce enough cash flow to at lease replace her income—correct?" I said looking right at Linda.

"At the very least," Linda replied, suddenly sitting upright in her chair.

"So even if you could qualify at the bank for a 5% down purchase, if the property didn't have positive cash flow as a result, then it wouldn't fit your model would it?"

"Absolutely not," she was quick to reply.

"This is a great example of the difference between an investor who is following a plan and focused on results versus an individual who is trying to stretch a few dollars over as many doors as possible. The same individual who bought four properties in 2007 with zero down and negative cash flow because his bank or broker told him he qualified to do so, now has properties that have dropped 20% in value and he's losing money." I could see that some of the men in the room were feeling a little uncomfortable in their seats, but surprisingly, Michelle was looking a little more comfortable. She was starting to see that there really was a plan and that Brian hadn't dragged her to a seminar on how to get rich quick. My sense was that she was starting to realize that if they followed a proper plan of action and got some good advice, maybe, just maybe, this wouldn't be as risky as Vegas.

"Now the other issue we need to be aware of is a component of cash flow," I started, wanting to be sure that everyone was clear on what the cause and effect of their options were. "The less money you put down, the less cash flow you will have; therefore, how will that affect your debt service limit and the left side and right side of the equation that formulated obstacle number one? We have to always be careful that we don't focus on one obstacle to the detriment of the other."

"So do you recommend that we never use high-ratio mortgages," asked Dr. Jasmine.

"Actually, that's not what I'm saying at all," I replied, addressing her and her husband directly. "What I'm saying is to analyze how putting less money down will impact your cash flow and impede your ability to qualify for the next mortgage. In fact, if I were to look at your scenario, buying a few properties with less than 20% down with a private money source may well be a good idea, depending on where you were buying them. If, for example, you were to buy properties in a place like Fort McMurray or Grande Prairie or certain pockets in Ontario, where the cash flow is so good that you are break even or positive even with only 15% down, and your personal income is sufficient to qualify for the mortgage, then yes, in that case, there is nothing wrong with getting a private second mortgage to help stretch your down payment dollars further." As I explained this, Dr. Gill seemed to get a more relaxed look on his face.

One last note for you, the reader, is to remind you of the lunch conversation with Neil Shopsowitz. The class examples above refer to residential real estate. You may recall from Neil's conversations earlier that the maximum mortgage that CMHC will ensure on a commercial loan is 85%. So regardless of whether you use CMHC insurance or a second mortgage through a private lender, you will need a minimum of 15% down for a commercial multi-family purchase.

Option Four: Sub-prime Mortgages

"Moving right along," I began, shifting the focus to the next option. "Option number four is sub-prime mortgages." As I said this, there was a puzzled look on some of the faces as if I had just said a bad word.

"I know a lot of you have heard the term 'sub-prime' bandied about over the past few years, but it is important to make the distinction between what is sub-prime in Canada as opposed to the colossal mess it became south of the border." I needed to clarify what has been an often used and misused term over the past few years. "To begin with, we need to understand what the term 'sub-prime' means. I remember I had a guy come up to me in Toronto after a workshop asking how he could get one of those 'sub-prime' mortgages. I was a little surprised that he actually wanted one and asked him why. He told me he wanted to save money on his mortgage, and that's when I realized he was confusing the word 'prime' with the prime rate. I explained to him, 'the rate isn't sub-prime, the client is.'" The class chuckled as they imagined the guy's disappointed look. "Prior to the sub-prime crisis in the U.S., most Canadians had never heard of the term and then, suddenly, it was all over the news and people were sitting at cocktail parties saying, 'isn't this sub-prime crisis awful?' So what exactly is sub-prime?" I asked the class trying to see how many really understood.

"Well, that's when banks were lending mortgages to people with no jobs," Brian said.

"That's part of it." I went on to explain, "the term 'sub-prime' typically refers to either the borrower or the mortgage as not being 'prime.' The term 'prime,' in this case, is not to be confused with the 'prime rate' that we refer to when you get a variable rate mortgage. It means that either the client is not a prime candidate or the mortgage is not a prime mortgage, thus the term sub-prime. At the risk of oversimplifying an entire industry, the reason we ended up with a sub-prime crisis in the U.S., that spilled over into Canada and the rest of the world, was because of two things.

"First, the U.S. banking industry became overly aggressive with new and creative ways to allow everybody and anybody to borrow money at the peak. This was ultimately epitomized by a product in California called the 'NINJA' mortgage, which meant, No income, No job, No assets, No problem. The sub-prime market in the U.S. grew to as much as 25% of the U.S. mortgage market. That means that as many as one in four people who bought a house at the peak of the market in 2007 should never have qualified for a mortgage in the first place.

"Second, this was further compounded by a marketplace that was being fuelled by greed and a constant hunger for higher returns. It's bad enough that loans were being given in the first place to people who really didn't qualify for them, but this was further complicated by the fact that a sub-prime loan should, by definition, be more expensive. In other words, the rates are higher. So how do you help someone who doesn't have a job afford a mortgage rate that is higher than normal? Easy, use the 'don't pay now' method. I know it sounds crazy, but the majority of these loans were set up exactly that way. They had a teaser period that 'deferred' the interest to a later date. So let me ask you a question: if the average person who has no job at the height of an economic boom cannot afford the mortgage today, what is the chance they will be able to afford it one or two years later when the mortgage rate is reset and their payments will virtually double?"

"Sounds like a recipe for disaster to me," said Liz.

"So what does all of that have to do with you as a real estate investor and down payment option number four?" I asked.

"Don't get a sub-prime mortgage?" said Sean half seriously.

"Well, not necessarily. The real reason I wanted you to know more about the type of problems that were developed in the U.S. is so that you can understand what is fundamentally different here in Canada," I said wanting to make sure they understood that Canada didn't have nearly the kind of mortgage issues our neighbours to the south had.

To begin with, at its peak, the sub-prime market in Canada represented less than 5% of the entire Canadian mortgage market, compared with 25% in the U.S. And, more importantly, the sub-prime programs that were available in Canada, although aggressive by Canadian standards, did not push the envelope nearly as much as in the U.S.," I explained. "So in the end, Canada's recession was not a born-at-home sub-prime issue that created a housing bubble waiting to burst. In fact, it was our very stodgy, conservative Canadian banking system with all of its protective measures that not only kept us out of a sub-prime mess, but is today the envy of other countries."

"Having said all that," I continued, not wanting the class to think that our system is perfect, "some would argue that we were indeed going down the same slippery slope and it would have been only a matter of time before we were exposed to our own version of NINJA-type products. The fact is, there were a few American banks who had entered the Canadian marketplace by 2006, such as Wells Fargo and American Home Lenders, who along with Xceed and a few other home-grown sub-prime lenders were aggressively looking for market share in the sub-prime marketplace and offered zero-down options on rental properties with 40-year amortizations, and in some cases, 'stated-income.' Now, it wasn't the zero-down option or 40-year amortization that I worried about—CMHC was already offering that through conventional lenders. It was the 'stated income' products that concerned me." As I explained some of the history around the sub-prime issues, I wanted everyone to understand what the danger is with these programs so that they were not lamenting the fact that they were no longer around.

"Stated-income," I continued, "was created for the self-employed individual who wrote everything off on their tax returns, and therefore did not have sufficient 'verifiable' income to qualify for a conventional loan—does everyone remember the left-side, right-side conversation in the previous section?"

"All too well," Ryan said with a hint of "don't remind me" in his voice.

"The idea of the stated-income mortgage was that banks knew there are legitimate self-employed individuals out there who do make more money than they declare, and many of those individuals are not a risk to default on their mortgage. And so a variety of sub-prime mortgage programs were developed and designed to allow the borrower to 'state' their income. As long as the 'stated income' was deemed to be reasonable to the lender based on the business they said they were in, then the lender did not ask for the income to be verified."

"I could see where that would make things a lot easier than having to kill two trees just to provide all my business statements," said Jeff, who obviously had gone through the process of trying to qualify for a mortgage after having just started a new company.

"It certainly makes it a lot easier for a self-employed borrower who makes good money but has trouble verifying it all. But it also makes it a lot easier for someone who has no money to say they're 'self-employed' and use it as a loophole to get a mortgage. Now does anyone remember the statistics regarding fraud that I shared with you to start the day?" I asked, hoping to link back to what I taught earlier in the day.

"Yeah, isn't it something like 70% of investors commit fraud or something like that?" answered Shelley.

"Not exactly, Shelley. Seventy percent of the fraud that occurs within the banks is with real estate investors—there's a big difference. Those who actually commit fraud could be as little as 5% of all investors, it's just that banks find more fraud, foreclosure and default among this segment of the market. And then you introduce a zero-down, stated-income option—and it's like you're asking them to lie," I said half joking, half serious.

"The point I'm trying to make here is to show you where things were and where things have subsequently settled," I stated, wanting to wrap up option number four. "Before the credit crisis there were indeed a handful of sub-prime options open and available to the Canadian real estate investor. However, we did not often recommend them for one simple reason. When you use a sub-prime mortgage to try to avoid having to put 20% down on a conventional mortgage, you will pay higher interest rates and fees. Now, having just walked through obstacle number one this morning, what do you think will be an obvious problem with having a higher mortgage amount and a higher rate? What is the cause and affect?" I quizzed the class.

"Cash flow!" announced Brian, very proudly.

"Exactly," I answered smiling, as I knew Brian was really understanding the issues. "If you're having trouble finding a good, positive cash flow property with 20% down, what happens at zero down with a higher rate?"

"You have to stick to somewhere like Fort McMurray," answered Chad.

"You're right, with the rare exception of places like Fort Mac, the majority of quality investment properties simply won't cash flow on that basis, and the last time I checked, all of you had a gap that required positive cash flow." As I said this, I could see that anyone who was holding out for that magic bullet of a zero-down mortgage was starting to realize that even if it were available, it would not likely be a mortgage that would fit their objectives and investment goals. "And not only that," I continued, "does anyone remember my story about Randy, one of my first investor clients? You may recall that I set him up with a sub-prime mortgage on his first deal. He got the mortgage all right, but how did it impact him from a 3,000-foot view?'

"He couldn't qualify for the next one," answered Dr. Gill.

"Correct. So again, I want to remind each of you to always be thinking of the portfolio approach instead of the transactional approach so that you never fall victim to someone trying to push you into a product just so they can earn a higher commission or you can get that one property," I said, supporting Dr. Gill's answer.

"Ever since the sub-prime crisis," I continued in conclusion, "virtually every sub-prime lender that was active before the crisis is now either gone from the Canadian marketplace or has re-invented themselves. Xceed, for example, has applied for a bank licence and is now playing in the prime lending sandbox offering fully discounted rates insured by CMHC. But as for actual sub-prime lenders that you in this room can access as an alternative source for down payments, there are a few players left who will go up to 85%, but again, that changes monthly and for all the reasons I just mentioned, you're typically better off finding a different option. And speaking of options, let's look at the next one."

An important note for you, the reader, is to remind you that most sub-prime lenders are in the residential sandbox. There are a few commercial lenders who could be considered sub-prime, but much like their residential counterparts, the Asset Backed Commercial Paper (ACBP) crisis of 2008 made credit much tighter, and the majority of these options disappeared or borrowers simply turned to private money as an alternative.

Option Five: Private Money

"When all the conventional lender options have been exhausted, there is still one more alternative out there that many investors forget about— private money," I began, explaining the next option.

"Isn't that a very expensive alternative though?" Kathy asked, wondering if there was some information she didn't know about private money. As it turned out, she had spoken with a private lender in the past and found it to be very expensive.

"It certainly can be," I answered. "But at the same time, private money is, in my opinion, the most misunderstood and underutilized option. The reason for this is obvious—it is typically an option of last resort and a much more expensive alternative to conventional financing. Properly used, however, it can be a very effective tool. In fact," I continued, "under the right circumstances, the use of private money can not only be a viable option, but a strategic partner in your portfolio development, as long as it is used properly. The key is your exit strategy," I emphasized.

"But why would anyone want to pay higher rates than they need to?" asked Michelle, with an almost indignant look. "Hey, if we can't get the money from the bank, I'm certainly not going to let Brian get indebted to some loan shark for the rest of his life."

"I agree completely," I responded, as Michelle looked surprised that I was agreeing with her. "I wouldn't want him to either. So the key here is for you to learn and understand the difference between borrowing from a legitimate private lender versus a loan shark." I then turned to the whole class to explain. "At the heart of Michelle's question is a basic lack of understanding of the role that private money can play and that is precisely why it is so underutilized," I stated at the risk of insulting Michelle, though luckily she looked more curious than insulted.

"Now let's be clear. Private money is not for everyone. In fact, I own a Mortgage Investment Corporation (MIC) myself and the first thing we do with every client is exhaust every means possible to help the client get cheaper, conventional money. But if they can't and they have a good purchase opportunity with a solid exit strategy, then the use of private money can be invaluable." I continued, "Let me give you a few examples of what I'm talking about. I personally had a situation whereby I had an opportunity to buy the building that you're sitting in. At the time, I didn't have the money I needed to tie the building up prior to completion, but I had some other properties with equity in them. It would have been overly complicated to approach a conventional lender to put a blanket charge over three or four of my other rental properties, so I approached a private lender to grant me the blanket mortgage and I used those funds for the deposit on the building.

Once the building was complete and we moved in, I was able to arrange a conventional mortgage and pay out the private one. Was the private money more expensive—yes, absolutely. But for me, the end result was well worth it, because this building now plays a critical role in my personal real estate action plan."

"I would never be able to sleep at night with that weighing over my head," Michelle was quick to respond.

"Well, like I said, it's certainly not for everybody," I conceded.

"If you own an MIC, why didn't you just lend the money to yourself?" Marc asked me.

"Good question. The fact is you can't do that," I answered, happy to clarify. "MICs are highly regulated by the provincial bodies to protect the consumers, in this case, investors in the MIC, from having their funds used inappropriately. In fact, every MIC has an offering memorandum and in it, they will outline their risk parameters, which include the maximum loan to value (LTV) they will allow on any one deal. Which reminds me," I said, remembering another very important misunderstanding among investors. "Don't confuse private money with a zero-down option. Just because the money comes from a private source and not a bank doesn't mean that they don't worry about risk. Some private lenders worry more about security than the banks—they just tend to have the ability to use more common sense sometimes. But in any case, most MICs will go up to 85% with 90% being quite rare."

"Gee, every time I think I have the solution, you keep throwing in these twists," Ryan lamented.

"Yes, but at least I'm telling you the truth, not just what you want to hear," I said, grinning back at him. I knew Ryan was starting to realize that this whole private jet thing might be harder than it had seemed after watching a few late-night TV shows.

"Here's another example of a good use of private funds," I continued. "Suppose you find an ideal apartment building in northeast Edmonton that has great potential, but the current owner just had a rent change in the past month. You know that the current rents are under market value, but you will have to wait a year before you can impose any rental increases. At present, CMHC will only grant you a first mortgage for up to 55% of the purchase price based on their DCR calculations. If you are very confident that you are getting good value on the purchase price and that you will be able to raise the rents within a year, then taking advantage of private money may very well be a great short-term solution, as opposed to walking away from the purchase altogether." I could tell that this example certainly got the attention of a few of the students looking to buy multi-family units.

"I need to provide a major disclaimer at this point," I emphasized. "Please note that in the previous example, I used the word *if*. *If* you know that the rents will go up . . ." I needed to remind everybody that the key to successfully using private money is to have a strong exit strategy that is based on fact, not hope. We saw many instances in the 2008 Alberta market where investors who bought at the end of 2007 had a game plan that was 100% reliant on the market continuing to go up in a straight line forever. Well, we all know that no market will do that, but advice is a cheap commodity when doled out in hindsight. That certainly didn't stop a number of investors from acquiring buildings with expensive private money that did not necessarily fit the fundamentals. The exit strategy for many was to simply flip the property to the "greater fool" who would come along in six months, pay more than they did, pay off the expensive private funds and pocket the difference. Great plan until the train came to a grinding halt in September 2007 and values started to drop. Now the investor (who was really more of a speculator) is left holding the bag—which, in this case, is a large apartment with vacancies and an expensive private mortgage that the rent doesn't cover.

"That's the downside," I said, not wanting to scare them too much. "The upside is that there are just as many successful stories of individuals who have been able to use private money over a short period and then replace it with conventional funding when it became available—especially if you're thinking of doing 'flips,'" I added, knowing that although I personally am not a big fan of trying to 'flip' property, it is something that a lot of investors have an appetite for. "The word 'flip' is another word that often gets misused," I continued. "A true flip to me is when you buy a house today and put it up for sale the next day, or perhaps within a week after some paint and new carpet. It's very important that you all realize that no bank will be interested in dealing with you if this is your game plan. However, private lenders love that kind of business. Since they charge lending fees up front, most MICs have no problem with you paying them back sooner, so flippers make good clients for a MIC," I explained.

"I was going to ask you about flips and how they fit into this whole picture," said Linda.

"Well, the answer to that is easy," I began, as I realized this was important enough to touch on. "Let me ask you a very simple question. Did you have a gap number when you did your analysis this morning?"

"Yes, of course, I need enough money to replace my income," she answered with total clarity.

"Great, and how much cash flow do you make on a monthly basis when you 'flip' a house?" I asked, knowing that she knew where I was going with this.

"I know, I know, zero, but still, what about the fact that you can make a profit—where does that fit into the plan?" she responded not wanting to acquiesce just yet.

"Great question, Linda, and this is something I want everyone to know," I said, looking up trying to get everyone's attention. "Linda just made a very good point. Many of you may have the ability or desire to find properties where you either negotiated a great deal, or perhaps you're like Brian here and have the ability and skill to add more than just paint to the house to add some legitimate value. In those cases, you can make very good money by doing a relatively quick flip and pocketing the profits. But here's the thing; don't confuse that with a long-term strategy for cash flow. Flipping for quick cash is a great, albeit a more risky way of raising capital and, in keeping with our current theme, potential source of down payment capital. Just keep in mind that at some point, the business of flipping houses will need to turn to a buy and hold strategy in order to accomplish the cash flow goal you established during the gap analysis this morning," I explained much to Linda's satisfaction.

"Oh please, don't be giving him any more ideas," Michelle said with a chuckle.

"I'll leave that one alone," I said, noticing Brian's glare at her. "Again, financing for flips is another good example of where private money can be used effectively," I concluded. "It is an option that you should be aware of and not simply ignore as an expensive last resort. But, again, it is a short-term alternative that requires a solid exit strategy."

NOTE

Private money is typically made available through an MIC, which represents an amalgamation of private investors' funds that have been handed over to an MIC for the purpose of investment.

Any individual is free to lend their own money to other individuals in the form of a first or second mortgage. In fact, many Canadians view this as a great investment alternative to putting their money in the stock market. They can typically get between a 7% and 14% return on the investment, and their money is secured by real estate through either a first or second mortgage. The downside with doing this, as an individual, is that you have placed all of your proverbial eggs into one basket. If the person you lent the money to defaults on their payment and you have to foreclose on the property, your interest payments will cease. This can become an even more sensitive issue if the borrower was a friend or relative.

The advantage of using an MIC for investing in mortgages is simply the fact that your money is pooled with dozens or even hundreds of other investors' capital and, much in the same way a rental pool protects an investor in the event that he has a vacancy, the pool of capital in an MIC mitigates any singular loss resulting from a mortgage gone bad. Within an MIC, your investment dollars are not lent directly to one individual borrower—they are part of what's referred to as a "syndication of funds."

The operators of the MIC have to answer to their directors but, unlike a bank, their decision-making process is not restricted to "bank" policy. Typically, they will lend on the strength of the property rather than the strength of the borrower. Most private lenders today will only go as high as 85% financing on a deal with the odd one going as high as 90%. But don't expect to pay the same rate and fee at 90% as you did at 75%. The bottom line for a private lender is that the deal has to "make sense" and they will need to see the borrower's "exit strategy." In other words, the borrower will need to be able to explain how they plan to repay the loan. If the MIC determines that the borrower's exit strategy is based on an "unreasonable expectation" (e.g., I'll be able to sell off three of my properties this month at above-market prices), they will pass on the deal.

Option Six: Vendor Take-back Mortgages

"Option six is another example of a term that is thrown around a lot, but not well understood—the vendor take-back mortgage or VTB," I began as we jumped right into our sixth option for down payments.

"Okay, that's a term I've never heard," offered Nicole, who had been fairly quiet up to this point in the afternoon.

"Don't worry Nicole, you're certainly not alone in that boat," I responded. "It's one of those terms that a lot of real estate investors think they know a lot about and use it to impress others." I smiled, and she felt a little better for not knowing anything about vendor take-back mortgages. "Besides, when I look at your goals over the next 15 years, believe me, you won't need anything beyond options one and two, but I'll cover that with you later when we start developing your actual action plan," I said, knowing that most of this would have little or no relevance for Nicole and Marc. But for the others, there was a little myth-busting that was desperately needed.

"I always hear people say that you should ask every homeowner if they are interested in a VTB, but I never really understood what that meant," Barb said, showing a keen interest to learn.

"To begin with," I explained, "a VTB is essentially a second mortgage that is arranged by the vendor (seller). It works like this. Suppose you found a property that you wanted to buy, but you didn't have the full 20% to put down or were looking to stretch your down payment dollars further. You could approach the seller and ask them the following question: 'What are you planning to do with the proceeds of sale from this transaction?' Now, after they tell you it's none of your business, you can simply offer the following: 'The reason I ask is that if you do not need the entire amount of the proceeds of sale for a subsequent purchase and were looking to invest the funds, I was wondering if you would consider offering me a second mortgage on this purchase?'

"You could then explain that the seller (vendor) can 'take back' or grant you a portion of the down payment (say 10%) in the form of a second mortgage—i.e., a VTB." As I laid this out in more basic terms, I could see the majority of the class understood it.

I then used my PowerPoint to show the following example of how it would work:

- The purchase price is $100,000 (let's keep the math easy).
- You have $10,000 to use as a down payment.
- You arrange a first mortgage for $80,000 from a chartered bank at fully discounted rates.
- You are $10,000 short, so you ask the vendor to grant you the $10,000 in the form of a second mortgage charge against the property.
- You offer to pay full list price today and 10% interest-only payments for one year on the $10,000 you borrow from the vendor.[1]
- The vendor accepts your offer because their alternative use of the funds was to place it in a GIC earning less than 4%, and they know that if you default on payments they can foreclose on you and get their house back (hypothetically).
- You make payments to the bank for the first mortgage and payments to the seller (vendor) for the second mortgage, and you have purchased the property with only 10% down.

"Although this is a viable option for overcoming your down payment obstacle," I began to caution.

"Let me guess, there's a reason it's not a good option," interjected Ryan, who was still looking, or shall I say hoping, for a way to buy all the doors he needed with as little money down as possible.

"No, Ryan, there's actually four," I said knowing this information wouldn't make him feel any better. "Well, they're not *reasons* it's not a good option, so much as *issues* you need to be aware of. Remember, this whole day has been about being consistent and honest, and not fooling

---

[1] These are random numbers used for illustration purposes only. The amount you choose to offer to pay for both the house and the interest rate are subject to what you are able to negotiate.

yourself into thinking there's an easy way out," I stated in a more serious tone.

"I'm starting to get that point," Ryan replied as the class chuckled with him.

I then explained the following four issues to keep in mind when trying to use a VTB:

1. A VTB is essentially a second mortgage charge on the property and not all lenders will allow a second mortgage to be registered behind their first mortgage. This is especially true for commercial lenders who seldom allow seconds to be placed behind their first.

2. Those that do allow a second mortgage will carefully scrutinize the deal to ensure that there is either sufficient cash flow from the property to carry it, or sufficient income from the borrower to service the debt. There is currently no Canadian bank that will allow the VTB to be as high as 20%. This is not to be construed, therefore, as a loophole to buy real estate with nothing down.

3. As I have indicated before, any time you put less than 20% down on a rental property, your cash flow will be impacted. This strategy should only be considered if the cash flow from the subject property is quite significant. Does the phrase "cause and affect" ring a bell?

4. Vendor take-backs are difficult to obtain if vendors aren't overly motivated, especially when they're getting offers $10,000 to $30,000 over their list price. Vendors would only be motivated to do this if they were having difficulty selling. So a VTB is often only an option in a "buyer's market" with motivated vendors.

"Oh yes, there is one more point that is not an issue so much as a clarification," I added. "Banks that do allow VTBs on a rental property will typically only allow 10% of the mortgage to be a VTB. In some cases, they will allow up to 15%, which, if you have a first mortgage up to 80%, now constitutes 95% financing, but this is rare and you should expect a lot of paperwork when it comes to income verification."

"What if my first mortgage is for 75% and the vendor is willing to offer me a 25% VTB? Wouldn't that be allowed?" asked Kathy.

"Sorry, not any more," I replied. "There was a product like that a few years ago, but after the credit crunch, it disappeared."

"As you can see," I summarized, "although a lot of people may throw the term around, a VTB is far from a slam-dunk simple solution to our down payment obstacle."

"I'm beginning to think that none of these are,'" Chad muttered, with a definite tone of disappointment.

"Well, Chad, to a certain extent, that is the point I'm trying to make." I responded in a serious tone. "My job is to manage your expectations, not fill you full of false hopes that will only lead to disappointment and frustration down the road. Think about it, remember the statistics we spoke about earlier for real estate investors?"

"You mean the high percentage of fraud and defaults?" John offered.

"Yes, those less-than-flattering statistics that some less-than-scrupulous investors have burdened you with. Let me ask you to put yourselves into the bank's shoes for a moment."

"That's a little uncomfortable, but I'll try," joked Marc.

"Imagine a real estate investor walks into your office and tells you he wants to buy 20 properties over the next five years. Now imagine that you have just received an audit report from your boss that morning that stated 70% of the fraud, foreclosure and defaults your bank has experienced over the past year have been among real estate investors. And further to that, your boss reminds you that we have just come out of a credit crisis and global recession; therefore, credit or money is tighter this year than last. As such, he asks you to be more cautious than ever in your day-to-day mortgage lending. Then you turn to the young investor in front of you only to find out that the investor wants to know how many of those properties he can buy with as little down as possible using high-ratio insurance and VTBs. Would your perception of risk for this client go up a little?"

"I'd say no bloody way I'm lending you anything," Nicole blurted out.

"And the majority of bankers in this country would feel the exact same way," I responded. "And that is exactly why you are learning how to elevate yourself above the average investor today."

"Yes, but so far the only thing I've learned is that it's going to be very hard to come up with the money I need for the down payments," Barb stated in a manner that only Type A personalities can.

"I did tell you earlier that I had 'good news and bad news,'" I said, hoping to coax a smile out of her, but to no avail. "The truth of the matter is that there is no band-aid easy solution. But that doesn't mean that there is *no* solution. Again, I told you at the beginning of the day that there is no such thing as a realistic or unrealistic goal. Your goal is an inanimate object. It is your willingness to do what it takes in order to accomplish your goals that is realistic or not. And that brings me to our next and final option for down payments—joint venture partners.

Option Seven: Joint Venture Partners

"The biggest theme you should have noticed by now is how obstacles number one and number two interrelate to each other. Every time you look for a shortcut or band-aid solution to your down payment obstacle, the cause and effect of your decision-making process impacts your cash flow, which was a critical component to overcoming obstacle number one: qualifying at the bank," I began. "You have a fundamental clash between the investor who clearly doesn't have enough cash to accomplish their goals and a lending environment that is not overly motivated to help you find creative solutions. The bottom line is simply this: instead of constantly looking for short-term solutions to stretch $1 into $2—why not learn how to find the second dollar in the first place?" As I challenged the class, I could see a wide range of looks on their faces.

"That, in my opinion, is exactly what option number seven is— using a joint venture (JV) partner. A JV partnership can be structured in many different ways, but a basic outline would look something like this:

- You become the real estate expert and put the deal together.
- You then package it and present it to an individual who has the money to invest, but lacks the time and expertise that you have.
- The two of you enter into a JV agreement, whereby you provide the "deal" and your partner provides the cash.
- Both parties are on title and both are responsible for the mortgage.

- The JV agreement can be for whatever percentage you negotiate. A typical JV agreement would split both the monthly cash flow and the net proceeds from a future sale 50/50, after all initial expenses paid by the cash investor have been returned.

"Learning how to structure JV agreements and attract JV capital can be the magic key to the proverbial vault, but it is not as easy as some may make it sound," I cautioned.

"I could never see myself doing something like that," Liz remarked.

"That is why there are seven options. This is simply one of them," I responded, knowing that although it wasn't for everyone, I could guarantee it would be in the back of their minds for the rest of the day.

"When looking for a JV partner," I continued, "make sure they have something to bring to the table that you don't have. Basically, the bottom line is that JV partners could be the most powerful tool to 'help you go when your car runs out of gas.' In fact, a JV partner could be the most critical component to help you get to the next level. But learning how to do it properly is so important, that I will be devoting an entire section of this workshop to it later today."

After reviewing all the down payment options, you may have realized that it basically comes down to three options: liquid assets; real estate equity; and joint venture partners. Everything else in between requires diligence on the cause and effect. We will talk more about these three solutions in our next section as well as how to incorporate them into your personalized action plan.

"Again, now that we've summarized our down payment options, we're at a point in the day where we need to pause for a bit and reflect on what we've just done. We all agreed that there are two major obstacles standing in the way of you being able to buy the number of doors required to accomplish your goals. Those were qualifying at a bank and coming up with the down payments to be able to buy the real estate. The point you should find interesting is that what you do in one area can have a significant impact on the other."

"There's one major obstacle that I'm surprised you haven't covered," Brian said, sounding a little disappointed.

"What's that?" I asked, although I was quite certain I knew what he was going to say.

"I've never bought real estate before and I don't know whether I should be buying in my own hometown or maybe another province. I mean I'm not sure where to even begin," Brian stated with a sense of frustration.

"I was thinking the same thing," Shelley said, echoing Brian's sentiment.

I wasn't surprised by the questions; in fact, I had expected someone to bring this subject up much earlier in the day.

"That's a very good question and a legitimate concern," I answered. "Knowing where to buy and what to look for is critical. However, it is beyond the mandate of this workshop. The purpose of this workshop is to help you build a financial business plan so that you can identify why you are buying real estate, identify your financial obstacles and build a business plan around how to overcome them. Identifying markets and how to know when, what and how to buy real estate is obviously a critical part of the entire process. So important, in fact, that it requires much more than the cursory overview that I would provide."

Real estate is not a "get rich quick" game and involves an investment of your time as well as your money. To truly do it justice, I would recommend that you look into joining a reputable real estate investment network such as REIN (www.reincanada.com),[2] which is operated by Don R. Campbell. REIN not only has an annual "boot camp" that teaches investors about the economic fundamentals for buying real estate along with the top ten towns in each province, but it also provides ongoing monthly workshops in key metropolitan centres with guest speakers who offer unbiased knowledge and research into how, what, where and when to buy quality real estate for investment purposes.

"I just can't believe how much there is to learn and how much I never even thought of before," Dr. Gill marvelled as his wife and others nodded in agreement.

---

[2] REIN is not the only network in Canada and there are certainly other organizations and networks that can provide you with great information and education on the fundamentals about how to buy real estate. But I caution the reader to be careful to only seek out groups that offer unbiased advice. Some groups are more interested in selling real estate to you and as such, you need to question their bias. Always look for the motivation behind what is being taught from stage.

"Don't feel bad," I responded encouragingly. "Remember, this is what I do for a living. I make a science out of it. It's my job to think of these things so that you don't have to."

"I'm glad you are," he said with some assurance.

"And on that note, it's time for us to take a short coffee break before we come back and dive right into actually building your real estate action plan. So get up, stretch your legs, and grab a java and maybe even some fresh air. Because when you come back, we have a lot of work to do." And with that, the group began to disperse and conversations started to spring up around the room. They certainly had a lot of information to digest and the best was yet to come.

As I made my own way over to the coffee urn just outside of the classroom, I came across Michelle and Brian in what appeared to be a deep conversation. It's not unusual at this point in the day for many couples to start having deeper and more intense dialogue. The day starts out with the creative visualization process and everyone is either excited about accomplishing their goals, or extremely guarded about getting caught up in a fantasy or worse yet, concerned they've been roped into some motivational seminar that will end up costing them more money. It usually takes this long—three-quarters of the way through the day—before both sides start to meet in the middle. After analyzing the obstacles, the over-exuberant dreamer is starting to come to the realization that this real estate thing may not be as easy as they thought. The skeptic is beginning to realize that I'm not offering any get-rich-quick solutions designed to fuel the fire and pick the pocket of the former. And so, the one key ingredient upon which a business relationship is built, or for that matter any relationship, *trust*, begins to form.

This was evident when I joined Brian and Michelle's conversation. Brian had started the day itching to start buying real estate and Michelle was equally anxious that he not get distracted by yet another money-losing, time-sucking venture. But as the day had progressed, Brian had started to temper some of his enthusiasm with a serious dose of reality—it may not be as easy as he had thought. Meanwhile, Michelle was starting to come around—thinking that if indeed they were following a properly structured plan and were aware of the obstacles, that perhaps the idea of buying a few properties was not so crazy after all. In fact, Michelle was quite anxious to find out what was next in the process. My guess is that she will be surprised to discover that her goals are not as far out of reach as she may have thought.

Brian and Michelle are not unlike most couples I meet across Canada, with the rare exception of the small percentage of Canadians who have joined a real estate networking group. But even among those groups, it is unusual for both the husband and wife to be totally on the same page when it comes to goals. If you are reading this right now and have not already done so, I encourage you to share your goals with your spouse or significant other. Ideally, they will read this book as well and you can do the exercises together. At the very least, I encourage you to sit down with your spouse one evening and have a serious discussion about how you want to live your life five or ten years from now. You might be surprised by what you hear if you just take the time to listen. . . .

Part II

THREE-PHASE
ACTION PLAN

Chapter 9

Phase One—Seed Capital

As everyone settled back into their seats, I wanted to once again remind everyone of what we had learned so far. "Well, we've actually covered quite a bit today. Remember, everything we do today is about living your life on purpose, which means we always need to be aware of the cause and effect of our actions.

"At the beginning of the workshop, you'll recall, we talked about how the majority of investors are defined by the cash flow they produce. And that cash flow ends up producing the lifestyle they live. After five years, most Canadian investors are living a life by default, not a life lived on purpose," I paused to let the concept of a life lived on purpose sink in again.

"We all agreed that the real reason we were buying real estate was to produce results, and those results were required to ultimately live the life that we wanted to live. Therefore, we will need a certain amount of cash flow to live that life," I continued. "So, each of you calculated how much that was for you, and deducted from that amount your expected cash flow in five years, to arrive at your 'gap' figure. And with that 'gap' number as a target goal, we could calculate the type and nature of real estate, or at least the total number of doors you would need to purchase based on an assumption of X dollars per door, which we called your 'gap doors.' Once you knew how many 'gap doors' you would need to buy in order to create the total cash flow required to live the lifestyle you want, you had to identify the obstacles standing in your way of accomplishing your goal." As I recapped the morning portion of the workshop, I could see nods from most of the class.

"And after identifying the two main obstacles, outside of your own personal limitations or inhibitions," I continued, "we walked through the ways to overcome them."

"The first obstacle was qualifying at a bank. Who remembers how to overcome that obstacle?" I asked, making sure that they were paying attention.

"The impact of cash flow and how to balance out the left side and right side to make sure your DSL is higher than your personal monthly debt," Barb stated very proudly.

"You nailed it, Barb. And if you're self-employed and simply don't declare enough income to qualify with a conventional lender, what are your options?" I continued, looking to see how many of them were actually retaining the information.

"You could use private money," Dr. Gill threw out, a little less convincingly.

"Yes, that's one option, what else?"

"Bring in a joint venture partner to help you qualify," Ryan said enthusiastically, as if he had been grasping onto it as an option all afternoon.

"Yes, working with a JV partner is definitely another one, but there's one more," I said, scanning the group to see who was going to bite.

"Shift your focus to multi-family purchases," Linda said with confidence.

"Exactly!" I responded, not surprised that she had that answer.

"So remember, we talked about the cause and effect of your decision-making process and how decisions you make today can impact your ability to purchase real estate in the future," I continued. "And with that we moved into obstacle two, which was coming up with the money for the down payments that you would need to purchase all of this real estate. After going over seven options for down payments, what was a common theme that we saw throughout them?"

"That there's no quick and easy solution," Ryan offered with a degree of disappointment.

"C'mon Ryan, don't tell me you were looking for the zero down answer all morning?" I razzed him a little, knowing he could take it.

"Well, not necessarily zero down, but I was looking for at least one magic bullet," he responded with a smirk on his face.

"Don't give up just yet, the day isn't over," I answered smiling. "Anything else that you learned from the seven down payment options?"

"Well, basically there are a few high-ratio options out there, but every time you put less money down, it impacts your cash flow," Brian answered showing that he was really starting to understand the concept of cause and effect. I could see a slight smile on Michelle's face as if to say, "I'm glad he's learning how to do this the right way." They were ready to go to the next step and start developing their plan.

By now, you, the reader, should also be clear about:

- Why you are buying real estate;
- What result real estate has to produce for you;
- How much cash flow and/or net worth will be required to create the end result;
- How much real estate you need to buy in order to create the end result;
- What your obstacles are and, more importantly, you know specifically what part of those obstacles are pertinent to you; and
- What the strategies are that you can use to overcome whatever obstacle you've identified as important to overcome to reach your goal.

The next step is to put all of this together and develop your own personal three-phase action plan.

PHASE ONE: 18 MONTHS

"You've now reached the point where we can start to build your own three-phase action plan," I announced to the class. "If I were to say to you today, what is your plan for the next five years, you might find that very difficult to answer. The problem with looking at five years as one huge block of time is that it is quite intimidating, and it drives most people into a state of procrastination. So instead of looking at your goal from a five-year or ten-year perspective, we're going to break that down into three manageable chunks of time." I began explaining why it was necessary to break five-years into three 18-month phases. Obviously, it's necessary to have the long-term goal of five to ten years, but of equal importance, is the need to break that goal down into smaller tangible blocks of time. I have always found it easier to think in terms of "what do I need to accomplish or focus on over the next 18 months" rather than the next five or ten years. The other important component of this is that each of you will evolve towards your goal. In other words, what you do in the first 18 months may be very different from what you do in the 18 months after that. Something that is even more important, though it is less obvious to you today, is that "who you are" will be different at each phase of this journey.

A critical component to the accomplishment of your goal is your personal growth through the process of attaining your goals. Although difficult to visualize at this stage, your personal evolution will change your ability to accomplish the things you currently think are beyond your reach. Standing there in the workshop that day, I knew that people like Brian and Michelle, Shelley, Chad and many others were about to undertake a journey, not only of creating wealth, but one of personal growth that they were not even cognizant of at the moment. And that, for me was the most exciting part of the process.

SEED CAPITAL—ACCESSING EQUITY

"As a real estate investor, the first rule of business is for you to treat this like a business from day one," I began, speaking to the class in a tone that emphasized the importance of the concept. "Think about the results that each of you are expecting from your real estate and then ask yourself a simple question: Outside of winning a lottery or getting lucky on a hot stock pick, what else would you need to do in order to create the same results over the same period of time?"

"I'd have to start up a new business venture," John said in his very "matter of fact" tone.

"I would have to double the effort in my current job and work longer than I want to," Dr. Jasmine said as her husband nodded with a pensive look on his face. I could tell Shelley was thinking hard, but hadn't come up with any ideas yet. Brian was no doubt thinking about how much harder he'd have to work installing kitchen cabinets.

"Is it safe to say that, at the very least, you should treat your real estate business with the same level of respect that you would treat a part-time job or any new business?" I asked rhetorically. "And again, with a few exceptions, isn't it customary to start a new business with a certain amount of capital or start-up money?"

"It just cost me sixty grand to start up my company, and that doesn't include inventory," Jeff was quick to offer.

"Absolutely, and yet it amazes me the number of people who look at an opportunity like real estate and don't respect it as a business, yet are wondering why they aren't getting any results. For our purposes today, I want to focus on a component of starting a new business; something I refer to as your 'seed capital.'"

"Seed capital is the amount of money that you are emotionally willing and/or able to invest to start your real estate business. Remember, just because you have money in savings or equity doesn't mean that your spouse is going to be supportive of you spending it all on your next real estate purchase."

If you already own real estate and are reading this book to learn how to avoid a brick wall or want to take your investing to the next level, then for you, seed capital is the money you will need to take your business to that next level.

"Seed capital," I explained, "can be acquired through many of the same means that we discussed earlier in the section on down payment options. The most commonly used are liquid assets and real estate equity.

"As previously discussed, liquid assets can be cash, savings or any investment that you are willing and able to 'liquidate,' such as stocks, bonds, mutual funds, etc., but typically would not include RRSPs. On the rare occasion that an investor is in a low tax bracket due to self-employed earnings, they could choose to liquidate a non-performing RRSP, but it is not a strategy that I personally recommend. Once you determine which assets you are willing to liquidate and combine those funds with the amount of cash or savings you have available, you can determine the total amount of liquid assets that you are willing to invest in real estate."

As the reader, you should now take the time to do the same calculation that I asked the class to do:

_____	+	_____	+	_____	=	_____
CASH	+	SAVINGS	+	LIQUIDATED ASSETS	=	TOTAL LIQUID ASSETS

"Do we include equity in our home as a liquid asset?" Sean asked.

"Glad you asked, Sean. As a matter of fact, we are just about to talk about accessing equity," I answered. "Your seed capital will be the combination of your total accessible equity and your total liquid assets. Which, to answer Sean's question more specifically, leads right into the next section in your workbook."

How to Access Equity

I now had the class work on some basic formulas for determining how much potential equity they could access. Many of you reading this may find the following calculations very basic and simple, but it is important that you do the exercises. The remainder of the action plan builds on these simple calculations. It is not my intention to introduce to you new and exciting formulas, but rather show you very basic formulas that you may already be familiar with. The key is not in the formula, but in how you apply the answer.

Many people are unaware that virtually every bank in Canada will allow you to use the equity in your principal residence as a source of down payment on a rental property, as long as you can qualify to borrow it (see Chapter 5). The fact is that equity in your own home is typically the easiest and most cost effective way to access money for down payments. So how do you know how much you can access? Well again, assuming that you would qualify at the bank to do so, you can do the following:

1. Take the market value of your principal residence and multiply by 80%. If you're not sure about the value of your home, just ball-park it.

2. Personal equity is the value of your home multiplied by 80% minus any mortgage or secured line of credit (LOC)[1] you currently have.

By LOC, I mean the amount of money used on an LOC, not the amount of money you have access to. If you have a $200,000 LOC but you

---

[1] Don't confuse a secured LOC with an unsecured LOC. A secured LOC is a line of credit that is secured against the equity in your home. Banks will allow you to access this equity and use it as a source of down payment. An unsecured or personal LOC is a source of capital that a bank will create for you if you have strong personal credit, but is not secured by any assets. As such, the bank will view this form of debt quite differently than they will a secured LOC. An unsecured LOC typically cannot be used as a source for a down payment on real estate.

haven't accessed it, then you don't count it here. If you have a $200,000 LOC but you've accessed $50,000, then you put in $50,000.

• • •

Use the formula below to calculate the potential accessible equity from your principal residence:

Market value of principal residence = $ _____

Current balance on mortgage or LOC = $ _____

(_____ − _____) = _____

(Value of home × 80%) − (Mortgage + LOC) = Potential personal equity

"You should note that I use the word 'potential' equity. The above formula simply reveals to you how much equity you have access to. In order to actually access any of that equity, you will, of course, still need to qualify at the bank. And, more importantly, you always have to remember the 'cause and effect' of your actions. Remember that any equity that is taken out of your principal residence will increase your personal consumer debt on the left side of the balance sheet when we calculate your 'impact of cash flow.' Decisions can never be made in isolation. This simply requires you to be aware of these issues before making a decision.

"As a rule, I don't like to teach people to access all of their potential equity for the purpose of creating seed capital because you could leave yourself vulnerable to market fluctuations and the danger of being in a negative equity position in your home," I continued. "Remember the examples we discussed that occurred from 2007–2009, when the markets dipped by as much 20% in some cases. People who had only put 5% down or had refinanced up to 95% were stressed and panicky. The key point I want to make to you, as a sophisticated real estate investor, is why put yourself and your family through that kind of stress when you don't have to? Building this business will bring about its own stresses, and there is no need to bring the water line right up to your chin voluntarily. Understand the difference between what is within the world of possibilities and what is fiscally responsible for you and your family." As I finished, I almost expected Michelle to give me an "Amen Brother." But instead, she just elbowed Brian and said, "Are you catching any of this?"

"There are people such as yourselves who could easily qualify to access that extra capital, but again, I would only consider it if you had a very solid 'deal' or game plan to replace the equity in the short term," I added, knowing that in some cases, a very good deal could justify the additional risk exposure. "By the way, that reminds me of another thing I want to tell all of you about," I continued, as I thought of a key component of the risk involved in spending your seed capital. "I'd like all of you to write the following two words on the bottom of your page: 'what if.'"

The "What If" Clause

"I know for sure that for the majority of you, the equity in your home is something that has been given to you by the market not earned through your hard work. Although I'm sure there are some of you who have not recognized that it is the market that has blessed you with equity and not your own 'brilliance.' One of the things I've noticed over the years is that if it hasn't been 'earned' per se, then there is a greater fear of 'losing it.' So it is not uncommon for the 'temperature to rise' a little when the topic of spending house equity comes up, especially with couples. Remember men, most women are strongly attached to the security that a lot of equity in their home brings, so don't be surprised to see a bit of a backlash if you suddenly come home with a grandiose scheme to spend it all." At the risk of sounding sexist, I wanted to speak directly to some of the men in the room. It is a fact that we men tend to be more of the big picture 'dreamers' in a relationship and, quite often, we don't appreciate our spouse's need for security. For us, that 'sure thing' exciting investment could be the source of total anxiety for our spouse. Again, I've witnessed this dynamic in so many workshops across Canada but having said that, it's not always the men who are the big dreamers. I have often seen these roles reversed with the wife wanting to create a vision, while the husband was completely spooked by the concept.

"You're really not helping me here, buddy," Brian laughed.

"Actually, I am. You see, this is exactly why you are building this plan today," I continued, hoping they were all getting my point. "It's one thing to take your hard-earned (or should I say lucky) equity out of your house and take a long shot on buying real estate. It is a completely different thing to come here today and build a solid business plan based on facts and strategy, and leverage your equity to create long-term wealth." Brian nodded as both he and Michelle started grasping the importance of the plan.

"But even the best-laid plans don't always go according to plan, that's why I created the 'what if' clause," I carried on. "The 'what if' clause was created to offset false assumptions. As I conducted my workshops, I continually saw people who were beginning to stretch their assumptions into some risky territory. Again, this was rampant from 2004 to 2008. People started to slowly move their investment decisions away from the fundamentals towards goals that could only be accomplished if certain assumptions held true, like the following: As long as the market keeps going up another 10% to 20%, I'll be able to refinance this and pay off those expensive second mortgages; or as long as I have no vacancies, my cash flow will be fine. The reason I knew these assumptions so well was that I was just as guilty of getting caught up in the euphoria of the market in 2007 as everyone else was, and I had made a large commercial purchase based on a few assumptions that did not actualize. The only thing that saved me from disaster was my 'what if' clause.

"The 'what if' clause asks: What if all the assumptions I made don't pan out? What if I don't get a tenant right away? What if the market shifts and I can't refinance? In my case, the plan was to refinance the building as soon as it was fully leased. I closed in August 2008, but the decision I made was based on the market in May 2008. In September 2008, the leasing market in Canada virtually dried up, and I had to sit on a half-empty building for virtually a year before it slowly recovered. The key to my situation not becoming a disaster was because I asked myself back in May 2008: What if it doesn't get leased out and I have to carry this for an entire year? My ability to answer that question and live with the 'worst-case scenario' allowed me to create a back-up plan, avoid disaster and go into 2010 with a fully leased building and positive cash flow due to refinanced mortgage terms. If I had not prepared for my 'what if' clause, I would have lost a lot more than just the building due to some false assumptions, and, more importantly, a reliance on conditions beyond my personal control.

"It is very important to figure out your 'what if' clause before you spend your seed capital, and make sure you can live with the 'worst-case scenario' if your assumptions were not accurate or did not come to fruition. If you can live with the worst-case scenario, then you will have a very solid investment that is likely to perform well during good times and bad. And more importantly, you'll feel far more confident about spending your seed capital."

"So does that mean we shouldn't plan for things like equity appreciation?" asked Marc.

"Well, in your case Marc, you have a 15-year timeline, so it would be unreasonable not to expect some equity appreciation. But for someone who is making a short-term plan, I would keep the focus on buying for cash flow from day one, because that is something you can control, whereas appreciation is something you can't control. If you do get it, great, that's a bonus. But don't bank on it—no pun intended. Remember, the theme we've been working on all day is building your plan based on realism and being honest with yourself. Hope for the best, but have a back-up plan for the worst. If you do that, both you and your spouse will sleep better at night." As I explained this important concept, I could see more than one spouse leaning over to whisper to their partner.

"Okay, now back to your seed capital. Before you create a plan on how to spend it, we need to know how much you have." I shifted gears back to the topic at hand, identifying how much seed capital everyone had available to them. I explained to the class that they should fall into one of the following three scenarios:

1. They know exactly how much accessible equity is available in their home.

2. Their current mortgage is high ratio, therefore there is no equity available in their home.

3. They have no principal residence and therefore no equity.

If you are in category one, write down your potential accessible home equity: $ _____.

If you are in category two or three, then your seed capital is limited to your liquid assets at this point, and we'll address how to overcome that obstacle in Chapter 11.

"Now that you have calculated the accessible equity in your principal residence, you can follow that same formula to calculate the potential accessible equity in your real estate portfolio if you already own rental properties." I knew that some of the class, such as Barb and Kathy already owned some properties, while others such as Brian and Michelle were just starting out.

Please refer to the worksheets on our website at www.peterkinch.com to access a Rental Cash Flow Analysis/DCR spreadsheet to help with the calculation of your total values.

(Total value of property in portfolio × 80%) − Total balance of outstanding mortgages/LOC = Total potential accessible equity

(_____ × 80%) − _____

= _____

As everyone was busy pulling out calculators and spreadsheets beginning their calculations, I reminded them of the following:

- Don't include properties in your portfolio that you own with a joint venture partner unless both of you have agreed to withdraw equity together.

- If you have a high-ratio mortgage, you likely don't have access to equity in that property.

- In this exercise, you can't have a negative number; it just means you have no equity available to access at this time, so your answer is just zero.

At this point, you should have the following numbers calculated:

1. Total amount of liquid assets: $_____
2. Total amount of potential accessible home equity: $_____
3. Total amount of potential accessible portfolio equity: $_____
   The sum total of all three of these is your seed capital.

Seed capital: $_____

"Everyone should now be aware of the total amount of seed capital that you potentially have access to," I announced as I watched the majority of the class finish up the last of their calculations. "Again, these numbers will, for the most part, be all over the map. Some of you will have a large number, while for others you may have zero. Remember it cannot be a negative number. But regardless of what that number is, every one of you should have one by now."

"I don't have a principal residence yet and the only property I own I was able to get with only 5% down last year. So how does that work for me?" asked Ryan with a look of concern on his face.

"In that case, you would have zero for accessible equity. What was your amount for liquid assets Ryan?"

"I had $20,000 down for that," he responded rather sheepishly.

"That makes your total seed capital $20,000 then. Don't worry, it is what it is. Remember, there's no point in sugarcoating anything today. We need to work from a point of total honesty. A false premise leads to a false future."

I was glad Ryan was at the workshop today because he represents a classic type of investor that I often meet in my travels. He's young and ambitious, which I certainly don't begrudge, but investors like Ryan are often prone to wanting to "shortcut the shortcut." Being able to build a real estate portfolio and retire well before you're 65 is entirely possible and realistic—especially for someone with the intelligence, willingness and ambition that Ryan had. But all too often, I find these young investors in their 20s, who could easily knock 20 years off of the usual retirement age, are intent on trying to find an even shorter, quicker solution. If only they could see their lives from a 3,000-foot view, they would realize that there is so much potential within their grasp—if only they could be patient enough to do it properly. Unfortunately, investors like Ryan also fall victim to brokers and bankers who take the transactional approach rather than the portfolio approach to acquiring their first property. It was, therefore, not surprising to hear that when it came time to purchase his first property, Ryan had walked into the same branch that he had been dealing with for years. They were able to work wonders and get him a mortgage for only 5% down without ever asking him about his long-term goals. The fact that the 95% financing on the property created negative cash flow and severely hindered his future purchasing power was not relative at the time. They got the mortgage done—end of story. What Ryan didn't know was that all he had created was a band-aid. I knew it would take some work, but there was still a way for him to accomplish his goal.

Here are some key points to remember while calculating the total amount of money that you can access in equity:

- You still need to qualify at the bank to access that equity—remember the left-side, right-side balance?

- You need to look at the cause and effect of your decisions. How will refinancing the mortgages in your portfolio impact your cash flow? Remember my story about Joseph in an earlier chapter?

- If refinancing a property up to 80% creates negative cash flow— what about only going to 75% or even 65%?

- If you have a solid plan and are very confident in your investment strategy *and* you have enough personal income to support a negative cash flow or you are buying real estate in an area that has great cash flow or your overall portfolio will help to compensate for one negative cash flow property, then, and only then, can you consider refinancing beyond 80% and accessing equity on a high-ratio basis.

- Whenever possible, use an LOC instead of a mortgage when refinancing for the purpose of accessing equity and also take full advantage of using a re-advanceable mortgage strategy on both your principal residence and rental properties, so every time you or a tenant make a monthly payment, you are building up equity that can be used for future down payments.

- Certain properties such as recreational cabins, time-shares, quarter shares or raw land will not fit into these calculations. Depending on the nature of the recreational property, they generally cannot be easily refinanced beyond 50% of the value. Time-share and quarter-share properties fit into a totally different category and should not be included at all for these purposes. Raw land is also difficult to finance beyond 50% of the value.

Chapter 10

Utilizing Your Seed Capital

THE FIRST 18 MONTHS

"Now we need to put all of this together and build your three-phase action plan," I announced as everyone finished calculating their seed capital. "As I said before, the idea of looking at a five-year goal can be quite daunting and ominous, so we're going to break it down into three 18-month segments. Thinking about the next 18 months seems a lot easier to me than to think about the next five years.

"It's really important to point out," I paused to make sure everyone was listening, "that the majority of the time we spend today will be in phase one of our action plan. This is because you will spend more effort getting your plan up and running than you will spend guiding it to fruition. I once heard that it takes 90% of a rocket's fuel just to get it off the ground, but with the momentum that is created by the initial burst the other 10% will take it to the moon and back." I mentioned this for two reasons. Firstly, I knew that we would spend the majority of the remainder of the day on phase one and secondly, the truth is, once you complete phase one and set things in motion, the rest becomes a combination of math and managing certain variables that we simply can't account for 18 to 36 months from now.

"You have calculated your seed capital, which was a combination of the accessible equity in your real estate and the liquid assets that you are willing and able to invest, so how much real estate are you capable of buying today?" I asked, shifting the class focus back to buying real estate. "To answer this, take a look at the amount you calculated for your seed capital and multiply that number by five, and you will have the maximum amount of residential real estate you can buy today." I could tell immediately that some of them got it, while others were wondering why they were multiplying their seed capital by five.

$$\text{Seed capital} \times 5^1 = \text{Maximum purchase price (MPP)}$$
$$\underline{\hspace{3cm}} \times 5 = \underline{\hspace{5cm}}$$

Remember, your seed capital is the total amount of accessible equity, plus any other liquid assets that you are willing and able to invest.

"So why did I ask you to multiply your seed capital by five?" I asked, seeing how many had clued into what I thought was an obvious answer.

"That represents a 20% down payment," Barb answered quickly.

"Exactly. Let me give you an example. Let's say that I have $50,000 in liquid assets and $150,000 in accessible equity. That gives me $200,000 in seed capital," I responded, as I wrote out my example on the board. "If I multiply my seed capital by five, I will have my maximum purchase price of $1,000,000." I knew that as soon as everyone started to fill out the equation for themselves, there would be a range of answers and correlating emotions around the room. The responses ranged from disappointment to flat-out disbelief. As expected, Ryan was a little disappointed, after multiplying $20,000 by five, he wondered what he could possibly get for only $100,000. I explained that I would walk him through his options in the next chapter on joint venture partners.

Drs. Jasmine and Gill were busy re-calculating their number because they kept thinking they had made a mistake.

"Is this right?" she kept asking. They had a total of $500,000 in seed capital, so yes, they could conceivably go out today and purchase $2.5 million worth of real estate, assuming they put 20% down and the properties had at least a breakeven or positive cash flow. They had never done this exercise before and were quite shocked that they actually had that much buying power. The next step was to teach them how to spend it in a way that would be consistent and congruent with their goals. They weren't the only ones who were surprised. Nicole and Marc discovered that between liquid assets and equity in their home, they had $250,000 in seed capital, which, if used as a 20% down payment, would allow them to purchase $1.25 million worth of real estate. Actually, Marc was surprised; Nicole was

---

[1] Multiply by three instead of five if you are buying commercial/multi-family real estate.

shocked. The thought of going out and being able to buy that much real estate was quite scary to her.

"Don't worry, Nicole," I reassured her. "You don't need to go buy all of it tomorrow. Remember, this is purely an exercise in becoming aware of what is possible. But having said that, you guys are a lot closer to your goals than you may have thought at the beginning of the day."

"Wow, I would never have guessed this when I came here today," Marc said with a sense of quiet confidence. I had suspected from the outset that Nicole and Marc would have no problem accomplishing their goals. They had conservative but very achievable goals. They wanted three properties that would produce $3,000 positive net cash flow at the end of every month, and they were giving themselves a 15-year window to accomplish this. Now that they knew how much they could potentially buy, the next step was to determine their comfort level in spending that seed capital.

"I'm a bit surprised too," said Brian, still not convinced that the number he used for calculating his seed capital was the number that Michelle would agree to, but nonetheless, he now had a better understanding of what was potentially possible. "So, if I've done this correctly, I could, or I mean *we*, could go out there tomorrow and buy $750,000 worth of real estate?"

"Not so fast there, Tarzan," Michelle was quick to jump in. I knew she was making a point, but at the same time she was saying it with a smile on her face, so I knew she wasn't 100% against the idea either. In fact, I was even getting the sense that she was actually warming up to the concept.

I leaned over Brian's shoulder and saw that his seed capital amount was $150,000, which meant that they could indeed purchase up to $750,000 worth of residential real estate.

"You are technically correct, Brian. The key for you is your self-employed income; you would need to make sure that whatever you bought created a positive cash flow. If it did, then you would definitely qualify for the mortgages—especially when we incorporate Michelle's income as well." I wanted to make sure that she saw herself as an important part of the equation.

"What if we wanted to buy a multi-family commercial building?" asked Kathy. "Barb and I were thinking of shifting our portfolio into some small multi-family units."

"That's a great question, Kathy, and it reminds me yet again that we always have to make the distinction between residential and commercial. If you are buying a multi-family building, then your down payment can range from 15%, if your purchase has sufficient cash flow to qualify for CMHC insurance, to as much as 35% if you need to go conventional. So, as a conservative rule of thumb, you should multiply your seed capital by three to calculate your maximum multi-family purchase amount. The real number is three point something, but to make things easy, just round that off to three and you'll have a good idea as to what you can afford."

"That certainly makes a difference," Kathy murmured as she recalculated their purchasing power. Barb and Kathy had $125,000 in seed capital between them, so their maximum commercial purchase could be as low as $375,000 or as high as $833,000 if they found a property that could qualify for 85% financing and CMHC insurance. They already had a modest portfolio of residential real estate that they had purchased together, which ate up the majority of their existing seed capital, so the next step for them would prove critical in determining their ability to accomplish their goals. I knew we would have quite a bit to discuss in the next section of the workshop.

As the reader, you should now know exactly how much seed capital you have and, therefore, the maximum amount of real estate you can purchase depending on what percentage you use for a down payment. Please write that total in here:

Maximum purchase price (MPP) = _____

"You'll recall that in the hypothetical example that I used earlier, I had $200,000 worth of seed capital," I reminded everyone. "Imagine that I came home and announced to my wife, 'Hey honey, look at this seed capital we have. That's a million dollars of real estate that we could purchase. Let's go buy a million-dollar building'."

"Sounds like someone I know," Michelle grinned.

"Believe me, I'd get the same response in my household as well," I said, imagining my own wife's response.

"Before we go out and start spending our hard-earned and valuable seed capital, I need to remind you about our friend who went into the hardware store to buy a drill and came home with a power saw instead. Some of you are excited because you just discovered all this money you now have available to spend, while the rest of you are still concerned about losing the equity in your home." The truth is this is exactly the situation many couples find themselves in—polarized between the possibilities on one hand and fear on the other. For that reason, I wanted to bring them back to the core of what I had been teaching all day—their goals, the reason they want to buy real estate in the first place.

"How do you make sure that you don't end up spending your seed capital on a power saw when what you really need is a drill?" I challenged them.

"The answer lies in your goals. The way you protect yourself from making a poor buying decision is to ask yourself: what is the purpose of buying real estate? You need to be very clear about your goal and purpose, and ensure that every decision you make is congruent with that goal. Some people are a walking inconsistency to their stated goal or purpose. They have a written goal, but through their actions they do the opposite. Every decision you make from today forward will either move you a step closer to or a step further away from your goal," I explained.

"The most common question I get is, 'Do you think this is a good investment for me or not?' My answer is always the same: What is your goal? What does real estate have to do for you? I challenge each of you to ask yourself the following question before you make your next purchase: Will this purchase move me a step closer to or further away from my stated goal? Nine times out of 10, you will be able to answer your own question, and, more importantly, the answer will allow you to start investing with confidence—not fear. And, if you do this as a couple, it should help the two of you to be on the same page in terms of comfort level."

These were very important points that I wanted to get across, because I knew that significant gaps existed between some of the couples, and part of my objective for the day was to help narrow at least some of those gaps.

As you read this, I challenge you to think about these things as well. By now, you should know what your vision is. You should know why you are buying real estate and more importantly, what end result real estate needs to produce for you. And you also know how much real estate you can potentially afford to buy. *How* you spend your seed capital is a critical component of your business plan.

The following story illustrates exactly why you need a plan and the importance of sticking to your plan.

Spending Your Seed Capital—The Importance of a Plan

A number of years ago, we created a real estate action plan for a couple living in Vancouver.

Together, we came up with their five-year plan. Their lifestyle goal was to spend the next two years travelling on their sailboat down the coast to Mexico and beyond. They were planning to sell both their home and business and use those funds to finance their lifestyle vision. By working through exactly the same exercises that you have completed here, they derived a plan of action. The end result was to generate enough monthly cash flow from real estate investments to have cheques or money orders meet them every month in a different port.

In order to do this, they needed to calculate: a) how much money they would need on a monthly basis; and b) how many doors at X dollars per door would be required to generate that much money on a monthly basis. We could easily calculate their seed capital based on the projected net proceeds from the sale of their house and business. The next step was simply to determine how many doors they needed to buy.

When we finished our planning session, I felt excited for them, knowing that we had just mapped out a plan for them to accomplish what was a life-long goal of living on their boat for two years without the worry of where their next dollar was coming from. The plan was perfectly laid out; they simply had to execute it according to plan.

However, three months later, one of my senior brokers came into my office and said that she had just received a call from the husband. One of the benefits of doing your real estate action plan with our office is that we not only do the plan for you, but we also provide a level of accountability, should you choose to use our services for your mortgages.[2] My broker then explained that the couple had just put an offer in on a $1.5-million chalet at a ski resort and wanted our help in securing a mortgage for them. The broker said that getting the mortgage would be very easy, given the amount of money they had available for a down payment; however, after reviewing their real estate action plan, the purchase of a ski chalet was inconsistent with their stated goal and would not allow them to accomplish their goal of sailing down to Mexico.

So I contacted the husband myself, and reminded him that when we last spoke, the plan was to buy a certain number of doors at X dollars per door in order to finance living on their boat for the next two years. I was very certain to explain that it didn't make any difference to me whether they chose to spend their money on a ski chalet or stick to the original plan, but I reminded him that there would be little or no positive cash flow from the ski chalet and, as such, spending his seed capital in this manner would not allow him to accomplish his previously stated goal. I asked him directly: "Have you and your wife changed your goals or did you just lose your focus for a while?"

He immediately told me he needed to talk to his wife again and would call me right back. A day later, we received a call saying that they had chosen not to buy the property. Understand that I wasn't trying to tell him what to do, I just wanted to make sure that their purchase decisions were consistent with their goals and that they had analyzed the cause and effect of their decision-making process.

Shortly after that, they went back to their original plan, and we helped facilitate the purchase of multiple rental properties in accordance with their plan. Eighteen months later, I received a card from them letting me know

---

[2] One of the features of doing the real estate action plan that is less obvious is the potential for ongoing coaching through our PK-Approved broker program. Once you've completed all of the exercises in this book (which you can easily download from our website at www.peterkinch.com), simply fill out the summary available on the website and forward a copy to us via e-mail. We will be able to put you in touch directly with the PK-Approved broker nearest you in your province. The broker is trained to provide you with a portfolio review/consultation based on the information from your real estate action plan. The broker can then provide guidance and consulting (free of charge) in an effort to help you stay consistent with your goals in the same manner as the above example. This is our way to ensure that, after reading this book, you will have the personal contact you need in order to stay true to your goals.

that they were just about to set sail. The last I heard, they did fulfill their dream. They lived on their boat for two years and were able to buy a place to return to at the same ski hill—just a smaller version. Today, they live on the mountain; they've fulfilled a life-long goal to sail for two years and they still earn money on a monthly basis from their real estate investments.

That's the difference between making a plan and sticking to it versus straying off course because you lost focus of your goals.

"This story illustrates that staying true to the goals you set will minimize the chances of making poor investment decisions that will endanger your hard-earned seed capital," I summarized.

"I'm glad you clarified that for me," said Shelley, who had been quiet for most of the afternoon. "I'm sitting here doing these calculations and I see what my maximum purchase price is if I access all my potential equity. But as a mother of two with no spouse to rely on, it freaks me out. I mean, if I make a poor investment, I'm not confident that I have the ability to recoup that equity again. I'd have to wait for another housing boom like the last one and there's no guarantee that we'll have another one soon. But thinking about purchasing in this way does give me a bit more confidence."

I knew that Shelley had about $170,000 in potential accessible equity built up in her house. That would afford her a maximum purchase of $850,000. I also knew that she had bought her house in late 1999, and was the beneficiary of a great rise in the market. She was like a lot of people in her position: they were house rich and cash poor, and their newfound wealth was the result of good timing rather than brilliant decision making. And that's exactly why she was so afraid of making a mistake.

"Shelley, you're absolutely right and that's exactly why I share these stories," I answered. "Don't feel bad about being concerned over the potential of losing your equity. In fact, being concerned is prudent. The difference is, your concern can be transferred into proper due diligence as opposed to paralyzing fear. Many Canadians feel the same way that you do, but they let their fear paralyze them and they never act." I empathized with her, knowing exactly how she felt. "As we progress with the final exercises Shelley, I think you'll start to see your confidence grow."

Everyone now knew how much money they had to spend; the next question was what were they going to spend it on? In other words, how many doors could they afford to buy with their seed capital?

AFFORDABLE DOORS

"How many of you have been out there looking at some properties or have an idea of the type of real estate you are thinking about buying?" I asked as 80% of the room raised their hands. I then asked them how much they were paying for their average purchase. The answers in the room varied from a three-bedroom townhouse in northeast Edmonton at around $225,000, to a single-family home in Kitchener for around $350,000, to a house in Calgary for over $600,000. Anyone looking at multi-family apartment buildings were starting in the million-dollar range.

"The next exercise is to come up with a rough calculation as to the average purchase price per door that you are considering. If you have been out there shopping, then you should have a good idea of what this number needs to be. If you are sitting there with no idea, then simply choose a number for the purpose of this exercise, but make a note to adjust that number once you determine what it really is," I announced, knowing that there would be a wide range of answers in the room, including those who had never thought of it before.

The reader should write this number down as well. Again, you either have a clear understanding of what this number is or you are making a best-guess estimate of what you think it would be. Remember that it is a number per door. That means if you are targeting a million-dollar apartment building with 10 units in it, then your average purchase price per door would be $100,000.

What is your average purchase price per door?

Average purchase price (APP) per door = $ _____

"Once you've calculated the average purchase price per door that you are targeting, you can now calculate your total current affordable doors. In other words, how many doors can you afford to buy today with your seed capital?" I asked, as we moved on to the section of the plan where we will shed some light on exactly where you are today and, more importantly, how far away you are from your goals.

We were now entering my favourite part of the plan. Up until this point, everyone could hold onto their visions and goals and what they thought they could do with real estate. But the next exercise, although very simple, will no doubt expose a few individuals in the room along with a few readers. The intent of this part of the workshop is to be blatantly honest with yourself. I am not concerned with how ambitious your goals are; I'm concerned that you are being realistic with respect to what is required for you to accomplish those goals. To date, I have never met a client with a goal—no matter how ambitious—that I have not been able to draft a plan for. But it should be noted, some clients haven't always liked the answers or weren't willing to buy into the amount of work required for them to actually accomplish those goals. And I knew that today would be no different. There were some people in the room who would find it very easy to reach their goals, whereas others would need a dose of reality. Either way, everyone was moving a step closer to designing their business plans.

"Now let's see how many doors you can afford to buy today, based on your average price per door. In order to calculate the total amount of affordable doors, simply follow the following formula," I told everyone as I wrote the formula on the board.

$$\text{Total current affordable doors} = \frac{\text{MPP (or seed capital} \times 5)}{\text{Average purchase price}}$$

I described the following hypothetical example to the class using the same numbers that I had been working with the whole day.

CALCULATING TOTAL CURRENT AFFORDABLE DOORS

- I have $200,000 seed capital.
- The average purchase price in the area I'm interested in is $200,000.

Maximum purchase price = $1,000,000 (calculated by multiplying seed capital × 5) ÷ $200,000 (average purchase price)

My total current affordable doors = 5

Those 5 doors can be 5 separate apartment units or townhouses totalling $1,000,000, or one five-plex for $1,000,000.

"You'll probably end up with a weird number like 3.7 or 1.9, or 0.2, depending on what and where you're buying. Do not expect an even number," I said as I walked around glancing over everyone's shoulder as they did their calculations. As expected, there was a huge gap in the number of doors various people were in a position to buy. Drs. Jasmine and Gill were in a position to buy 10, whereas Ryan was struggling to see what he could possibly buy with only $20,000 in seed capital. The person that I was very curious about was Chad. I'd had a good feeling about Chad from the start of the day and a good sense of how to help him achieve his goal. Remember, his goal was very aggressive ($30,000 a month), but he only had $80,000 in seed capital. Since he was targeting $350,000 townhouses in Fort McMurray, he was not in a position to even buy two. I knew that there would be no way for Chad to accomplish his goal without engaging joint venture partners, so the key for Chad was not how much money he had, but rather, how he spent it.

CALCULATING THE SHORTFALL

"Now that you have the total number of doors you can afford, go back to one of our first exercises and write down the number of doors that were required to fill your gap." I was moving right along to the next exercise, even though Barb and Kathy were well ahead of us and had already completed the calculations.

The shortfall is the difference between the number of doors you can afford to purchase right now with your available seed money, and the total number of doors you need to generate the cash flow required to live the lifestyle you want in five years.

What about you? What is your shortfall? Are you surprised? Excited? Or disappointed?

Gap doors − (# of doors you already own*) − (Affordable doors) = Shortfall

_____ − (_____) − (_____) = _____

*This does not include your principal residence.

CALCULATING YOUR SHORTFALL

Here are my numbers from my hypothetical example:

- My gap was $4,000, which means I require $4,000 a month cash flow to live my ultimate lifestyle.

- I need 40 doors at $100 per door to bridge that gap.

- The total number of doors that I currently own is four.

- The total number doors I can currently afford is five.

- Therefore my shortfall is 31 doors.

I need to find a way to buy 31 more doors once I spend my seed capital, in order to accomplish my goal.

What is your shortfall? _____

"You can see from my example, I have a shortfall of about 31 doors. That's a pretty serious shortfall. Is there anyone else in the room that had a shortfall?" I asked with amusement, as I knew virtually everyone had a shortfall and some of them were much higher than mine. Actually, the only couple who did not have a shortfall was Nicole and Marc. They had $250,000 in seed capital and their goal was to generate an additional $3,000 a month, but over a 15-year timeline. If they chose the right type of house or duplex, they could quite easily make three purchases today of properties in the $400,000 range and, within 15 years, have enough of the mortgages paid off to net $1,000 a month from each of the properties. Quite simply, with the right choices, they could be all set to accomplish their goal. Marc was quite excited, but Nicole still was trying to grasp the concept of going out and buying over a million dollars of real estate, although she was starting to warm up to the idea.

Many of you may have a significant amount of equity available and are in a position to purchase the number of doors necessary to generate the results you need. If so, you are the person that I worry about the most, because the more money you make, the easier it is for you to make a mistake. Moving forward, you need to remember my hardware store tale and make sure your purchases can create the results you need. Make sure it's a "good deal" because it fits *your* needs, not those of the realtor.

I realized Brian and Michelle were having quite a conversation. They both knew they could buy $750,000 worth of real estate, and they had agreed on an average price per door of $250,000 for the purpose of this exercise, which would allow them to buy three properties, but they still had not settled on their gap number.

"So now that everyone has calculated their shortfall, the next question is: how are you going to overcome it?" I threw this out as a challenge to the group because I am always curious to see if anyone had a solid plan coming into the workshop. But the truth is, I am continually surprised to find that although 99% of attendees at almost every workshop I hold have a shortfall, they almost never have a plan on how to overcome that shortfall.

"This is where the workshop gets really interesting," I began, as I shifted into what I felt was probably the most important part of the day. "Think of it this way; you start out on a trip with a full tank of gas. You know you have to drive a thousand miles and you know that at one point you will need to stop to buy gas. When would be the best time to look at a road map and think about where there might be a town with a gas station for you to fill up? Before you start or once you're already on empty?"

"With my husband, it would definitely be when we're on empty," Candice joked.

"It never ceases to amaze me how many real estate investors run their cars on empty, only to find themselves in the middle of a desert with no gas station in sight. You all know that your car is going to run out of gas at one point or another—so what is your plan?" I asked, again challenging the group.

"Think about it. We've come up with a few ways to overcome obstacle number one and get qualified at the bank, and now the only thing standing between you and your goals is this final obstacle. So, on a scale of 1 to 10, with 10 being extremely important, how important is it to find a solution to overcoming your shortfall?"

"Eleven!" shouted out Chad, and I knew he wasn't joking. Chad had totally understood my point. He knew that he could qualify easily, but what he lacked was the down payment. If he could overcome this obstacle, he knew he had the desire and ability to work hard enough at building a real estate business.

"If that's the case, then you've all agreed that this is the most important obstacle." I emphasized.

"I would think that if something is this important, you would have a whole load of solutions to help you overcome this obstacle. Why don't you shout out a few of them right now?" I asked the class in order to provide a graphic illustration of how few solutions people typically come up with. I do this at every workshop I hold and, to this day, I'm waiting for someone to come up with something new, but typically it's the same half a dozen ideas, only two of which are in your control—the others are completely dependent on factors outside of your control.

Here is the list of options the group came up with to overcome a shortfall:

1. **Equity appreciation:** This is a good source, but one that is controlled by market conditions. Do you have control over when and how much your equity appreciates?

2. **Liquidation of other assets:** This is a short-term solution, because once those assets are gone, they are not replenishable.

3. **Inheritance:** An always-popular answer, but how long will you have to wait? This is also an option that is out of your control—at least one would certainly hope so.

4. **Excess money from job or business:** For some, this is an excellent option. This is exactly how I got started in my real estate career. I was able to earn enough extra money from my mortgage business to start investing in real estate. However, the average Canadian is not making enough "extra" money to buy 10 or more properties, so the biggest issue with this option is that it may take too much time for the money to accumulate.

5. **Money from family or parents:** This may or may not be an option, depending on your personal situation. It could be a good option to help you get started, but again, it is dependent on the willingness of a family member.

6. **Creative buying strategies:** There are many strategies in the market such as "lease to own," "skip transfers," "flips," etc.,

and many cases where a Canadian was able to implement these strategies effectively and buy multiple properties with no money to start. However, I can assure you that it is not as easy as some programs suggest it is. These strategies are not a game for the faint of heart and the majority of investors will not, and should not, participate.

7. **Joint ventures (JV):** Learning how to attract joint venture capital is not easy, but it is the one option you can control that could open the door to an unlimited supply of capital.

8. **Lotto 649:** You can try to practice the law of attraction on this one.

"If we look at this list of eight options, how many of them do you personally have direct control over?" I asked. "I would say two, maybe three, if I include excess money from your job or business. Otherwise, outside of creative buying strategies, which is a little suspect for most of us, attracting and developing a joint venture partner is the only other option out of the eight that is sustainable and is within your personal control," I explained, knowing that all of the other options that had been presented were either dependent on market conditions or would require a longer timeline than most wanted, or in the case of liquidating assets, not a sustainable long-term solution.

"How many of you think that joint ventures is the best option?" About 80% put up their hands. "I would have to agree with you. But once you discover the power behind working with JV partners as a source of capital, it can be the key to the proverbial vault."

"I'm still not sure what that means," Michelle offered honestly.

"Joint venture is just a technical term for a partnership," I explained. "There is nothing written in stone as to how they are structured, but the most common partnership would be one where you become the real estate expert and source out the deals, while the other party is the partner who puts up enough money for the down payment and closing costs. You take care of everything to do with the transaction, right down to property management and tenants, and your JV partner doesn't have to lift a finger once the money has been paid. It's a simple 'hand's off' deal for them, and a way for you to earn your percentage of ownership without having to put any money into it. Typically, these deals would be split 50/50 on both the monthly cash flow and 50% of the proceeds of sale after the investor part-ner has been repaid his initial down payment."

"You mean someone's going to risk all their money up front and then give up 50% ownership in the property just because I found the deal? I can't see anyone in their right mind doing that!" Michelle said with quite an incredulous look.

"Well, Michelle, a number of years ago I would have said exactly the same thing. But let me share a story with you. About four years ago, a friend of mine, who happened to live in Fort McMurray, approached me with an offer. He had just found an apartment that he could purchase for $300,000. The existing owner wanted to buy a home in Calgary for his retirement, but he still had to work three more years in Fort Mac before retirement. He wanted to sell his apartment and use the funds to secure his retirement home early and, therefore, he was willing to lease the unit back for three years at $2,500 a month. Since he was the original owner, he would make an ideal tenant. The rent generated a monthly profit of over $600. My friend offered me the opportunity to participate in this with him. I put up $70,000 for the down payment and closing costs. He handled everything else. Since that time, I have not had anything to do with that property and my JV partner has taken care of everything. The property would likely sell for almost $450,000 today and the tenant has spent the past three years paying down the mortgage. I have personally enjoyed $300 a month income from the property, which we have put back on the mort-gage. By the time we sell it I expect to receive double what I put down. My joint venture partner will have earned his fair share by virtue of a) bring-ing a deal to the table that I would otherwise not have been able to source on my own, and b) taking care of all the logistics and details so that it was a 'hands-off' investment for me.

"Now, let me ask you, Michelle. Did my friend take advantage of me, or did he have a great deal that he let me participate in?"

I knew that Michelle was unfamiliar with a lot of the language used in real estate investment and I also know that there are many "Michelles" reading this book right now. The challenge is to separate the "late night" hype from what is real. A majority of the people reading this book will automatically jump to the conclusion that the biggest risk in buying real estate is to the person who puts up the money. However, I will demonstrate to you why and how your time is equally valuable in the transaction. I also knew there were a few people in the room that day who needed to learn this as well.

Here's the bottom line. If you have a shortfall, then you need to come up with a plan to overcome it. Go through the list of eight options that we have provided or feel free to add your own—remember this is *your* business plan. Now ask yourself a very honest question. Which of those options is going to work best for you and will it be enough to allow you to purchase the number of doors you need to fill the gap and allow you to generate the cash flow necessary to live your ideal lifestyle?

If you've been able to choose an option other than JV partners— fantastic. Do the math. If you need a JV partner, then the next chapter is critical to you.

Chapter 11

Attracting Joint Venture Capital

For a majority of readers, this may well be the most important chapter of this book. If it's late and you're feeling a little sleepy while reading this section, then go get a cup of tea or coffee or go for a walk—whatever it takes for you to wake up and pay attention; it could have a dramatic impact on your future investing career!

If you are reading this right now, you are probably in one of two camps:

1. You have gone through the calculations and exercises in the book and concluded that you either have the required amount of seed capital to be able to purchase the requisite number of doors to achieve your goals, or you are confident in your ability to utilize one of the seven other options to overcome your shortfall and, therefore, you have no need to worry about attracting or utilizing JV partners; or

2. You are like the majority of investors that I meet across the country and your goals outstretch your current ability to achieve them. Your ability to attract and utilize JV partners represents your best option to accomplish your goals.

If you are a member of the first group, then I will ask for your patience as we spend this chapter focusing on those people in the second group. For members of group one, your business plan should be starting to come into focus now. You know what your goal is, you know what results real estate has to produce for you, you know how many doors at X dollars per door you will need to purchase in order to create the cash flow required to finance your ideal lifestyle, and you now know how much seed capital you have available to spend on acquiring those doors. You are now set to complete phase one—which, for you, will be the buying phase. But before we go there, we need to spend some time with the members of group two and help them to create a plan of action to overcome their gap shortfall.

I would first like to preface a discussion about JV partners by sharing some of my personal observations over the years. As a speaker and educator to various real estate investment groups across Canada and in the numerous workshops that I have conducted, the term "joint venture partner" is probably the most overused and misused term tossed around today. It would not be an exaggeration to say that over 90% of the individuals and couples that I meet and consult with have no financing alternative other than using JV partners if they truly hope to accomplish their goals. I am not being cynical or negative—I am simply stating a fact. Personally, I have no problem with using JV partners. In my investment career, I have been on both sides of the fence—both a money partner and a deal finder. I believe that learning how to create, attract and develop a proper JV partnership can indeed be the "magic bullet," the secret gem to creating real estate success. If you learn how to do it properly, it truly can provide you with the keys to the proverbial vault. I have witnessed this personally and professionally many, many times.

So, that's what I like about the concept of using JV partners. Here's what I don't like. Far too many people are walking around seminars and workshops today throwing out the term "joint venture" as if it were a simple magic bullet that will solve all your real estate needs.

"Don't have any money?" Don't worry, use a JV partner. "Can't qualify for a mortgage?" Don't worry, use a JV partner. "Don't know how to buy real estate?" Don't worry, use a JV partner. . . .

The result: too many novice investors are running around under the false belief that this is a simple, magical solution to all their woes. In the process, they do one of three things:

1.   They come across like they just got into the latest multi-level marketing (MLM) craze and annoy all of their relatives and friends, asking them for money to invest in their next venture.

2.   They succeed in attracting some JV partners, but because they really don't know what they are doing proceed to make a poor investment and end up "educating" themselves on someone else's nickel.

3. Their general demeanour, poor track record and late-night TV sales pitch, gives the entire industry a bad name, ruining opportunities for those who do know what they're doing.

Then there are the majority of investors who don't fit into any of the categories above, because they conceptually understand the need to use JV partners, but no one has ever actually sat down to show them how and, therefore, their real estate dreams and goals have been put on hold as they sit in the realm of analysis paralysis—not sure how to do it, deathly afraid to and, in the end, totally inactive.

This next section will address these individuals and show you how to use your seed capital to attract JV partners and still keep your friends.

ATTRACTING JOINT VENTURE PARTNERS—THE PARADIGM SHIFT

"Before I start talking about attracting JV partners, let's address the white elephant in the room," I began, knowing that half the room was completely dependent on using a successful JV strategy, 20% didn't know what it was, 20% knew they would probably need to use it, but the concept actually frightened them and then there was John and Liz, who had no intention of teaming up with anyone else, although that might also change. The first step that day was to address the painfully obvious.

"How many of you are totally comfortable with the idea of working with, or even talking to, another person about giving you their money to go buy real estate?" I asked, as only two hands went up. I knew that this was a topic that is talked about a lot in real estate investors' circles, but it is also one of the most misused terms. The average person is very uncomfortable talking to others about this topic without coming across as a salesman.

"And how many of you find that the whole idea just kind of freaks you out?" Not surprisingly, there were a lot more hands going up after this question.

"Count me as one of the 'freaked-out' ones," Shelley stated. As a single mom, I knew that her goals were achievable, but would most likely require some help from JV partners. "I mean, I barely understand this well enough myself to feel comfortable spending my own money, let alone being responsible for somebody else's," she continued. "Every time I go to a workshop, I hear people talking about using JV partners and I kind of figured that I would probably need to do that if I wanted to reach my target, but when I actually think about talking to people I know, yeah, it freaks me out."

"Shelley, you've made an excellent point and that's exactly why I've broken this down into three 18-month segments," I explained. "I know that's how most of you feel, and that's why I don't want anyone trying to use joint venture partners during phase one, if you can avoid it. However, phase two is 18 months from now, and who you are today may not be the same as who you will be then," I answered to a few confused looks.

"Remember the analogy I used earlier of your car running out of gas?" I asked the whole class, making sure everyone was on the same page before I moved forward. "Well, right now I want to create a paradigm shift in your mind. I want you to picture your real estate goal as a thousand-mile journey and your biggest obstacle is simply a lack of gas. All you need to do to reach your goal is to plot out how and where to find the gas stations along the road map. Now the problem is, if you don't have a map and you're simply looking out the front window hoping you'll stumble across a gas station along the way, the odds of you running across a gas station at the exact same time you are about to hit empty are remote."

I explained that this is exactly how most real estate investors approach using JV partners. They wait until they run out of money or options and then turn to it as a "last resort," with little or no preparation.

"What if instead, you were able to take a 3,000-foot view of your journey? What if I could move you forward into the future and show you exactly where your car would run out of gas and exactly how and where you could fill the tank? What if you had the ability to look into the future and know precisely when you would run out of your own money and just what you would have to do to attract more? Well, that is exactly what you have the ability to do—and that is the paradigm shift you will be making today." I paused to make sure everyone was listening carefully, because I knew this was the most important point for everyone in the room to understand— and for you the reader as well.

"The paradigm shift is simply this: From today forward, I want each of you to change your perception of what your seed capital is going to do for you!" I could tell by the looks on their faces that there were more than a few people who were not sure of the point I was trying to make.

"You see, the majority of real estate investors will look at their seed capital and simply try to figure out how much they can buy with it. I want you to use the same seed capital and figure out who you can become in the process of spending it."

That is my key message. The average investor will spend their money focusing on how much they are making in the process. Then, when their car runs out of gas, they start worrying about how to deal with finding a JV partner. They typically have not prepared themselves, or their portfolios, to properly attract JV partners. Their car is empty so now they begin to look for a gas station.

What I was teaching that day was this: You already know exactly where and when you're going to run out of gas. We just completed that calculation. You know what your seed capital is, you know what your maximum purchase price is and you know what your average purchase price is. You already figured out today how many doors you can buy and you know that once you've spent your seed capital you will need to attract JV partners. So when is the best time to start thinking about what will be required to attract JV partners?

What if instead of focusing only on what kind of real estate you are going to buy over the next 18 months, you shifted your focus to thinking about what a potential JV partner would want to see in you? What if you projected yourself 18 months into the future and asked yourself the following question: Who would I need to be in order for someone to believe enough in me to trust me with their money? Are you that person today? Is there anything you need to change in order to become that person? What if, in the process of spending your seed capital, instead of concentrating on what you are buying, you focus on *becoming* the person you need to be in order to attract JV capital in the future? It is important to understand that you don't need to be that person today—you need to *become* that person. When you start thinking this way, it will change the role and purpose of your seed capital. Seed capital is now no longer simply cash for a down payment. It's the tuition fee that allows you to develop into a sophisticated real estate investor who is well positioned to be able to attract JV capital in the future. In order to understand this, you need to learn about CCI—Confidence, Credibility and Integrity.

CCI—THE SECRET TO ATTRACTING JV CAPITAL

"Over 90% of all the real estate investors I have worked with or spoken to over the years eventually come to the point where they turn to joint venture capital as a solution to their lack of seed capital," I continued as everyone digested the concept of how to use their seed capital.

"I have taken a good hard look at why some people succeed while others do not. And in the process I boiled it down to one simple thing—character."

Again, the looks on the faces in the room suggested this was not the answer they were expecting. I explained that I had learned that investors who focused on trying to "sell" their deal to a potential investor always stumbled; but those investors who have strong characters, who were able to garner a sense of trust and confidence, were successful. I came to the realization that your ability to attract JV capital had more to do with a person's character than the deal itself. This is why I developed and started to teach the concept of CCI.

"You can do all the calculations in the world and spend all your time putting together the greatest PowerPoint presentation ever created in an attempt to convince your prospect of why they should invest with you; but in the end, if the person on the other side of the table isn't 'buying' into you—then nothing else matters." I went on to explain, "Your character and the ability of the other person to trust you is everything. If you exhibit confidence, credibility and integrity, which allows the other person to trust you, then your presentation can be on the back of a napkin at a restaurant and you will be more successful." I could tell by the nodding heads that everyone was starting to understand, and I knew that it was making sense to Shelley now. She was beginning to realize that just because she couldn't see herself talking about real estate to people today, didn't mean that she wouldn't be able to 18 months from now.

"Have you ever sat across from someone who was trying to sell you something, or perhaps they had just joined the latest 'thing' and wanted you to sign up, but no matter what they were saying, you just weren't buying into them?"

"Yes, my brother-in-law did that last weekend at my sister's fortieth birthday," Candice said with a sense of distaste.

"Exactly, and were you totally focused on what he had to say or more irritated by his approach?" I asked.

"Totally irritated. First of all, we should have been focusing on my sister's birthday and secondly, Stu has been involved in so many different things over the years that have just flopped, and this sounded like just one more," Candice went on to explain.

"That's very typical and exactly what a lot of real estate investors sound like. Think about it. If you are not 'buying' into the person, does it really matter what they are selling?"

I'm sure that you are probably thinking of a time when you experienced something similar yourself, while reading about Candice's brother-in-law. And it's exactly for this reason the focus needs to be on developing character, rather than simply your portfolio.

"What if, instead of going out and spending your seed capital on a few more properties, you asked yourself today, what could I do over the next 18 months to develop my CCI? How can I spend my seed capital and in the process, develop my CCI?" I challenged the class to think about this and provided them with the following example to illustrate what I was talking about.

A typical scene that gets played out all over the country is where a young guy (I'll pick on the Ryans of the world—because they actually are capable of accomplishing their goals, but all too often go about it the wrong way) attends a seminar or watches a late-night TV show that extols the virtue of OPM—other people's money—a term I dislike. The very tone of "other people" gives me the sense that they don't care—they just want to "risk" someone else's money, not their own. And so you've got Joey running out of a seminar looking for "other people's money" to use.

Imagine the following scenario:

Joey has just finished the seminar and approaches John, because he knows John is fairly successful and probably has some money. Joey approaches John in a timid, almost scared voice:

"Hey John, I just went to this workshop on how to buy real estate and I'm really excited. And what I would like to do is buy some real estate, but I don't have any money for the down payment. So, if you have some money you'd like to invest with me, we could become like partners. I'll go out and do all the work and go find the property. And I would like, if you don't mind, for you to simply be the money guy and come up with the down payment. You provide the down payment and I'll do all the work of finding the deal and all that, and if it works out well, then we'll split it 50/50. What do you think?"

"John, what would your response be to someone approaching you like that—even if you knew them really well?" I asked, sure that I already knew the answer.

"No bloody way!" he responded without hesitation.

"Of course I'm exaggerating the character to make my point, but even if our friend Joey had a great presentation but no results, what do you think Liz's response would have been?" I asked, to a round of laughter.

"How much confidence did Joey show?"

"Not much," was the unanimous response.

"How much credibility did Joey have?" I asked.

"None that I could tell," said John.

"You're right, he probably didn't have any, and he was probably trying to gain it on your dime," I mused. "And finally, how much integrity did Joey have?"

"It's hard to tell. We probably wouldn't have gone far enough to tell," John offered.

I explained to the group the key points of CCI and my personal philosophy:

- You get *confidence* by doing.
- You get *credibility* by having some results—some fruit on the tree.
- You get *integrity* by using your own money to earn your stripes and not by using someone else's money as your tuition fee.

"Let me ask you a question," I again challenged the class to think. "What can you do over the next 18 months, during phase one of your business plan, to develop CCI and attract JV capital for you?"

Next I gave the class an alternative scenario to Joey's novice investor approach.

"Imagine instead that Linda (Linda will be the one building their real estate portfolio while Jeff focuses on his regular business) spent the next 18 months using her seed capital in such a way that she developed her CCI." Jeff and Linda were a great example. They had a goal to build a portfolio while Linda was still working, so they could use her income until the cash flow from the real estate hit the point where she could retire. By that time, Jeff's new business would be up and running, so they would be able to maintain their family's current lifestyle without two working parents. Jeff wanted to focus on his new business and real estate was going to be Linda's 'project.'"

Jeff and Linda had $250,000 in seed capital. I knew that if they used it for a 20% down payment, they would be able to buy up to $1.25 million worth of residential real estate. Their gap was $4,000 a month. Assuming $200 a door of net cash flow, they would require 20 doors. If their average purchase price was $250,000 a door, they would be able to buy five more doors with their current seed capital. Along with the three rental properties they already own, they will still have a shortfall of 12 doors once their seed capital is spent. I knew that Linda would be a prime candidate for needing to learn how to develop CCI. For Linda, the obstacle was an emotional one, not a physical one—she simply had to learn how to step out of her comfort zone.

"So, let's use Linda as an example. Linda, you and Jeff have already bought some real estate beyond your principal residence, right?"

"Yes, Jeff tried his hand at a raw land deal, which we subsequently sold. Now we have three rental properties," she responded.

"Have you learned anything from that experience? I mean, if you look back to your very first purchase, do you know more now than you did then?" I asked, again confident that I knew what the answer would be.

Linda could hardly answer through her laughter. "We had no clue what we were doing then. I look back now and can't believe how much we've learned."

"So it's safe to say that if you actually became cognizant of that learning process over the next 18 months as you spend your seed capital, you could almost learn exponentially?"

"Oh, without a doubt." They both answered almost in unison to what sounded to them like a rhetorical question.

"Let's suppose Linda spends the next 18 months working with Jeff to use their seed capital to buy five more properties and, during the process, she develops confidence, credibility and integrity. Now let's also suppose that during this time she knows John as an acquaintance or friend. Over this period of 18 months, the two of them have several conversations about real estate. Linda never fishes for money and never comes across as desperate. She is simply excited about what she and Jeff are doing, and while sharing her excitement, she runs into the 'Johns' of the world. John had at one time or another expressed an interest in getting involved in real estate, but was too busy to learn how, what and where to buy. Linda always listened and simply shared some of her success stories when appropriate. But after completing phase one, she could then approach John and the conversation might sound something like this:

> "Hey, John, as you know, over the last 18 months Jeff and I have been going out and developing our real estate portfolio. In fact, we've been focusing on this one specific area and really studying the core fundamentals of real estate investing. We've been focusing on this one area so much that we've actually become experts there." (Note that an area of expertise can range from a geographical area or a specialization such as townhouses or apartment buildings).

> At this point, I would pull out a rental cash flow analysis and show John my numbers.

> "Here's a look at our portfolio and here are the numbers. These are the results we've gotten over the past 18 months. We're now at a point where we are continuing to grow our portfolio and we're starting to bring on some investment partners. In fact, I've just identified a few more investment opportunities in this area that would be perfect, and we'd be interested in doing a partnership with the right investor. Now I remember a few months back where you said you'd like to get involved in real estate but you didn't have the time. Well, if you're still willing to or want to get involved, we have

an opportunity where you can participate in our next real estate investment."

At this point, I would also show John a copy of a pro forma or a spreadsheet that broke down all the numbers on one of the next purchase opportunities complete with the return on investment (ROI) numbers so that John could see exactly what ROI he could expect.

"If this is something you would like to get more information on, great. If not, no big deal. Maybe you'd be interested in one of our future investments."

No pressure—take it or leave it, and then walk away.

"Now Linda, could you see yourself having that type of conversation 18 months from now—not today, but 18 months from now?" I wanted to make sure she understood that there would be massive personal development in the interim.

"Absolutely. In fact, I already have someone in mind," she responded with total confidence.

"John, what would your response have been if Linda had approached you in that manner?"

"A heck of a lot more positive than with Joey," he laughed.

"Of course we'd have to do more research, but we'd definitely be interested," added Liz.

"Definitely," I said, "people aren't going to simply write you a cheque because you memorized some lines, but let me ask you: Did Linda have confidence and, if so, how could you tell?"

"For sure," answered Brian, who was finding this entire section fascinating. "She spoke with confidence and was willing to show John her results."

"Did she have credibility and, if so, how could we tell?"

"Her credibility came from having spent her own money—oh sorry, Jeff—*their* money, to build a portfolio and they had some good results." added Chad, who had been quiet up until now. I was glad he was getting this. Ever since I first looked at his numbers, I had a plan for Chad to accomplish his goals, but I knew it would involve his willingness to use JV partners. I was looking forward to showing him how to put it all together in the next section.

"And lastly, did she have integrity and, if so, how do we know?"

"She wasn't desperate," Shelley answered. "'First off, they spent their own money to get results, and they were willing to be totally open with their results, which makes me think she has nothing to hide. And finally, she had a take-it-or-leave-it attitude. It made me think that she knew it was a great deal for John and it was up to him to see it or not."

"Exactly Shelley, and if he didn't see it, she would simply move on to the next potential investor. Are you starting to see what I mean when I say that we are talking about the future you—not the person you are today?" I asked, happy to see Shelley interacting.

"Yeah, I'm starting to see that now," she was quick to respond. "I see there is a lot to learn and that I will actually be getting an education as I spend my seed capital." I knew from Shelley's response that she was understanding the concept and I was getting excited about helping her to develop a plan to accomplish her goals.

"Bottom line guys, it's more about character than it is about details, and the sooner you learn that the more successful you'll be. Your seed capital is simply a tool that you can use to create or develop that character," I said looking to summarize the section.

"But what if you don't have enough seed capital to create CCI on your own," Ryan asked with a sense of despair in his voice.

"That's a great question. Obviously there will be many investors who want to get involved in real estate but simply don't have the capital to get started or not enough to do what we just described."

"I'm not going to sugarcoat it. Not having enough seed capital will make things more difficult for sure. You'll have to find a way to use your inner sphere of influence to help you get started. You may actually have to take your seed capital and pool it with a close friend or family member— someone with whom you already possess CCI," I explained.

"Well, my dad has told me he might be willing to help out," Ryan replied.

"That's great,'" I responded, "but remember, your job is to treat your dad's money as if it is gold and make sure he gets more from the investment than you do. If you have to use someone else's money, don't ever worry about how much you are making in the deal. Focus on what you are learning in the process and ensure they make the money first."

There may be many readers in the same situation as Ryan. In Ryan's case, he only had $20,000, but a willingness to put all of it on the line would show his dad that he was serious. The next step for Ryan would be to truly become a real estate expert in terms of studying regions and economic fundamentals, in order to minimize the risk of making a poor decision with his dad's money. If you are reading this and thinking, "That's good for Ryan, but I don't have a father with tons of money to lend me," then you will need to become the consummate "deal finder" and learn how to present excellent investment opportunities to people you know who have expressed an interest in buying real estate but don't have the time or knowledge. You provide the time and knowledge, and they put up the money. My suggestion is that if you are in this situation and you cannot develop CCI with your own money, then don't ask for a 50/50 split on the deals until you feel confident you have earned it. I would happily take 30%, 20% or even 10% of a deal if it meant I had the opportunity to learn and it didn't cost me anything but my time. But again, the key to your success will be your ability to help the other person make money and then turn them into a raving fan of your service. That's how you will attract other JV partners in the future. Like I said, it's not easy doing it this way, but it can be done—just as Ryan was about to experience.

Using Seed Capital to Create CCI

You should now have a good sense of the importance of learning how to attract JV capital. Assuming that you don't already have enough capital to reach your goal, you will need to bridge the gap to overcome your shortfall. I realize this may be a topic that is uncomfortable for some of you, but hopefully you're starting to see that this may be something you are willing to approach 18 months from now. The next step is to focus on spending your seed capital in a way that allows you to develop your CCI.

Let's go back to the example where I had $200,000 and could purchase a maximum number of five doors. I am going to use that seed capital to buy my next five doors while developing my CCI in the process. To do this, I need to become a student of the process. While it might be attractive to take the easy route, I encourage you to embrace the challenges you will face along the way and really use the experience of each purchase to "earn your stripes."

To be a student of the process you need to become proficient at the following three things:

1. Finding the deal—the property;
2. Finding the JV partners; and
3. Bringing the two together.

Finding the deal and finding the JV partner require two different skill sets—and you need to learn how to master both. Become adept at turning every conversation into a real estate conversation, as long as it is natural. The more "real estate" conversations you have, the more people you will attract in the future—I guarantee that as you start the process of spending your seed capital and buying real estate, you will have people watching and judging you. Be excited about what you are doing, become a total expert at it, develop your CCI and 18 months later, you can renew some of those earlier conversations.

JV Partnerships Are Like Potlucks

The final stage of teaching the class how to develop confidence in their ability to attract JV capital was to help them understand their own importance. In order to do this, they had to know their role in the process.

"A JV partnership," I began, "is just like a potluck—it's only successful if everyone brings something different to the table. It's important to know what the other person is bringing to the table, but it's even more important to know what you are bringing to the table. If I agreed to come over to Brian and Michelle's house tomorrow for dinner and decided to pick up an apple pie on the way, then arrived to find that Michelle had spent the whole time baking a chocolate cake, it wouldn't be much of a dinner would it?"

"I'd be okay with that," Brian chuckled.

"Yes, we'd all be excited for a short time and then we'd crash." I added. "I know that sounds silly, but that's exactly what I see real estate investors doing all the time. Let me give you a perfect example. I met a young gentleman at a real estate event and he came up to me all excited because he wanted to make real estate his full-time job. He proceeded to tell me that he had just quit his job and how he now had the time to really focus on buying real estate. I said, 'Well, that's great that you have all this free time now, but you're forgetting one important thing. With no job and no money, qualifying for a mortgage and coming up with the down payment will be a slight issue,' trying not to sound too sarcastic. He then went on to tell me that wasn't a problem because he had a partner who was going to help him build his new business. I then met his partner, hoping to hear about his wonderful job and how he was going to provide the capital etc., only to find out that his partner was the same age and had also just quit his day job to focus on building their real estate business. My first reaction was—great, two cupcakes—they both brought dessert to the potluck." As the class shared a laugh over the story, the point was clear. Know what it is that you bring to the table and partner with someone who brings a complementary skill set to the partnership. Now as it turned out, the two young friends did indeed succeed in building a fairly large portfolio in the end, but not without going through a great deal of heartache and headaches over finding the right JV partners to offset their shortfalls. They succeeded because of their commitment and determination, but it is certainly not a path that I would recommend for the average investor.

The bottom line is, you have to be clear what it is that you bring to the table and you need to be equally clear on what you are looking for in a JV partner. I see a lot of people running around talking to people about being a JV partner and they sound as if they just joined the latest multi-level marketing company and they're hunting for prospects. The first step you need to take is to learn how to filter your list of potential JV partners. You need to know exactly what an ideal JV partner would look like for you.

"A question I get asked a lot is: Where do you find JV partners?" I began, hoping to illustrate the importance of knowing what to look for in a JV partner. "I always answer 'Of course they meet at the Elks Hall on Main Street every third Thursday of the month, just waiting for you to show up.' As I'm sure you know, it's not that simple. However, the more clarity you have in identifying what that JV partner looks like, the more you'll use the law of attraction to find them." I met a friend years ago who shared the perfect analogy with me to help clarify this for people, and I shared it with the class that afternoon.

The Basketball Challenge

A friend of mine from Seattle was coming up to visit for the weekend and he was bringing with him four basketball players from the University of Washington. He challenged me to a game of four on four with the winner taking home $15,000. I had 48 hours to put together a team.

"So, I now have 48 hours to put together a team of four players to take on these guys from the University of Washington." I then turned to Brian and said, "Brian, if that were you and there was $15,000 on the line, would you ask anyone in this room to play?"

Without any hesitation he said, "No."

"Wait a minute," I responded in a feigned tone of surprise. "Are you kidding me? You would exclude this group of people that quickly? I mean you didn't even take the time to ask them any questions. You didn't even have to think about it—you immediately disqualified every one in this room in an instant."

"Well, I thought about Chad for a brief second, but if these guys play for a university, we'd need some real basketball players," Brian said hoping that Chad wouldn't be insulted.

"Chad, are you insulted by that?" I asked bluntly.

"Absolutely not. I can't even play basketball," he chuckled.

"Is anyone in the room insulted?" I asked, again knowing the answer would be no. "So that's interesting," I continued, "because you have such clarity around what it is that you are looking for, you can quickly and easily discount certain people in a heartbeat. Now let me ask you Brian, how would you start your search for these four players?"

"Well, I'd probably go up to the university to start with, and begin asking people questions," he responded.

"Like what?"

"Well, 'Do you play basketball?' would be a good one to start."

"If I asked you all to break into groups right now and gave you five minutes, do you think you could come up with five very good questions to ask and a solid game plan to find a way to put this basketball team together to challenge these guys?" I asked the class, to which there was a resounding "Yes, of course!"

"Now isn't it amazing that this sounds so obvious when we're talking about basketball players, but when it comes to investors looking for JV partners, I still see a lot of people talking to their brother-in-law over Thanksgiving dinner and they can't figure out why no one is investing with them." I explained that as soon as they get that much clarity around what they are looking for in a JV partner, they would be able to recognize them as easily as a seven-foot basketball player.

WHAT DO YOU BRING TO THE TABLE?

"Before you know what to look for in other people, you need to be clear on what it is that you bring to the table," I explained, as it was now time for everyone to shift and study themselves, to determine exactly what they are good at and what skills they need to spend the next 18 months working on.

As you are reading this now, take the time to look at the following chart, which I handed out to the class. On the left-hand side are some of the things that a good real estate investor could bring to the table. On the right-hand side are things that you need to work on, assuming that you have not gained efficiency in that area. This will then become the list of things that you can focus on as you spend your seed capital over the next 18 months, developing your CCI in the process. Take a few minutes and do your own personal inventory.

Things to bring to the table:	Things I need to work on:
You've gained expert knowledge in your field.	
You've developed a good team.	
You have become an expert within the area of real estate that you are purchasing.	
You've got the time to do it.	
You've developed CCI.	
You've developed a successful track record.	
You've developed the ability to give a good presentation when you're sitting down with potential JV partners.	

After the class completed this exercise, I wanted to emphasize the importance of knowing exactly what it was that each of them needed to work on during the process of spending their seed capital.

"Here's another question for you," I began, choosing Brian again as my volunteer. "Brian, I want you to imagine that you just met Chad over here for the first time, which shouldn't be very hard, because you did just meet today. Now imagine that I have introduced Chad to you as a sophisticated real estate investor and suggested that it would be a great idea for you to give him your seed capital and let him invest it on your behalf and then benefit from 50% of the profit. Sound a little bizarre? What would your initial reaction be?" I asked, again pretty confident I already knew the answer.

"Probably no," Brian answered almost casually, but with a hint of curiosity.

"Now picture yourself trying to explain that to Michelle." This time, the answer was not so casual and even the entire class knew how that conversation was going to end.

"Yeah, that isn't gonna happen," Michelle was quick to add.

I explained that this is exactly the position we put other people in when we are asking them to trust us with their money. The fact is, there is a very large percentage of Canadians today who are sitting on a lot of equity in their homes and would love to learn how to invest in real estate and safely leverage that equity into wealth for their families and future generations. There are literally billions of dollars sitting out there in equity waiting to be better utilized, but it is guarded by the millions of homeowners who either lack the knowledge or trust to be able to access it. And if you recall the statistics I used at the beginning of the book, of all the mortgages in Canada, only 4% are for real estate investments. This suggests that a majority of Canadian homeowners are sitting on untapped or under-utilized equity in their homes. So does the potential exist to find a few JV partners out there who would be willing to partner with you if you could show them a way to safely leverage their equity to create more wealth? The answer is obviously yes, but the key to tapping into it is your ability to create CCI in yourself and better understand what they need to see in you.

"If you were Brian and Michelle, what would you need to see in Chad before you would ever consider giving him your seed capital?"

"A track record for sure," Dr. Gill said.

"CCI," Shelley offered.

"Honesty," said Sean.

And the list went on. I asked the class to take the next 10 minutes, either alone or in a group, and make a list of the 10 things you would need to see in somebody else before you would ever consider giving them your seed capital to invest on your behalf.

Please take some time yourself to make the same list. Remember, this is your seed capital and you will be trusting someone else to invest it for you. What 10 qualities or elements would you need to see in a person before you could entrust them with your home equity?

1.

2.

3.

4.

5.

6.

7.

8.

9.

10.

Once everyone had completed the list, I told the class what many of them had already figured out. The list you just made are the qualities that you need to develop in yourself. Whether you realize it or not, you have just created a list of 10 things you need to focus on and be cognizant of developing in yourself over the next 18 months as you spend your seed capital. As I said before, this is a journey and it is as much a journey of personal growth as it is of wealth creation. In my life so far, I have found one seldom comes with out the other.

THE ONE QUESTION THAT CAN KILL A DEAL

Everyone now knew what they needed to work on personally in order to develop their CCI, but I knew that there was still one major hurdle for many of them in terms of attracting JV capital—their ability to see their own value. I also knew that no matter what I said that day, 99% of them would eventually be asked the one question that could bring about complete failure. Everything comes down to their ability to answer this one question.

"So, now that you know what you need to work on, there's one more thing you need to be able to tackle before we move on. No matter how much you study or learn about real estate, the day will come when you sit down with a potential JV partner and they will ask you the one question that kills 99% of all deals. That one question will make your hands sweat and your heart beat fast," I paused to see if anyone could come up with the killer question.

"How much are you putting into the deal?" Linda jumped in with the voice of experience.

"Bingo! That's exactly the question that virtually every investor fears when sitting down with a JV partner, and it's the question that will invariably cause you to stutter, pause, fumble around for words and boom! Right there you've lost the deal." I stated this emphatically, hoping to drive home the point. "And yet, all of you can probably predict that question will be coming, right? So, as a sophisticated investor who can look into the future and anticipate the question before it arrives, wouldn't it be important to have an answer beforehand?" I asked, once again challenging the class to really think ahead.

"Here's the thing. When someone asks you that question, what is the underlying assumption that they are making?"

"That their money is more important than our time," Barb said.

"Exactly, and can you blame them?" I responded, again hoping to get people thinking rather than just assuming. "I mean really, isn't your money important to you? It was important to Michelle when I suggested that Brian give it to Chad. If money isn't the most important or valuable part of the transaction, what is?"

"My ability to find a good deal," Kathy offered. "You can have all the money in the world, but if you don't know how or where to invest it, it won't help you," she continued.

"That's right, but if you are offering someone the opportunity to invest with you as a 50/50 partner and they are putting up all the money, you better darn well be able to explain what your role is in justifying your 50% of the deal."

To help the class get a much clearer understanding of this, I again asked them to split into groups, making sure that at least one person in each group had bought investment real estate in the past, and that person had to make a list of everything that was involved in buying their last piece of real estate.

As the reader, take the time to do this now as well. If you currently own a rental property, take a moment to create a list of what was involved in the process of buying it. Be as detailed as possible, putting down every step from the day you first sat down to look at the MLS listings to getting a tenant and arranging for property management. Make your list so thorough that you could take it down to the local college and teach a course called the "step-by-step guide to buying a rental property."

If you haven't yet bought a property, then make this a homework assignment for your first purchase. You should know how much seed capital you have now, and you are probably in the position to make your first purchase soon. When you do, simply grab a notepad and log every single step along the way—what you had to do, how much time it took, what was involved in the process. Again, be as detailed as possible.

The following is an example of the answers that the class came up with that day:

Requirement	Notes and Explanations
Identify the target area Identify the property type	Find one area you'll have expertise in. Use a filter system to determine the criteria for the property type that matches your needs. Go through your different filters until you find the right property. For example, you want a property where the annual rent is at least 7% of the purchase price.
Go on MLS	Search MLS listings to find properties that meet your criteria.
Determine exit strategy	For example, is it buy, rent and hold; fix and rent; etc.
Put together your team	Engage a real estate agent, find a mortgage broker, a lawyer, etc. What you could do is pre-position yourself with your mortgage broker ahead of time, letting them know you are thinking of buying this property. For example, you might ask your broker something like, "I'm looking at buying this property. Given my current left-side, right-side numbers, and if the property has

(continued)

Requirement	Notes and Explanations
	negative $250 a month, will that be an issue? Yes or no. Do I need to make sure it's positive cash flow? Yes or no. How much do I need to be reliant on my JV partner, their income?"
Pre-qualify your JV partner	Many times JV partners do not want to provide their personal information, especially if it's a close family friend. So, you may want to let the potential partner know up front that you've set up a system that avoids confidentiality conflicts—you advise the partner that they can submit their information to your mortgage broker and only the mortgage broker will see both parties' information. The only thing the mortgage broker will disclose is whether the deal will work or if there are issues that would require a different JV partner. This saves time and protects confidentiality.
Write an offer	Also negotiating an offer. Remember, you will often have to put in multiple offers.
Arrange for deposits	Once your offer is accepted, you will want to have the required deposit money available. Deposit requirements for commercial properties can be expensive.
Down payment money	Also have your down payment money handy. The last thing you want is to wait until the last moment, then announce that you still need to set up an LOC for the down payment.
Find a tenant	That means hiring a rental agent, a property manager or posting ads, then qualifying the potential tenant, i.e., background check, credit scores, etc. This also includes coming up with an effective rental/lease contract.
Get insurance	Insurance is important and requires an understanding of the different types of coverage such as fire insurance, flood insurance, liability insurance, etc. You need to understand what is, or is not, covered.
Property manager	Hiring a property manager may be the best money you'll ever spend.
Lawyer	It sounds simple, but signing documents with a JV partner and trying to co-ordinate the task and everyone's schedule can be challenging. Make sure the lawyer clearly explains everything.
Get an appraisal	All conventional residential mortgages will require an appraisal. Commercial properties require much more due diligence than residential, and can take up to six weeks to complete.

Requirement	Notes and Explanations
Property inspection	When you put in your offer, ideally you should ask for seven days for subject approval. You write, "subject to finance and subject to inspection." Never buy a property without these subjects. Don't feel pressured by a realtor telling you, "Oh, in this market if you come in with conditions, I don't think you're going to be able to get the deal." In that case, get a new realtor, because you have no idea what may be wrong with the property and, at the very least, getting an inspection is probably the most important thing you do.
Condo docs review	Make sure you receive the condo/strata docs. You may want to hire an expert to review them for you, especially if you are not familiar with what to look for.
Closing	Signing closing documents, taking possession, then inspection on the day of possession.
Renovations	Renovate or arrange for renovations if necessary.

Note: These are not necessarily in sequential order and are only examples.

The above list is by no means intended to be exhaustive and yours may well be longer as there are endless minor details that you can include. After completing the exercise, everyone got the point I was making.

"Holy cow, that's a lot of work!" exclaimed Chad.

"Absolutely. It's certainly not a one-hour project is it? And this is just the time and energy spent on the property you bought. What about the number of places where you put in an offer but didn't close? It's a lot of time out of your regular day-to-day life on top of your job and your families. Now here's the million-dollar question," I started and paused to make sure everyone was listening. "If you were to become an expert at doing everything on this list and all your JV partner had to do was write a cheque and let you take care of all the rest, is that worth 50% of the deal?"

"No way. I'm increasing my percentage to 80," Chad said boldly. "This is the hard stuff."

"You're right Chad. Being able to learn how to handle and deal with everything on this list is far more difficult than writing a cheque. And remember, I've done both and, quite frankly, I'd rather just write the cheque and let the other guy do all the work—assuming that I trusted him or her and that they were able to exhibit CCI to me."

"But the thing is," I continued, "I could spend all day long telling you this and it would be in your head, but until you actually write this list out for yourself it will always remain a concept in your head. The day you can move it from your head to your heart and own it," I said pointing to my chest, "is the day you will be successful. So the next time someone sits down with you and asks you, 'How much are you putting in?' you'll be able to pull out this list, point to it and say something along the lines of, 'You know what, Bob? Here's a list of everything that is involved in bringing this investment opportunity to you. Now the reason that I'm giving this opportunity to you, Bob, is that last month you told me that you would love to get involved in real estate, but you didn't have the time or knowledge of where to start. Well, I'll take care of all of the details for you and you'll be able to leverage your investment and get a better return than you are currently getting. Now, if you're in a position where you have the money and the time to do all of these things on the list, then by all means, you don't need to partner with me at all and I wish you the very best. I was just thinking that this would be a better fit for you.' Now that beats the heck out of stuttering doesn't it?" I asked rhetorically, ending my mini lecture.

"That makes total sense," said Shelley. "I could never see why someone would put the money up and only take 50% of the deal, but now I'm starting to see that the money is only a small part of the process."

"Even if it's a big part of the process, the key here is to never underestimate your own value and what you bring to the table. And remember, if you're new or just getting started, you're not having this conversation tomorrow. This will be after you have spent your seed capital and developed your CCI." I reminded Shelley loud enough so everyone could hear.

I can't emphasize enough how important this exercise is for the reader. Again, if you have never bought a rental property before, make sure that you keep your diary including the time it took from A to Z to close on your next deal. By doing so, you will have total clarity as to what is involved in the process. You will know how much of your time will be required, and more important than anything else, you will be completely aware of the value you bring to the table.

Most people that I have met sell themselves short. They underestimate the value they bring to the JV partnership. If you have purchased more than three properties on your own (especially if they are commercial), and you have developed great relationships along the way with your team of professionals (lawyer, realtor, broker, etc.), and if you know how to find the deal and deliver it packaged on a silver platter so your JV partner only has to sit down with you and review the deal for an hour and write a cheque, who has earned more in the deal? Now keep in mind that your JV partner is not going to be thinking this way, simply because they don't know what they don't know. If they have never gone through this process then they do not yet have the ability to understand what value you bring to the relationship. But because you know your value before you start, you can be the "Jedi master," managing their expectations along the way and educating them throughout the process, which will garner even more trust in the relationship.

The bottom line is *know your worth* and do not sell yourself short.

For further information on joint venture partnerships, go to www. realestateinvestingincanada.com, where you'll find Russell Westcott's home study course "JV Secrets." It is an excellent in-depth program designed to teach you anything and everything you want to know about joint venture partnerships. Russell's wisdom on this subject can also be found in the book *Real Estate Joint Ventures for Canadian Investors: A Proven and Powerful Step-by-Step System* (publication date is Spring 2011), which he co-wrote with Don R. Campbell.

Chapter 12

The Halfway Point

The energy and confidence in the room had completely changed. I could tell the majority of people, even those who were previously closed to the concept, were now looking at the idea of using JV capital differently. Keep in mind that it is not my intention to try to convince you or any of the students that day that they should be using JV capital. Far from it. My goal is twofold:

1. Make sure that your actions are consistent with your goals and that you are being honest with yourself. Don't say you want to buy 50 doors but you don't want to use JV partners, unless you have a solid, legitimate alternative plan.

2. If you are going to use JV partners, and I suspect a large percentage of you will, then learn how to do it the right way to be successful.

I could see a lot of excitement return to some of the faces in the room as they envisioned, possibly for the first time, that it might be possible for them to use JV money to accomplish their goals. But for many people, the task still seemed a little daunting. I needed to present one more question to the group to help them think a little deeper.

"Suppose you're sitting here today and thinking, 'Wow, my target was for 40 doors and now that I've spent my seed capital, I've only been able to buy four or five. I've got a long way to go.'" I moaned in a whiney voice and looked directly at Barb and Kathy. I knew that they only had $125,000 in seed capital, but had already purchased a number of properties between the two of them. Their seed capital would likely allow them to make two more purchases, which would bring their total doors to seven before needing to shift to working with JV partners.

"So tell me, if my target number of doors is 40, when am I halfway there?" I asked, knowing most of the class was waiting to find out if it was a trick question.

"Twenty," said Barb, looking at me as if she now understood why I had been an English teacher and not a math teacher in my previous life.

"Well actually, I'd say it's somewhere in between seven and ten," I responded, knowing full well she was thinking that I'd lost the plot.

"Does anyone here work in construction?" I asked, as Ryan shot his hand up.

"Well, if I were to build a 40-storey building, how many floors down into the ground would I need to go just to build the foundation?"

"Probably around five or six," Ryan replied with a fair sense of confidence.

"So once I start digging in the ground to create the foundation, is it possible that I might hit something like bedrock that I did not anticipate, and it could cause a delay until I figured out a solution and a way to get around it?"

"Absolutely, that happens all the time."

"Then, once we get going again and finish the foundation, is it possible that we would have more delays by shifting from the foundation to the ground floor and having to adjust how we were doing things—i.e., working with joint venture partners for the first time?"

"Sure."

"And once we start adding floors, we would still run across the odd problem that we haven't seen before, which would cause us to stop and analyze the situation to come up with a solution. But wouldn't it be true that each time we encounter the same problem it would get easier to fix? And then finally, once we are somewhere around the sixth or seventh floor, wouldn't it be less likely that we would run into a situation that we haven't encountered before? Wouldn't we simply be repeating the same process over and over with far fewer problems? And wouldn't the number of new problems we encounter diminish the further along we go?" I asked, rhetorically.

"Yes, each floor can present its own challenges, but for the most part, I'd say that's probably totally accurate," Ryan replied.

"Exactly. Just like every property and every new JV partner will present you with a new challenge, but after a while, the basics of the deal would become cookie-cutter as you develop your systems, wouldn't you agree?" I asked the class as they all nodded their heads.

"So the definition of halfway is when you stop doing something for the first time." I paused again to give them time to think about this.

Halfway is the point when it is no longer your first JV partner, no longer your first issue with this or that. Halfway is the point where you really start to have confidence that you know what you are doing and it shows. And for most of you, halfway will be accomplished through the process of spending your seed capital. So in reality, buying doors eight through to forty should be easier than doors one to seven. The problem is that many people quit after their seventh or eighth purchase, thinking that they were so far away from being done, when they really were already halfway—far closer to the end than they realized.

I reiterated to the class the importance of being a student of the business and following a system. The more you systematize your process, the easier it will be the next time you encounter the same obstacle. You will overcome it and learn what to anticipate the next time, already having a solution in place. This is what makes you valuable to future JV partners.

Summary of Phase One

I'm sure there are at least a few of you thinking, "Gee, he sure is spending a lot of time on phase one. When are we going to get to phase two? Well, you may recall my rocket ship analogy from earlier in phase one (Chapter 10) Building phase one of your real estate action plan will consume about 90% of your fuel—developing your CCI, becoming a student of the real estate business and building the foundation for your portfolio. That's why 90% of Part II of this book is focused on it. Once your real estate ship is off the ground, you will only have to make minor adjustments. Just like building a 40-storey tower, you need to start with a solid foundation.

"Before we wrap up phase one, it's time to get back to doing some math," I announced before letting everyone go for a short coffee break.

Take a moment to do the following calculations:

- How many doors do you currently own? _____
- How many doors can you purchase with your seed capital? _____

- What was your original number of gap doors? _____
  (see page 54, Chapter 4)
- What is your remaining shortfall? _____

# of current doors + # of doors purchased with = Total # of doors purchased
          seed capital   at end of phase one

_____ + _____ = _____

# of gap doors − Total # of doors at end of phase one = Shortfall

_____ − _____ = _____

Now remember, phase one is the time in which you spend your seed capital. That could be any time frame that you choose, but for the sake of argument, let's say it is over the next 18 months. At this point, you should fall into one of the following categories:

1. The amount of seed capital that you have available is sufficient for you to purchase the required number of gap doors. You will spend phase one using your seed capital to acquire the doors you need. If that is the case, you will spend the majority of phase two shifting to a debt reduction strategy.

2. You have recognized that the amount of seed capital you have is not enough to enable you to purchase the required number of gap doors, but you have been able to utilize one of the seven options for overcoming your shortfall other than using JV partners; hence, you have either completed the process of buying the required doors or will complete that process in phase two, since one of your options required some patience in order to refinance or access an asset.

3. You have recognized that the only way you will be able to purchase the required number of gap doors is by using JV partners. During phase one, you spent your seed capital in such a way that you were able to develop CCI and you are now much more sophisticated than when you started. You are now ready to begin working with JV partners in phase two.

4. You do not have the money to purchase the required number of gap doors and you recognize the need to find JV partners, but do

not have sufficient seed capital to create or develop your CCI. You have spent phase one as a complete student of the process of buying real estate and rely on third-party credibility to associate yourself with credible partners, having joined a real estate network to further develop your knowledge and contacts. You have been 100% reliant on working within your own sphere of influence with close family or friends to help you get started. You were willing to give up as much as 90% of the deal, just in order to get off the ground on your first deal, and you have now purchased enough properties in that manner to allow you to develop the CCI required to branch out. You will spend phase two attracting JV partners who are not necessarily within your sphere of influence.

I suggested that everyone take a quick 10-minute coffee break, because I knew that we were now going to shift to the final two phases of the day and everyone would have questions about their particular situation. The coffee break allowed me the chance to chat with some of the participants. I also knew that going through phases two and three would be much quicker for two reasons:

1. Every portfolio gets to a point where it is just simply a matter of math. You either keep doing what you're doing or you shift your focus to debt reduction; and

2. The ability to predict unknown variables beyond two years out makes it virtually impossible to know what decision to make in advance.

It was a good thing we took a break when we did—everyone was in the mood to chat and they had a lot of questions.

I caught up with Chad as he was pouring some cream into his coffee mug. I was anxious to see where his thought process was at this time in the day.

"How are you enjoying the day so far Chad?"

"Oh, great. It's really got my head buzzing," he answered as he stirred his coffee.

"Well, I've got an idea I've been waiting to share with you all day that might get your head spinning even more," I offered.

"I'm all ears," he answered, as his eyes widened like a child on Christmas morning.

I explained to him that he was sitting on a virtual goldmine, but probably not even aware of it—as are many of you who are reading this book right now. But just as Russell Conwell's book, *Acres of Diamonds*, suggests, many of us spend our entire lives searching the world for something that has been right in front of us the whole time.

Chad works in a very interesting industry—the oil fields in northern Alberta. It wasn't the oil fields that interested me; it was the nature of the workers. I shared a few things with Chad that he already knew.

"Chad, describe the average single guy up in Fort McMurray right now, who is working in the oil fields and is about your age."

"Oh, that's easy. They come from all over because of the good money. All of them have visions of making lots of money, but because there's not much to do up there, most of them blow their money partying on the weekends. They have a great time, make a lot of money and then have little or nothing to show for it after two or three years," Chad explained, thinking back over the past three years of his experiences there.

"So what makes you different?" I asked, trying to challenge him to recognize what I had seen in him first thing in the morning.

"I don't know," he paused, really starting to think about it. "I'd say the biggest thing I see is that most of these guys are acting like the easy money will keep flowing forever. You know, I keep thinking that this is a lot of hard work and I don't want to be breaking my back at age 50. But most of them aren't saving anything. It's like, hey, the weekend's here and I just got paid, so why not blow half of it on the weekend?" I could tell he was now voicing something that he saw every day, but had not put into words before.

"That's totally common, Chad, and guess what?" I asked, again spiking his curiosity. "Most of those guys are simply going through the motions and the truth is, a lot of them would change their habits in a heartbeat if someone was able to show them an alternative. But as long as their peers all keep making the same decisions, they will follow. What I want you to see is the opportunity in that." I could see as I was talking that the proverbial penny was dropping for Chad.

I have met a lot of Chads in my time. They are bright young men who actually "get it." They are the few among the many who recognize that, although they are making great money today, it may not last forever, but they are surrounded by people who seem to think it will. I've seen this with stunt men in the Vancouver film industry; I've seen it with young professional athletes who think the flow will never end. And every once in a while, you'll see one of them step out from the crowd like Chad and look back from the outside to see what is obvious to everyone else—don't take for granted the money you're making now and assume that it will never end. Just like the young hockey player who is one bad knee away from heading back home to work on the farm, there are many young people today making relatively great money in the short term, which may or may not be sustainable in the future. I told Chad that day the same thing that I tell my clients in the film industry, whose entire future in Hollywood North could be wiped out with a Canadian dollar above par.

"Chad, what if you took your existing seed capital, used it to create CCI, built a small portfolio that kicked butt on your current pension plan and then started sharing what you've done with some of the guys you work with?"

"That would be amazing!" he exclaimed as the vision became completely clear to him. "There's tons of guys I work with who would love to get involved in real estate, but they don't have a clue where to start."

"And they all make great potential JV partners. They have verifiable income, and with a little help and education, can easily save up the down payment money."

"Yes, and with all the connections I already have, I can help them buy some excellent positive cash flow properties," Chad said with a rising sense of excitement in his voice.

"Exactly, and the most important thing is, that you wouldn't need to feel the least bit afraid that you are taking advantage of anyone, because what you're really doing is offering them an opportunity. You know most of them waste a lot of money anyway, so what you're offering them is the ability to simply piggyback off of what you have learned and done. That's why it's critical that you spend your seed capital in a way that you build a good portfolio to start, develop your CCI and have something of value to offer your peers," I said as Chad started to really envision his future. "If you focus on developing that skill set to attract JV partners among your peers, I guarantee you Chad, the rest will all be simple math. How many JV partners do you need to reach your desired number of doors?"

"You know what?" he asked, looking like he just had an epiphany, "suddenly this entire day is starting to make sense and come together."

"I'm glad to hear that, Chad. Now let's get back into the room and wrap up the final two phases of your plan," I said as I corralled everyone back into the room for the last part of the day.

For those of you who are thinking that Chad might be "taking advantage of his friends" or that you are not comfortable talking to friends about the whole joint venture thing, keep the following points in mind:

- The majority of people you would be talking to should or would be considering an investment of some sort.

- The average Canadian investor is very happy getting a 10% return on their money if they invested it in the stock market.

- If you took $100,000 and made a 10% return in the stock market, you would have $110,000.

- If you took the same $100,000 and invested it with a sophisticated real estate investor in a JV partnership, bought some real estate and it only increased in value by 5%, your return on your initial investment would be as follows:

  - Assuming you used the money as a 20% down payment, your purchase price would be $500,000.

  - If the real estate increased in value by only 5% (half as good as the stock market), your real estate would be valued at $525,000.

  - If the increased equity was split 50/50, the JV partner who simply put the money up would have earned $2,500 more than an alternative investment on the stock market, even though the real estate only grew by half of what a stock investment did.

  - This does not include the fact that there may have been positive cash flow generated from the real estate and the fact that the tenant would have been effectively paying off your mortgage every month.

It is important to note that most investors hesitate to offer these opportunities to potential JV partners because they are comparing a 50/50 real estate investment to the returns that the individual would have made if they had bought the property themselves. However, you are forgetting two things:

1. They likely would not be able to buy that same piece of real estate themselves. It is only because of your expertise and the experience you gained through spending your seed capital that you are in the position of buying a good quality investment. Don't underestimate your value in that regard.

2. The majority of Canadians that you talk to would end up making an alternative investment in the stock market or other vehicle that would not allow them to leverage their money. They would be happy with a 10% return—and that is what you should be comparing your return to. Don't underestimate the power of leverage.

If someone is in the position where they can make their own real estate investment and really don't need your help, then they are not the JV partner you are looking for. Or, if you do find someone like that, you can always go 50/50 and both put equal amounts of money down, which will allow you to double the amount of properties you can buy with your seed capital, thus doubling the value and experience you bring to the table.

Chapter 13

Phase Two of the Three-Phase Action Plan

As we moved to the final stages of the day, I felt it would be useful to remind everyone of where we had started and how far we had come. Throughout the day (and throughout the course of reading this book), we have completed multiple exercises—none of which have been particularly complicated or earth shattering. As I've said all along, the beauty of building this plan lies in its simplicity. That said, if you've ever read Malcolm Gladwell's book *The Tipping Point*, you'll know that a series of small, insignificant events may have little or no consequence by themselves, but when put together they can add up to significant change.

Let's review the following:

We began the day acknowledging that it's not the real estate we want so much as the results that real estate can produce for us. Real estate is simply our investment vehicle of choice. The results from our real estate investments will produce the cash flow necessary for us to live our ultimate lifestyle. Therefore, we needed to visualize and define that lifestyle or end result before we could possibly move forward. Once you had a clear vision of what that end result needed to be, you could then work to create a budget to identify exactly how much money it would take to live the life you want to live. Working through the following steps, we:

- Identified the gap between what we need versus what we are likely to earn five years from now;
- Discussed the cause and effect of our decision-making process;
- Determined what results our real estate has to produce in order to bridge that gap;
- Figured out how many doors at X dollars per door we will need to buy in order to bridge that gap;

- Identified our two major obstacles:
  1. Qualifying for a mortgage; and
  2. Coming up with the down payment;
- Learned how to qualify at the bank by learning about our DSL, the impact of cash flow and how to balance the left side, right side equation;
- Looked at seven different options for down payments;
- Identified our seed capital;
- Identified how many doors we can afford today and what our current shortfall is;
- Analyzed how to use our seed capital to develop CCI to be able to attract joint venture partners; and finally
- Developed an action plan to help overcome that shortfall to be able to purchase the number of doors required to generate the cash flow necessary to live our ultimate lifestyle.

Once you know why you are doing what you are doing, the rest becomes a matter of how to make it happen.

PHASE TWO

Once again, I could see by the looks on some of the faces in the room that more and more of this was starting to click with each of them. Couples like Brian and Michelle were starting to share notes and actually agree on some things; others like Drs. Gill and Jasmine were almost giddy as they looked over their math, while others had a quiet confidence about them. Although everyone had a unique situation, there were also quite a few similarities, but as the day moved on, the gap between those similarities started to widen.

As you ended phase one, you calculated your remaining shortfall. Please carry that number from page 212 forward here:

Shortfall at the beginning of phase two = _____

At this point it is important to remind the reader that you will be in one of two camps, either:

1. You have a shortfall; or

2. You do not.

Your actions in phase two will be dictated by whether you are in camp one or two.

The most important thing to remember is that phase two is the second 18-month period of the plan. One of the biggest challenges for you, the reader, or for those attending the workshop that day, is that a lot can change in 18 months—especially if you are planning to be this active. That means, as we discussed before, the person you are today may not necessarily be the same person you are 18 months from now, which adds an unknown variable into the mix. But based on my experience, both personally and with my clients, that change is most often for the better. If you have followed all of the steps provided here, you are likely more confident and significantly more knowledgeable and experienced. You will have become a much more sophisticated real estate investor and developed your CCI. At this stage in your plan, you may be able to make decisions and take actions that you do not conceive as possible today—for that, you'll have to take a leap of faith to believe it can be done.

The second 18 months of your real estate action plan will be used to modify your plan to either shift into a debt reduction mode if you fall into category two above, or evaluate ways to continue to overcome your shortfall if you are in category one. As we have already mentioned, you have likely spent 90% of you energy in phase one developing your CCI, learning the real estate business and building the foundation for your portfolio. Once you are at this stage, it will only require 10% more to bring the rocket ship safely home.

"As you move into phase two of your business plan, you will have three or four options depending on where you are after spending your seed capital in phase one," I began as I outlined the options.

Option One

If you still require additional doors to accomplish your goal, you will now need to use JV capital to purchase the required number of doors. Remember, by this point you will have developed CCI and you are 18 months further along than you are today.

I could see by the look on his face that Chad was starting to visualize this option. But he wasn't alone, Ryan, Drs. Gill and Jasmine and even Shelley, although to a slightly lesser extent, were also seeing the JV option as a distinct possibility. I also found it interesting that Brian was starting to see a different option from the one he first envisioned. When we first met, Brian had told me his goal was to buy one property a year for the next 20 years. Of course, when I asked him why, his answer boiled down to, "It seems like a reasonable goal to me." But like so many Canadians, it was not a well-thought-out goal with a targeted end result; rather, it was an intangible goal based on the sense that if buying real estate is a good thing, buying more is better. I have found that the less tangible the goal, the harder it is to get the support of a spouse who may not be fully on board. And this is exactly where Brian and Michelle were at the beginning of the day. They had now spent the better part of a day working together to build a business plan that was based on a tangible goal. They were still far apart in terms of what that end result would be, but I can guarantee you that Michelle was getting much more comfortable with the idea given that Brian would actually be following a plan.

By the end of phase one, Brian had calculated that they had roughly $150,000 of seed capital. That would allow them to purchase up to $750,000 worth of real estate. Assuming they can find properties they like that have positive cash flow for around $250,000 each, they will have been able to buy three properties in phase one. In the process, Brian will have created and developed CCI. He also will have had a lot of people he knows watching him through this process. He will share a lot of stories (both good and bad) about his journey with those who are interested, and by the time he reaches phase two, he will be in a good position to approach those individuals as potential JV partners. I knew approaching any JV partners was still a foreign concept for Michelle, but that was normal. After all, the idea of simply spending all of their equity to buy three properties was a stretch in itself for her. So here's what I proposed.

"Brian, when we started this morning, you told me that your goal was to buy one property a year for the next 20 years, but when you did your gap analysis, based on the life you ultimately would like to live, the gap you came up with was $5,000 a month."

"Yup, that sounds about right," he responded as he flipped pages in his workbook to double check his numbers.

"So really, the lifestyle that an additional $5,000 a month can afford you is your real goal, not the 20 houses over 20 years?" I asked, again trying to challenge his thinking and also making sure he was still paying attention this late in the day.

"Sure, I'd say that's accurate," he responded, wondering where I was going with this.

"Then do you mind if I use you as an example for the last two phases?" I asked, knowing that it would be hard for him to say no.

"Hey, if you can show us how to get those results, fire away," Michelle was quick to jump in.

"Well, let's follow this through then. Let's say Brian's goal is to create $5,000 a month over the next five years. If he is able to get $100 a door in cash flow, that would require buying 50 doors. However, Brian and Michelle only have $150,000 in seed capital; therefore, at the end of phase one, they have three doors and their shortfall is still 47 doors," I explained as I laid out their scenario as an example.

"Sorry, Peter, but if you're trying to get me excited, it's not working," Michelle said with a smirk that indicated she was still not buying in yet.

"That's the same math I came up with and it was a little depressing" Brian added. "I'm assuming that's where the JV money comes in?"

"Let's take a look at that. Remember, my job is not to excite you; it's to show you what is required in order for you to accomplish the goal you stated. I'll just tell you the truth and you can decide if you are willing to do it or not," I responded, reminding everyone that goals are neither realistic nor unrealistic, it is the actions required to accomplish them that need to be judged by realism.

"Everyone in Brian and Michelle's position will have to do one of the following:

a) choose to stay put and settle for the three properties they have bought;

b) use the CCI they developed in phase one to attract JV capital to continue buying more; or

c) adjust the timelines on their goal.

"Assuming the answer is (b), then Brian would spend the next 18 months of his plan specializing in buying certain properties with JV partners that fit his criteria and work towards reaching 50 doors," I said, as I explained option one in phase two. I knew full well that the thought of buying 47 more doors with JV partners was quite daunting to Brian and virtually out of the question for Michelle, but I wanted them to see what was truly required if Brian wanted to accomplish his goal in five years. I then reminded him that his original goal was 20 years and that we still had one more phase to go. He seemed content to "play along" and see how the plan would play itself out.

Option Two

"The second option for those of you who do not want to use JV capital is to utilize one of the six other options for down payments in order to continue buying more real estate until you've reached the desired number of gap doors. Examples of this would be waiting for equity appreciation to refinance or utilize extra savings from your job or bonus income."

Sean and Candice, for example, had a gap number of $10,000 a month. They had $300,000 in equity, so their MPP (Maximum Purchase Price) was $1.5 million. Depending on the type and nature of real estate they buy, they should have been able to purchase five properties in phase one. Assuming $100 per door in cash flow, they would still be 95 doors short of their target. However, there are two very important components to their plan that need to be taken into consideration. Number one, their goal was over a 10-year timeline, not five. Number two, they are both very good income earners with the ability to make large commissions at any given time. This second factor, combined with the fact that they do not need to accomplish their goal within five years, affords Sean and Candice the luxury of either buying more real estate with their excess income or accelerating the pay down of debt on their existing mortgages over the upcoming years, which in turn, would serve to increase the amount of cash flow per door. A combination of these factors over the next 10 years, along with some favourable equity appreciation, could very well allow them to avoid the use of JV capital in accomplishing their end goals. Keep in mind that I am using a very conservative number in calculating $100 a door. If they were able to increase the amount of positive cash flow to $400 a door within a 10-year time frame, they would only need 25 doors to accomplish their goal—not 100. That target was significantly more achievable for them.

It should be noted that I normally do not encourage anyone to factor equity appreciation into their strategy over a five-year time frame. Of course, if you do benefit from a sharp rise in values, such as we saw across Canada from 2004 to 2007, that's fantastic—but it is certainly not something you can predict or bank on. Equity appreciation should, therefore, be treated as a bonus and not used as a main strategy. Having said that, Sean and Candice have a 10-year goal, so it would be unreasonable not to anticipate a degree of equity appreciation over that time frame.

Option Three

"The third option is to create economies of scale by shifting your portfolio into small multi-family properties or commercial investments."

Some of the investors in the room that day, such as Barb and Kathy or Jeff and Linda, were not brand new to real estate investing, so in many ways, they entered into the day already half of the way through phase one. If they spent the balance of their seed capital developing a higher level of CCI, they would then be in a position to look at small multi-family commercial purchases such as a six-plex, 12-plex or even something as large as a 20-unit apartment building. The advantage of multi-family properties is that you are able to create economies of scale by only having one roof to replace or one boiler. If you find a good property manager to run your building, it could be a lot less time consuming than if you were to have 20 single-family units in different cities.

"If I wanted to have small apartment buildings and I'm using JV money, wouldn't it make sense to skip the first step of buying single-family homes and jump right into multi-family?" asked Jeff, with a sense of impatience.

"Well, yes and no," I replied, not trying to be ambivalent. "In your case Jeff, you and Linda may very well jump straight to multi-family. You have $250,000 in seed capital, so in phase one you would be faced with a dilemma. You could buy five more apartment or townhouse units at $250,000 each and continue to solidify your CCI. You would position yourselves to be qualified to attract JV partners, but then what would you be qualified to buy?"

"Small single-family units," Jeff was quick to respond.

"Exactly. If it is your intention to use the JV capital to buy multi-family, you would be guilty of using JV money for your education if you haven't already bought one yourself. You will recall from our lunch conversations with Neil that commercial real estate is truly a different sandbox with a different set of rules. So you might be better served in phase one to use your seed capital to buy a small multi-family property to develop your 'commercial CCI,'" I explained. "The challenge there is the simple fact that commercial property, by definition, is more expensive and may require a larger down payment. So, you will likely only be able to buy one. However, the experience gained in one commercial purchase will be substantially more than one residential, so one purchase combined with your previous experience should create sufficient CCI to allow you to attract JV capital in phase two."

"Once you start attracting JV partners, is it a good idea to skip the small buildings and go for larger apartment buildings such as a 30- or 40-unit one?" asked Kathy, who was as anxious to skip to the large properties as Jeff was.

"Well, in theory it makes sense," I answered, "but here's where I see the problem. The average investor who goes out to attract JV capital for the first time, is not likely to be super confident in the beginning. And they're usually very excited when someone offers to partner with them for $75,000. Now let me ask you, how much would you need to put down for a 30-unit apartment building in Edmonton?"

"A heck of a lot more than $75,000," Kathy replied, as she clued into the point I was making.

"Keep the old adage in mind—walk before you run. Please don't get me wrong. If, after spending your seed capital in phase one, you have the confidence to attract over $1 million in JV capital, then by all means, buy an apartment building if you are so inclined. But my experience has been that the first few people you partner with will probably be offering a little less than that," I explained, while not trying to discourage anyone.

"I'd say that's accurate based on the people I've spoken to already," Kathy responded.

"But keep in mind," I added, "you are constantly evolving during this process and by the time you reach phase three, you may be surprised by how much money you can attract. I remember sitting down with one of my clients four years ago and they had just lost their job. He wanted to buy a lot of real estate, but because of the lack of a job, he had to rely 100% on JV capital. He followed our plan, developed CCI through a combination of his own seed capital and partnering with a few close friends in the beginning, and slowly developed his portfolio. Now, four years later, he has a significantly larger portfolio and the last cheque he received from a JV partner was for over $1 million. So it really is a case of having faith. Remember, don't judge yourself in the future based on who you are today."

I love sharing that story, hoping that it helps people like Jeff and Kathy to see that it is possible, but they just need to be patient and wait for it to develop naturally. "The bottom line is, if you are thinking of shifting your portfolio to multi-family, just remember that the cost of entry will be higher and that you are dealing in a different sandbox with different rules. It may be better to earn your stripes on a smaller property before tackling a larger one, especially if you are working with a JV partner," I summarized.

A special note to the reader—if you are interested in buying multi-family properties, here are a few key points to remember in addition to what Neil shared at lunch:

- For commercial properties, there are three key variables that change with every deal and are dealt with on a case-by-case basis:

  1. The loan to value, or the amount of money you can borrow.

  2. The interest rate the bank is going to charge you.

  3. The lender and broker fees that you'll be charged.

- The following four factors affect and dictate the above three points:

  1. Age and quality of the building.

  2. The cash flow on that particular building.

  3. The prevailing vacancy rates.

  4. The borrower—an examination of the borrower's financials is still important, just not as important as with residential.

The first three points will *always* be dictated by the bottom four factors.

Option Four

"The last option in phase two would be to sit and hold, shifting your focus to a debt reduction strategy. Assuming that you were able to reach your desired number of doors through the expenditure of your seed capital in phase one, you would shift your focus in phase two to reducing your mortgage debt."

The best example of this was Nicole and Marc. Their goal at the beginning of the day was to purchase enough real estate so that 15 years from now, they could be earning an additional $3,000 a month to supplement an early retirement for one of them. They had $250,000 in home equity, which would allow them to purchase $1.25 million of real estate. This, in turn, would allow them to purchase three homes in the $400,000 range. It's likely that these homes would be a combination of single-family dwellings and/or duplexes, some with suites. The rental incomes would likely be in the range of $1,400 to $1,600 per month. Once the mortgages are paid off in full, the rental income, less expenses such as ongoing maintenance and taxes, should easily allow them to net the desired $3,000 from the three properties. Nicole and Marc are certainly in a position to make the purchases they need in phase one and then shift their focus in phase two to paying off the debt. If they were to set an aggressive debt reduction strategy that includes recycling all positive cash flow from the properties back onto the mortgages, they could very well have their mortgages paid off in 15 years. That would result in an additional income of $3,000 a month cash flow, not to mention that they would be sitting on over $1.5 million of free and clear real estate, in addition to their principal residence.

When I laid this plan out for them, Marc got very excited, but Nicole was still a little apprehensive. It made sense to her in theory, but the idea of actually going out and doing it scared her. My suggestion was that she not think about all three purchases at once. They agreed that they would buy one property to start, and then just see how it goes. My guess is that Nicole will be the one pushing Marc to buy a second property sooner, rather than later.

The only other couple who I thought might fit into this category was John and Liz. They had $450,000 in seed capital and already owned some lakefront recreational property along with a very nice home. Their seed capital would allow them to be able to purchase over $2.25 million of real estate, again depending on whether they chose residential or commercial. Their goal was for their real estate to earn them an extra $3,000 a month over the next five years, have $5 million worth of real estate and $1 million in equity, so that they could lay a foundation for future generations. Between the value of their principal residence and the cottage at the lake, they would be very close to their goal based on their current situation, but would fall just short over the next five years. Since they will both be retired and Liz wants to shift her focus to giving more of her time and money to charity, they will have limitations to being able to accelerate the debt reduction.

I knew that neither of them was very excited about going out and raising JV capital, so I suggested an alternative for John. Over the course of his career, John had developed a vast network of friends and colleagues who respected and trusted him. Many of them were in very similar situations as John and Liz, but John would feel uncomfortable about approaching them to buy real estate without putting any of his own money into the deal. However, he had no qualms about approaching a few of them and going 50/50 on purchases where both parties put up equal amounts of the down payment. This simple strategy would allow them to double their purchasing power and they could now entertain some larger commercial opportunities. The idea excited John and he made a point of making a list of friends who would qualify on one hand and a to-do list of what required research on the other.

You should now have a good idea of what your focus will be in phase two. Obviously, there will be multiple variables and certain issues that are unpredictable or beyond your control, such as the global recession in 2009. However, that should not stop you from making a plan. You now know how many doors you were able to buy at the end of phase one and, therefore, you should know exactly what your shortfall was starting phase two. You are either in a position to focus on debt reduction such as Nicole and Marc; utilize one of the other down payment options such as Sean and Candice; shift your portfolio to multi-family such as Barb and Kathy and Jeff and Linda will be doing; or like Shelley, Chad, Ryan, Drs. Gill and Jasmine, use the CCI that you developed through spending your seed capital in phase one to attract enough JV capital to purchase your desired number of doors. Depending on how large your shortfall was, you may or may not have been able to purchase all your doors in phase two. If that is the case for you, then you know exactly how to start phase three—at the exact same place you left off. Or perhaps you are like Brian and Michelle and, as a couple, you're not quite sure where to go next. I knew I had opened Brian's eyes to some new ideas and Michelle was certainly open to at least getting started, so I suggested that Brian create a business plan based on the premise that he will be using JV capital in the future, but for now, he would simply start with one purchase at a time until both he and Michelle were comfortable with the concept.

Wherever you are in the process, you should be continuing to address your shortfall (if you still have one) through joint venture capital or one of the other down payment options. Don't forget that throughout this process you are building your future on purpose. Never forget what your vision is—the lifestyle that you ultimately want to live. Continue to chip away at your goal through working with JV partners until you achieve the desired number of doors required to accomplish your goal. And lastly, always remember to consider the cause and effect before making any decisions.

Chapter 14

Phase Three—The Final Phase

As the day began to wind down, we were now ready to move into the third and final phase of our three-phase real estate action plan. Please note that phase three will begin 36 to 48 months from the time you begin reading this book. That means if you are reading this in 2010, phase three will take place sometime in 2013 or 2014. You will be three years older than you are now. Think about it! Take the time to jot down your age at the beginning of phase three—how old will you be? What will you have learned over the next three years if you have been following this plan? How have you developed? What has changed in your life? Have you developed your CCI? How have you changed as a sophisticated investor?

It is important to keep in mind as you write out the possible steps for the third phase of your business plan, you will not the same person you are today—you will have developed a much higher level of sophistication in terms of being a real estate investor and you will likely be capable of making decisions three years from now that you would feel very uncomfortable making in your current situation. To illustrate how much things can change for you three years from now, simply think back three years ago from today and take a small inventory of what has already changed in your life:

- How old were you three years ago?
- Where were you living?
- What was your net worth?
- How much has changed over the past three years?

Now imagine how much can change three years from now if you work the plan!

As we mentioned at the beginning of phase two, there will be multiple variables beyond your control that can easily sidetrack the best-laid plans, but that doesn't mean you shouldn't make a plan—just be prepared to be flexible with it. My personal philosophy is that you should always have a plan or a sense of the direction in which you are heading. However, if things change in your life or the world around you, you always need to be prepared to make adjustments to your plan. Some people use this as an excuse not to make a plan at all, but if you don't have the plan in the first place, how will you know what to adjust? You will simply end up reacting to the world and events as they unfold around you and end up living a life by default. Remember, the true goal of this book is to plan your future and live your life on purpose!

"Now that you have completed phase two of your action plan, it is time to pause and consider where you will be at this point in your development," I began as I introduced the final phase to the class.

"Again, as we move further along the timeline of your business plan, it becomes more challenging in some ways to provide specific steps due to the obvious factor that we will be dealing with variables in the future that are unknown to us today. Therefore, phase three of your business plan will deal in generalities for most of you, while for some of you, the steps will seem obvious and specific. In all cases though, remember that you will be three years older than you are today." This is a point that I find needs to be reinforced at every workshop I do.

At this point I reminded the group that the action steps and options in phase three are very similar to phase two. The key to what you do in phase three is, in fact, completely dependant on what you did in the second phase of your plan:

- Were you in a sit and hold pattern of debt reduction because you reached your desired number of doors in phase one?

- Did you continue to use JV capital to overcome your remaining shortfall from phase one? If so, do you now have the desired number of doors?

- Did you utilize one of the seven other options for down payments to accomplish your goal? If so, did you need to adjust your timeline to a longer-term goal?

- Did you create some economies of scale by shifting your portfolio into small multi-family commercial investments?

Whichever action you took, you are now three years into your real estate action plan. You should have addressed your shortfall through one of the above actions and you will be slowly gathering the right number of doors to generate the cash flow you need to support your desired lifestyle.

You should take a moment to analyze where you would likely be at the end of phase two as we move into the final phase. How many more doors would you have likely purchased and what is your shortfall at the beginning of phase three?

$$\underline{\hspace{3cm}} - \underline{\hspace{6cm}} = \underline{\hspace{2cm}}$$

# of gap doors − # of total doors at end of phase two = Shortfall

Please take the time right now to do this exercise. Remember, these are future projected numbers, so also take the time to make notes about any assumptions you are making.

My shortfall at the beginning of phase three = _____.

WHAT ARE YOUR OPTIONS?

As in phase two, you will once again be faced with similar multiple options. The first rule of thumb is "if it aint broke—don't fix it." In other words, if what you have been doing in phase two is working well for you—keep doing the same. Here are two of four options:

1. If you were able to reach the desired number of doors in phase two, you will move into a sit and hold pattern where your focus shifts from acquisitions to a debt reduction mode. If you don't need the cash flow immediately, you can use it to accelerate your mortgage payments so your debt is reduced more quickly and you pay off the mortgages faster. Nicole and Marc should be able to do this at the end of phase one and, my guess is, John and Liz will be in this position by the end of phase two.

2. If you still haven't acquired the necessary number of doors, just continue doing what you've been doing in phases one and two. Use the CCI you have developed and continue to attract JV capital. At this stage, it is really just a matter of simple math—how

many doors do you still need to purchase? Do the calculation and keep developing your skill set. The key is not to complicate things and certainly don't give up. Remember back in phase one where you learned that by the tenth floor, you've reached the halfway point? That hasn't changed. Once you've figured it out in phase one, you just keep doing what you're doing, whether you need to go from the 10th floor to the 50th floor or even the 100th floor.

"Chad, this is exactly the stage where you will really start attracting JV partners from among your peers," I mentioned, not wanting Chad to think I had forgotten about him. "You will now be three years into your portfolio development and have some results to show for it. In phase two, you would have already partnered with a few of your friends and associates to make some more purchases and, by now, they are the ones who are talking about you to their friends. Success attracts success, and you will soon be getting calls from people you don't even know who want to know if they can partner with you. This will be a very exciting time in your life and you will simply need to stay steady to the course." As I described a potential future for Chad, he couldn't help but break into a broad smile. I knew he had the potential and I was determined to follow up with him.

Ryan, on the other hand, was going to be slightly more difficult. He had the same ambitions as Chad, but lacked both the job income and the capital to get started. He did, however, have one potential thing going for him—a father who was willing to help him get started. Ryan only had $20,000 of his own money, so his plan in phase two was to work in partnership with his dad. His father was willing to partner with him, as long as Ryan was willing and able to do all the work. Their split would favour the father more than Ryan in the beginning (likely a 70/30 split). But based on what we had reviewed in the JV section, Ryan was well aware that it was worth giving up more in the beginning in order to create the CCI. By the end of phase two, Ryan should be in a good position to use the experience gained through partnering with his dad, to springboard into approaching JV partners with confidence. I also knew that with his boldness and personality, shyness would not be an issue, so I was quite confident that given patience and time (likely more than the five years he initially had hoped),

Ryan could very well develop into a successful real estate investor and accomplish his goals.

"The key for you, Ryan," I stated, as if I were a grade school teacher pointing out a pupil, "is to treat your father like gold. Don't ever get greedy and make sure he receives all the benefit and profit up front, before you do. Your dad is entrusting you with his hard-earned capital, treat it with the utmost respect. The purpose of the initial purchases with your dad is not to make you money—it is for you to get your education. If you keep your focus on doing what is right, the money will come as a by-product in the future."

"Absolutely. I totally get it," he said, as he sat a little more upright in his chair.

One of the most interesting situations in the class that day was Shelley's. Here she was, a single mom with tons of ambition. She simply wanted to use real estate to create a better future for both herself and her kids. She had $170,000 in equity from her house that she could use as seed capital, which would allow her to buy around $850,000 in real estate. Her gap amount was $3,000 a month and her solution was no different than many others, she simply had to spend the $850,000 in a way that created CCI in the process, so that she could start to attract JV partners in phases two and three. Shelley understood this, and certainly welcomed the challenge, but the real issue she was bound to come across was time. As a single mother who worked full time, she was all too aware that there were only so many hours in the day. Make no mistake about it—real estate is not a passive revenue stream although some people would have you believe that it is. If you are going to go out and build a large portfolio, it will take time to research the property, to make the purchases, to find the tenants and to manage your property managers. I don't recommend you self-manage after you've made three purchases. It all takes time and when you have a busy schedule like Shelley does, something's got to give and it should not be the time you spend with your children.

So my suggestion to Shelley was to get started on her own in order to gain the experience necessary, but after making enough purchases to "earn her stripes" start to keep an eye out for a business partner whom she could work with—much as Barb and Kathy did. Sometimes finding a partner can take a bit of the load off of you and make the journey more enjoyable and tolerable. Besides, there will be plenty of times along the way where you'll want to have someone to commiserate with. This idea came as a great relief to Shelley, as she admitted that she had been silently struggling with those thoughts all day.

Option Three

The third option in the final phase is to shift your portfolio to larger multi-family units, such as 20- to 25-unit buildings or even larger. By now you will have gained a significant amount of CCI and will likely be surprised that the JV partners you are attracting now have significantly more money than the ones you were able to attract at first. As you grow in confidence and become increasingly better with your systems, you will start to find the process becomes easier as well. Those of you who moved to small apartments in phase two, may now want to take on something bigger.

I looked around the room as I was explaining the third option to the class and caught the eyes of Drs. Gill and Jasmine. I knew they had grasped all of the concepts we had taught that day and were very excited about the plan they were putting together, and rightfully so. They had a very ambitious goal of $15,000 a month, but at the same time, they had roughly $500,000 in seed capital. This would allow them to purchase upwards of $2.5 million in phase one with their seed capital alone, and it also opened up the door to shift into multi-family properties sooner. They were active in a real estate network, so they knew exactly where they wanted to focus their purchases and had a good idea as to the type of properties they wished to target. Now they knew exactly what results those properties needed to produce for them. I explained to them that if they could raise the amount of profit per door to $300, they would only need 50 doors to accomplish their goal. This could be accomplished with two 25-unit apartment buildings. Dr. Gill's face lit up with the thought that they could accomplish their goal with only two buildings.

"The key," I emphasized, "is to get the purchases under your belt over the next two years, and then spend the rest of phases two and three using your surplus income to accelerate your debt reduction."

I also suggested they consult a real estate accountant who could give them the proper advice in terms of incorporation, which would help to minimize their personal taxation. As a rule, I don't generally encourage investors to incorporate, since incorporation only serves to complicate the mortgage situation. However, in this case, both of them were earning significant revenue from their practice, so it would not make sense to draw a larger personal income just to pay down mortgage debt on an investment. My job was to make sure they understood the concept. I knew they could always book an appointment with my friend, Navaz Murji, an expert in real estate accounting to get the detailed advice they would need. (Feel free to send an e-mail to clientcare@peterkinch.com for a referral to a real estate accountant in your province.)

In phase two, Drs. Gill and Jasmine would have the option to make further purchases if they had saved enough from excess income or they could easily start attracting more capital from their peers, who by this time, would be not only very interested in their recent success but also wanting to share in the opportunities. Doctors can be notorious for making poor investment choices and, as such, can make good JV partners when shown better alternatives. A couple like Gill and Jasmine were well positioned to spend their seed capital in a way that would attract their peers' attention—they would likely have no shortage of peers lining up to get their advice. The key, of course, is to always use your own money to make your mistakes and develop your CCI. Drs. Jasmine and Gill had a lot of options and lots of reason to smile. I thought about how their goal was to help build a foundation for children, and I was looking forward to hearing how their real estate ends up helping children around the world overcome their difficulties. I love to help people build a plan for success, but when I know that helping them accomplish their goal will, in turn, help other people in this world, I am especially gratified.

All in all, it had been a good day!

The Final Option: The Exit Strategy

The last option is truly optional—it is the exit strategy. The majority of investors will buy for the long-term and nurse their portfolios until the day comes when the properties are all paid off and the cash flow is where they want it to be. But others reach a point where they say, "You know what? I've worked really hard the past number of years, now I just want out." If you fall into the former category, then you simply have to follow the plan you built and wait for it to grow. If you are in the latter group, however, then you would want to start considering your exit strategies now, so that you can build and structure your portfolio keeping the end result in mind.

"At this point in the day, a lot of you may be wondering when does this start to become easier? Is there any way of developing an exit strategy?" I asked, as if reading half of the minds in the room.

"Let's now assume that you are at the end of phase three and you have spent the past five years building your plan and now want to know what your exit strategies are. How old would you be at this point?" I asked, hoping to get everyone to see themselves five years in the future.

"I'd rather not answer that question if it's all the same to you," Michelle quipped back.

"That's okay. You don't have to share, as long as you know the answer." I answered her with a smile.

I then reminded Brian that he agreed that I could use him as an example for the last two phases.

"I thought you had forgotten," he joked, half serious.

"No fear of that, my friend. I've just been waiting for the right time," I replied, which made him a little nervous and excited at the same time.

"Now, I want to clarify up front that I am recommending that Brian and Michelle start with just buying one property to test the waters and get their proverbial feet wet. But for the sake of this example, let's take some poetic licence and assume Brian and Michelle followed the option of spending their seed capital in phase one and developed the CCI they needed to attract JV capital in phases two and three."

"That would require some imagination, but let's go with it," Michelle added with a laugh.

"Brian, what was your gap number at the beginning of the day?"

"$5,000 a month," he responded quickly. He had his numbers ready this time.

"So based on $100 a door positive cash flow per month, how many doors would you need to own?"

"Fifty." He answered while shielding himself from Michelle's glance.

"Okay, so he needs to buy 50 doors over the next five years in order to generate the $5,000 a month required to finance his goal," I said to the class as I began to run through an optional exit strategy using Brian as my example.

"Now the following example is an optional exit strategy and I have two major disclaimers that I want to address up front:

1. Everything I suggest in this next segment is dependent on market conditions; and

2. You will need to consult a tax accountant regarding potential capital gains."

It is important for you to always consult with a qualified accountant before making any decisions with regard to capital gains and other actions that have tax implications.

"Now, by the end of phase one, Brian was able to purchase three properties and, by doing so, he developed sufficient CCI that he was able to attract the attention of some of his friends. He became a student of the business and, together with Michelle, they systemized the process, studied the business of real estate and became proficient at finding good properties and matching them with interested individuals. They were then able to progress throughout phases two and three working with JV partners to purchase an additional 47 doors. Now, let me ask you a question." I paused to make sure everyone was paying attention.

"Brian's goal was to earn $5,000 a month in five years. But if he was earning $100 a door in net positive cash flow, having made all but three of his purchases with JV partners, how much would Brian be earning five years from now if he had 50 doors?" I asked, knowing full well that someone had already done the math, just as you may have already figured out.

He'd be earning "$2,500, because he only owns half of them," Chad was quick to volunteer.

"Well, probably $2,800, since they own three outright, but yes, Chad's right. I knew some of you were wondering when I was going to get to this obvious and glaring flaw in my master plan. I mean, hey—if you buy your doors with a JV partner then you have to virtually double the amount of doors you need, right?" I asked as I looked at a mixture of concern and disappointment on some of the faces in the room.

"Okay, 50 doors was a stretch for me, but there's no way I'm going to be buying a hundred properties just to make $5,000 a month," Michelle stated very clearly.

"No, I agree," I answered, surprising her somewhat. "I mean, think about it. Here's Brian and Michelle and they have followed the plan perfectly. They've put in long hours, taken chances, put up with some bad tenants, worked through some vacancies, dealt with some poor JV partners who turned out to be a total pain. They did everything they were supposed to and managed to buy 50 doors in five years, but after five years they're still only halfway to their goal. And they're still wondering when any of this is about to become passive." I paused, as everyone in the class was able to create the mental picture of a frustrated real estate investor.

"And so, after five years of hard work, Brian and Michelle decide it's time to look for an exit strategy," I began. "Now remember, they are only making $2,500 a month on their current portfolio of 50 doors. So here's what they do. They use the optional exit strategy that I call liquidate and consolidate."

Liquidate and Consolidate Optional Exit Strategy

Please keep in mind that you will need to take in to consideration both the market conditions at the time and the implication of capital gains tax in implementing this exit strategy. The numbers are not intended to be 100% accurate, but rather used to illustrate the power of real estate.

Step One: Sell Half of Your Doors

- After five years, you should have some equity developed through a combination of debt reduction from the accelerated pay down of the mortgages (if they put all the cash flow back onto the mortgages) and market appreciation (again, the strategy is market dependent).

- Use the proceeds to buy out your remaining JV partners. The thought here is that you should have made enough profit from the sale of 25 units that you would be able to buy out the remaining partners.

- Brian and Michelle now have 25 doors left and, hopefully, few or no JV partners. They own the remaining 25 doors outright.

Note: If you know that this may be an exit strategy you would like to utilize in the future, when would be a good time to think about mentioning it to your JV partners? Up front. Simply put a "shotgun" or "buyout" clause in every JV contract you draft. The key is that your partner will need to be bought out at fair market value and they would need to be a willing party to the buyout. The secret is to make sure the net result for the JV partner was a positive one. Make sure they are not disappointed with the end result. This is the biggest reason why this strategy is so market dependent. If the property has no equity appreciation, then there will likely not be enough money from the sale of 25 units to buy out the remaining 22 doors. (Remember, Brian was able to buy three with his own money.)

Step Two: Sell Slightly More Than Half the Remaining Doors

- The next step is to sell 15 of the remaining 25 doors.

- The expectation in this step, as it was in the step one, is that there will have been enough equity appreciation and mortgage reduction to generate a profit.

- The profit from the sale of the next 15 units will be used to pay down the mortgages on the remaining 10 units. Again, keep in mind that there will be capital gains to consider.

As an aside, I would suggest selling the units that have high-maintenance tenants and JV partners.

"The remaining 10 units that Brian and Michelle own will hopefully have no JV partners and the majority of them will be virtually mortgage free." As I stated this to the class I started to see slight smiles return to some of the faces.

"But here's the real point. We started this entire process off with the assumption that Brian and Michelle would only be getting $100 per door in positive cash flow. Please refer back to the number for the amount of money per door that we calculated once the mortgages were paid off in full—again, a very conservative number." Everyone started flipping back to the exercise that was completed earlier in the day (readers will find it on page 57 of this book).

"$500!" exclaimed Ryan.

"So now Brian and Michelle have 10 doors left with no joint venture partners and no mortgages. They are earning $500 a door net positive cash flow, how much are they earning in total every month?" I asked with a wry grin.

"Five thousand," Brian answered with a broad smile.

"Wait a minute," I said with mock surprise. "You mean to tell me that you went from having 50 doors and all those joint venture partners who were a hassle to deal with and all those problem tenants and only making $2,500 a month, to only 10 doors—one-fifth the number of doors, no more partners, only 10 tenants and you doubled your money?"

"That's pretty amazing," Brian said, still trying to grasp the concept.

"I have to admit, even I'm impressed," said Michelle, almost begrudgingly.

"So, let me ask you this," I asked the class. "Knowing that you could have an exit strategy that looked like that, would the absolute hassle and hard work of building it in the first place be worth it?"

The resounding answer was yes!

Now I already know that some of you reading this right now can pick apart the numbers and argue about equity appreciation and capital gains etc., and tell me that it would never work that way—I know. But, I would ask you not to get caught up in those details as much as understand the concept. No, the numbers may not always work exactly that way, but the fact is that the above example shows you the power of real estate. Even if you only succeeded in paying down half the mortgages and half the JV partners, or if it took you ten years instead of five, the net result sure beats a lot of the current pension plans that exist out there today.

OTHER EXIT STRATEGIES

Remember, I have used very conservative numbers for the amount of positive cash flow in our planning. If you changed most of the examples for any of the characters in this book from $100 per door to $300 per door we could significantly decrease the number of doors required and, therefore, the number of JV partners. The key is to always be thinking about your portfolio like a chess game—two or three moves in advance. So let's look at some ways we can increase the cash flow per door through other strategies:

- Liquidate a smaller portion of your portfolio and pay down the mortgages on the units you own without a JV partner. Utilizing this strategy, I could actually create multiple variations of the same idea. For example, I could sell one property a year and slowly pay off all my mortgages.

- Set up a system whereby for every four doors you sell, you pay off one. You can keep reducing debt until you reach the cash flow you want.

- Take advantage of market conditions to sell off less profitable properties. Shift the money to a property where you increase your cash flow. This will also help you to qualify at the bank if you want to buy more properties in the future.

Please make your own list of ideas that you have for additional exit strategies:

_____

_____

_____

_____

_____

_____

I encourage you to think about what is possible and feel free to think outside the box. However, please be sure to check with your accountant regarding any tax implications prior to trying anything.

As a class, we went over some of these alternative exit strategies and discussed the pros and cons of various ideas. I then asked the participants what it was that Brian and Michelle gave up by selling 80% of their properties after five years.

"The ability to hold in there for another 20 and have 50 doors at $500 a door," Barb responded as she crunched the "opportunity cost" on her calculator.

"Exactly. If they held on for another 20 years to all 50 doors and all the JV partners and all the hassle tenants, then they could be making over $12,000 a month. My guess is that Michelle would rather take the five grand today and buy back some of her time. But again, my point is you have options." I noticed Michelle nodding with me as I spoke.

"Now, as we wrap the day up, there is one more very important exit strategy that I think is important to bring up," I announced to the class, making sure I had everyone's attention. "Something a lot of people don't realize is that if you have a million dollars in cash, there are a lot of investment vehicles in the marketplace that will guarantee you a 6% to 8% annual return on your money and ensure your principal is protected at the same time. Often, this kind of investment vehicle is not available to you with less than a million dollars, but let's take a moment to think about this. If you were to get to the point where you just wanted to "check out" and sell everything—how much money would you need to live off of for the rest of your life?" I challenged the room.

"One thing we haven't spent a lot of time talking about is equity and net worth. We have spent most of the time talking about cash flow, but I would be remiss if I didn't at least touch on net worth." The reason I typically don't talk about net worth is because you can't buy groceries at Safeway with net worth. At the end of the day, you need cash to live off of.

"So what if you built a portfolio of up to $4 million worth of real estate and focused on getting half the portfolio free and clear of debt. If you were able to sell it and bank $2 million netting an annual rate of return of 8%, how much would you be earning in interest every month?"

"That would be $160,000 a year, or over $13,000 a month," said John in a very surprised tone.

"What about only a million. Is there anyone here who could live off of $80,000 a year?" I asked.

"I'd be okay with that," Shelley was quick to offer.

"Well, think about it, Shelley. You have enough seed capital today to buy $850,000 worth of real estate. If all you did was focus on an aggressive debt reduction strategy over the next 10 years and the property values increased by 20% in that time frame, you would have a million dollars of equity in real estate." Shelley was busy writing that idea down as her smile widened at the thought.

The main point I was trying to emphasize was that building up a real estate portfolio will not always be easy, but it can definitely be rewarding and I have never seen a worthwhile goal that was easy to obtain. The key is to always know *why* you are doing it and to keep your eye on the prize. It is very easy in life to focus on the obstacles and that is why most people quit. Put reminders up around your house of what your purpose is—what your goals are. Be clear with yourself and your spouse and even your kids if you have any, why you are doing what you do. Life will not always be in balance when you seek to achieve great things. But if you set time limits to your goals, you can be out of balance on purpose for limited periods of time, as long as you know what those limits are and don't let the timeline become an indefinite period.

SUMMARY

We were now ready to wrap up the day. Once again I reminded everyone that the purpose of this workshop was to discover why you were buying real estate, so that you could determine exactly what results you needed your real estate to produce for you. Starting with the end result in mind, we were able to reverse engineer the process, determining exactly how much money you would need to live your ultimate lifestyle and then break that down into how many doors you would need to buy in order to create the necessary cash flow. Once you knew what you needed to buy, the next step was to look at the obstacles you would face in buying those properties. We reviewed how to qualify at the bank and, hopefully, you now understand the importance of positive cash flow and how to balance the left side and right side of your portfolio. You have learned the difference between a transactional approach to building your portfolio and a portfolio approach. We tackled the second obstacle—down payments and covered various down payment options, including the importance of using your seed capital to develop CCI to overcome your fear of working with and attracting JV capital. And we finished the day by building a three-phase action plan to overcome your obstacles in order to accomplish your goal.

"Ladies and gentlemen, that is the Canadian Real Estate Action Plan," I announced. "With these tools, it is my hope that you are all empowered to be able to go out there and purchase enough doors to fill your gap, to reach your lifestyle and live your dreams."

The workshop was over, but before I would let anyone leave I asked them to do the same thing I am going to ask you to do. Now that you have finished reading (and hopefully doing) the real estate action plan, take a moment right now to complete the following:

My next step is:

_____

_____

_____

_____

_____

_____

What are you going to do right now, tomorrow, this week, to make your ultimate lifestyle a reality?

As everyone finished writing out their next step and got up to leave, I was pleased that we had come to the end of the day, but I also felt like I was just getting to know everyone and a part of me didn't want the day to end. But I knew that this was definitely not an end in any way—it was really just a beginning. I was very excited to be able to watch everyone grow as they set out on the journey to achieve their goals and I was filled with a sense of pride knowing that I had the chance to play a part in helping each of them achieve something that I knew would have a positive impact on those around them. I reminded everyone that I am here to help along the journey. Just as I am here for you, the reader. Simply send an e-mail to clientcare@peterkinch.com at any time and a staff member will put you in touch with a PK-Approved broker closest to where you live, who is trained specifically to assist you with your real estate action plan.

As Brian and Michelle got up to leave, they both thanked me. I could tell that Brian, in particular, was very happy that they made the effort to be there that day.

"Well, Michelle, I noticed your arms aren't crossed any more. Did you find the day useful?" I asked, confident I knew the answer.

"Absolutely. Brian has been going on about buying real estate for years now, but I never felt as though we had a plan before. I still don't see the 50-door thing, but I can definitely see getting started," she said as she looked up at Brian with a smile.

"Now, Brian, the key is to start slowly. You know what the big picture can look like now, but remember, it's not a race. You never have to worry about missing the 'best deal ever;' there will always be another one just as good a month from now. Take your time and make decisions on purpose and together. Walk before you run and you'll find that everything will start to unfold as it should."

"Don't worry, I'll keep him in line," Michelle promised.

"No worries, I know exactly what my next step is," Brian told me. "I'm going to check out the REIN website to learn more about the top 10 towns and the economic fundamentals. Now that we have a plan for the finance side, I need to study up on the real estate side."

"Great plan, Brian. That's a very good place to start," I said and, with that, we said goodbye. I couldn't help but think about some of the conversations that would be taking place on the drives home and I looked forward to helping everyone accomplish their goals.

As you finish reading this book, my hope is that you have more clarity now than when you started. I trust that you have a stronger sense of what results you need from your real estate and that you are now empowered to achieve those results. The obvious area that I have not covered in this book is the details about where and how to actually buy real estate. I strongly recommend that you pick up a copy of *97 Tips for Canadian Real Estate Investors*, which I co-authored with Don R. Campbell, or Don's book *Real Estate Investing in Canada 2.0* as perfect companion books to this one. Don will teach you about the 12 fundamentals you need to know in order to buy any real estate. When used in conjunction with this business plan, you will have everything you need to succeed.

I wish you success in your life and, more importantly, I truly want you to achieve your goal. For every person in this world who achieves a worthwhile goal, they positively impact a minimum of 100 people within their sphere of influence.

Never doubt that a small group of thoughtful
committed citizens can change the world;
indeed, it is the only thing that ever has.

—Margaret Meade

Please share your goals with us and allow us to help you achieve them. Together we can make this world a better place by achieving one goal at a time—starting with yours.

Epilogue

Thursday, March 25, 2010

This book is about building a business plan in order to accomplish your goals. This book is not intended to motivate you to "get rich" in real estate. Although some of the characters in the book have very aggressive goals to make tens of thousands of dollars a month from their real estate, it is important to note that the planning process involved is just as effective for making one thousand dollars a month. In fact, after reading this book you may come to the conclusion that buying real estate simply isn't for you. If that's the case—fantastic. I would rather see someone read my book and decide that they don't think this "real estate thing" is right for them, than to not discover this until after buying a property for the wrong reason. Again, I'm not trying to convince anyone that they should or should not be buying real estate. What I am trying to do is provide a business planning model for those who have decided to use real estate as their investment vehicle of choice. And for those who do choose to invest in real estate, my hope is that this book will act as a roadmap for you, to help keep you honest with yourself and keep you true to your goals.

In the process of working your way through your plan, you will encounter various obstacles both internal and external. Life will no doubt throw you a few curve balls, and the economy is bound to have more surprises in store for us in the future. A perfect example of this is the fact that, at the time of writing, the Canadian government is in the process of implementing rule changes to high-ratio mortgages in Canada. If there is one thing we can count on, it is change. This book is designed more to help you with building and structuring your business plan than to provide you with a list of rules and guidelines that can, and do, change on an ongoing basis. The core of your plan will not be affected by rule changes though. The underlying belief in this book is that you must create a plan with the end result in mind, and the key to doing that is to develop a clear understanding as to why you are buying real estate and what results you need from the real estate you buy. Along the road to accomplishing those goals, you will encounter various changes in terms of how banks treat investors—that part is inevitable. In fact, the only way we could keep up with rule changes in a book format would be if this were a digital book with monthly updates. Well, since we can't do that, we've created the next best thing.

I know that every one of you who sits down to make a plan will need some ongoing coaching and advice from someone who is familiar with the process. For that reason, I created the concept of the PK-Approved mortgage broker network. A PK-Approved broker has been trained to take the "portfolio approach" to working with you. They will know how to "coach" you through the mortgage process as you develop your real estate action plan. And, more importantly, they will always be on the cutting edge in terms of rule changes and updates. I encourage you to work with the PK-Approved broker nearest you as you progress through your plan.

The other resource available to you is my website, which I encourage you to use as a tool. All the forms mentioned in this book are available to you to download. If you found that you related to any of the characters in the book and are curious about how their plans worked out, you can look this up on the website. I have made a list of all the characters along with their financial information and a summary of their worksheets. Perhaps their actions can help you with your decision-making. And, of course, if you have any questions along the way, simply send an e-mail to clientcare@peterkinch.com and we will do our best to answer your question and point you in the right direction.

Our goal is to help you achieve your goal. That may sound like a cute catchphrase or sales line, but the ultimate benefit I can achieve through this book is to help someone else accomplish their goal. No matter how big or small you think your goal is, it's important. It is impossible to accomplish a worthwhile goal and not positively impact the people around you in some way. So my goal in writing this book is not only to help you achieve yours, but to see how your goal and the goals of thousands of individuals positively impact people around them. In fact, just by buying this book, you have already helped impact others in a positive way—50% of the author royalties from the sale of this book will be donated to Habitat for Humanity and used to help fund local housing projects in Canada for families who need it the most. What I love about Habitat for Humanity is that it provides families with a hand-up, not a handout. The families who benefit from donations have the opportunity to own the roof over their heads but are still responsible for making monthly payments. This fosters dignity and pride not only in the parents but also in the children, which will have a lasting impact on generations to come. So thank you for making a difference.

As you take your journey we'd like to know how your plan is progressing, so please take the time to share your stories with us. Let us know what your goal is and tell us how you're doing along the way. I look forward to sharing some of those success stories five years from now and celebrating how a small group of investors really did change the world for the better.

I wish you much success,
Peter Kinch

Why visit www.peterkinch.com?

To get Canadian Real Estate Action Plan resource materials:

- From the website you can download all the forms necessary to calculate your numbers.
- All the forms that Brian and Michelle used in this book are available on the website.

To find PK-Approved mortgage brokers near you:

- On the website, click on the map of Canada, select your city, and we will put you in contact with the PK-Approved broker nearest you.
- A PK-Approved broker is trained on how to help you implement your business plan and apply a portfolio approach to your next purchase. Simply forward a copy of your summary page to them, and they can provide ongoing support to help you achieve your goals.

For information on the Real Estate Action Plan all-day Workshop:

- Across Canada Peter will be holding live, all-day workshops just like the one Brian and Michelle attended.
- If you would like to attend one, visit our website for details and send us an e-mail to find out when the next live workshop will be held nearest you.

For information on the Real Estate Action Plan Homestudy Workbook:

- Don't have time to attend a workshop? Listen to it at home. The Home-study Workbook is a live recording of the actual workshop, accompanied by a binder full of all the worksheets, so that you can do the course at home at your pace.

To hire Peter as a Speaker:

- Peter has spoken to groups in both Canada and the U.S. on real estate, mortgage topics and business success principles.
- Have Peter speak at your next event or function. Topics include:
  - Making Sense of Today's Financial Markets
  - "Start with the End in Mind"—a Reverse Engineering process of goal-setting for any business.

Acknowledgements

There are many people who need to be thanked when writing a book, not the least of whom are Don Loney and the staff at John Wiley & Sons for their patience and support throughout the process, Cindy Freiman from Dominion Lending for her editorial and writing skills, and Les Hewitt for his mentorship and coaching along the way. I would also be remiss if I did not acknowledge the extra time, effort and support that my staff at PKMT provided. It was because of them that I was able to block off the time required to complete this book. But a special thank you is owed to Don R. Campbell. Without his support, mentorship and, most of all, friendship over the years, I would not even be in the position to be writing this book today.

Above all else, I would like to thank my wife Gena, who, in addition to being an incredible wife and mother during the process, provided her invaluable editing skills to the final copy. I am truly blessed to have her as my wife and life partner. And I can't thank Gena without also thanking our kids, Pierce and Mackenzie. You see, in the course of writing there were times when I had to lock myself away for days or weeks at a time. Now that it is completed, there will be various promotional trips and book tours. Throughout the course of the past few years, I've had to miss a few ball games, dance recitals and effectively ask Gena to act as a single mom at times. Essentially, they have had to pay a small price in order for me to write this book and, to their credit, Gena, Pierce and Mackenzie were willing to do so because part of them understood that this was an important thing for me to do—although they didn't always understand why.

But it's the *why* that is truly important. Yes, there are all the selfish and personal reasons for writing a book, but there is a significantly more important reason. I know deep in my heart that if you have a vision for your life and you've chosen real estate as the vehicle to accomplish your goal, then this book will be invaluable to you. In fact, I am writing this book in the hope that it provides thousands of real estate investors across

Canada the ability to use the right tools to achieve their goals within the context of the rules of engagement. By doing so, my real hope is that through the accomplishment of your goals, you will positively affect the world. Because the one thing I know is that if you read this book and take action, it is quite likely that your world and the world around you (your children, your family and your community) will be a better place because of it—and if this book can play a small role in that process, then Gena, Pierce and Mackenzie will know that their small sacrifice helped to make the world a better place.

About the Author

Peter Kinch is the founder of The Peter Kinch Mortgage Team and the PK-Approved Dominion Lending Centres network of brokers across Canada. He provides mortgage education on financing and real estate portfolio development through educational seminars, workshops and presentations. Throughout his mortgage career, Kinch has worked almost exclusively with real estate investors and is considered the foremost expert in Canada for helping real estate investors develop their mortgage portfolios. Through his expertise in this niche market, Kinch has become a lobbyist for the investor community with many chartered banks and trust companies. He was recognized as the #1 volume-producing mortgage broker in Canada for 2008 by *CMP Magazine*.

Peter is the author of *The Mortgage Minute* and is currently a featured mortgage guest on CTV News Channel, a regular guest on various radio and television programs throughout the country, and a frequent contributor to the News1130 Business Report with Russell Byth, heard on Rogers Radio in Vancouver, BC.

In addition to appearing on radio and television, Kinch has written various articles on the mortgage market that have been published in a variety of magazines and periodicals across Canada. He is co-author of the #1 best-seller *97 Tips for Canadian Real Estate Investors* and is a highly sought-after speaker for real estate investment groups across the country.

For more information, please visit www.peterkinch.com.

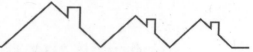

Canadian Real Estate Action Plan
Summary Page for Mortgage Coaching

Name:_____   Date:_____

E-mail: _____   Phone: _____

••

Monthly Cash Flow GAP $_____
                                                              A – (B + C)

GAP Doors *(# of doors needed to bridge your GAP)*   #_____

••

Monthly DSL (Verifiable Income x 40%) ÷ 12 $_____

Total Monthly Personal Debt $_____
(Taken from the Impact of Cashflow worksheet)

••

Value of Principal Residence $_____

Amount of Mortgage or Line of Credit $_____

Portfolio Value $_____

Amount of Mortgage and/or LOC on your Portfolio $_____

Liquid Assets (List what they are) $_____

_____   _____   _____

_____   _____   _____

Seed Capital (Money you're willing and able to invest) $_____

MPP (Maximum Purchase Price) $_____

APP (Average Purchase Price) $_____

Affordable Doors (MPP ÷ APP)   #_____

Short Fall (GAP Doors – Affordable Doors)   #_____

PETER KINCH MORTGAGE TEAM
#201 - 101 KLAHANIE DRIVE
PORT MOODY, BC, V3H 0C3
P: 604-939-8326 | TF: 1-866-988-8326
F: 604-939-8306 | WWW.PETERKINCH.COM

 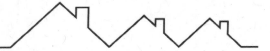

Additional Information:

Total Household Income $ _____

Principal Residence Mortgage (P+I+T) $ _____

Total Monthly Rental Income on Portfolio $ _____

Total Monthly Rental Mortgage Payments $ _____
(Mortgage Payments only on entire Portfolio)

••

Please fax or e-mail a copy of this summary page to Peter Kinch's office or a PK-Approved Broker™ before your next purchase so that we can coach you through the process.

Don't leave your future to chance!

By providing us a copy of this summary sheet you will give us the opportunity to analyze your next mortgage in the context of your goals.

Our goal is to help you achieve yours.

Toll free: 1-866-988-8326
Fax: 604-939-8307
E-mail: clientcare@peterkinch.com

PETER KINCH MORTGAGE TEAM
#201 - 101 KLAHANIE DRIVE
PORT MOODY, BC, V3H 0C3
P: 604-939-8326 | TF: 1-866-988-8326
F: 604-939-8306 | WWW.PETERKINCH.COM

Index